Performatism, or the End of Postmodernism

Performatism, or the End of Postmodernism

Raoul Eshelman

The Davies Group Publishers
Aurora, Colorado

Library of Congress Cataloging–in-publication data

Eshelman, Raoul, 1956-
    Performatism, or, the end of postmodernism / Raoul Eshelman.
        p. cm.
    Includes index.
    ISBN-13: 978-1-888570-41-0 (alk. paper)
    1. Arts, Modern--20th century. 2. Arts, Modern--21st century.
    3. Semiotics and the arts. 4. Aesthetics. 5. Subjectivity. I. Title.
    II. Title: Performatism. III. Title: End of postmodernism.
    NX456.E69 2009
    700'.41--dc22
                                    2007048472

Printed in the United States of America

1234567890

Contents

Acknowledgments

Most of the material in *Performatism, or the End of Postmodernism* has appeared previously.

Chapter One is based very loosely on my original article on performatism, which was written in German and translated into English for the journal *Anthropoetics*:

"Performatism, or the End of Postmodernism." *Anthropoetics* VI, 2 Fall 2000/Winter 2001 (*http://www.humnet.ucla.edu/humnet/anthropoetics/home.html*)

"Der Performatismus oder das Ende der Postmoderne. Ein Versuch." *Wiener Slawistischer Almanach* 46 (2000), 149-173.

Chapter Two (Literature) combines two articles. The first originally appeared in German in *Poetica* and was then translated and emendated for *Anthropoetics*; the second, "After Postmodernism," was written expressly for *Anthropoetics*:

"Aus der Epoche auschecken: Die Spätpostmoderne in Ali Smith's *Hotel World* und deren performatistische Überwindung in Olga Tokarczuk's Numery (Zimmernummern) und Miloš Urban's Sedmikostelí (Die Rache des Baumeisters)." *Poetica* 1-2 (2004), 193-219.

"Checking out of the Epoch: Performatism in Olga Tokarczuk's "The Hotel Capital" vs. Late Postmodernism in Ali Smith's *Hotel World* (with remarks on Arundhati Roy's *The God of Small Things* and Miloš Urban's *Sevenchurch*)." *Anthropoetics* 2 (2004 / 2005). (*http://www.anthropoetics.ucla.edu/ap1002/transhotel.htm*)

"After Postmodernism: Performatism in Literature." *Anthropoetics* 2 (2005/2006). (*http://www.anthropoetics.ucla.edu/ap1102/perform05.htm*)

Chapter Three (Movies) combines two articles, one written for *Anthropoetics* and the other for the internet journal *Artmargins*:

"Performatism in the Movies (1997-2003)." In: *Anthropoetics* 2 (2002/2003). (*www.anthropoetics.ucla.edu/ap0802/movies.htm*)

"Sokurov's Russian Ark and the End of Postmodernism." *Artmargins*, 30 July 2003 (*www.artmargins.com/content/cineview*)

Chapter Four (Architecture) is a slightly shortened version of an article that appeared in *Anthropoetics*:

"Performatism in Architecture. On Framing and the Spatial Realization of Ostensivity." *Anthropoetics* 2 (2001/2002) (*www.anthropoetics.ucla.edu/ap0702/arch2.htm*)

Chapter Five (Theory) will appear with small changes in a *Sonderband* of the *Wiener Slawistischer Almanach* in 2008:

"Performatism in Theory: The New Monism." *Festschrift für Igor' Smirnov, Wiener Slawistischen Almanach*. Sonderband 69 [in preparation].

Chapter Six (Art) is forthcoming in the 2007/8 edition of *Anthropoetics*.

Introduction

Some twenty years ago, Andreas Huyssen published an article called "Mapping the Postmodern"[1] whose cartographic imagery turned out to be ideally suited to describing the problem at hand. At the time, postmodernism was a murky, uncharted terrain whose existence was not acknowledged by many scholars and critics, let alone the general public. Apart from Lyotard's *La Condition postmoderne* (which had just come out in English) and Charles Jencks's *Language of Postmodern Architecture,* there were no book-length treatments of the subject and only a few noteworthy articles and essays. Now, more than two decades later, there is little question about the success of the cartographic venture launched by Huyssen. Students can draw on a well-regarded set of general works by authors like Hassan, Hutcheon, Huyssen himself, Jameson, Jencks, and McHale as well as on a vast body of more specialized studies. Today, few scholars and critics would dismiss postmodernism offhand as a mere fad or style, and you probably could, if so inclined, muster up a fair amount of agreement on a canon of typically postmodern authors and works.

A funny thing happens, though, when you try to use the map today. The reader perusing a novel like Yann Martel's *Life of Pi,* the cineast taking in Jim Jarmusch's *Ghost Dog,* or the pedestrian strolling past the Presidential Chancellery in Berlin[2] would have trouble connecting the standard descriptions of postmodernism with the works of art in question. *Life of Pi,* for example, makes you want to identify with a character who wants to believe in all major religions at once – a monist, faith-based wish not exactly in keeping with the pluralism and skepticism you would expect from a postmodern hero. *Ghost Dog,* for its part, is about a lone hero single-mindedly sacrificing himself in the name of an utterly rigid, hierarchical code of honor – also not exactly a plot device easily accounted for by postmodernist notions of decentered subjectivity and ludic regress. And, the Chancellery looks like a sleek anthracite hatbox with windows chiseled into it; it certainly doesn't resemble the playful, eclectically decorated buildings described by Charles Jencks in his classic work on postmodern architecture. Of course, you might want to argue that all these works are all in some way *ironic* – that they are ultimately just citing things alien to postmodernism and then twisting them around in order to renew and extend postmodernism itself. Even if you really believe this argument yourself, though, it's hard not to feel how strained it is. For with this simple formula you can assimilate literally *anything* back into the endless field of the postmodern episteme. The fact remains that, as of today, pulling out your trusty map of postmodernism doesn't always help when explaining contemporary books, films, and architectural objects. There are simply too many narrative strategies and motifs that go unexplained, too many artistic devices that diverge from the expected postmodern patterns.

Given these striking deviations from prevailing postmodern norms, you would think that there would be a groundswell of interest in finding out whether they have something in common or if they might all be leading in a similar direction. The case is quite the opposite, however. In spite of a widely held feeling that both postmodernism and its theoretical adjunct, poststructuralism, are on their way out, there is little or no interest in inquiring about what a succeeding epoch might look like or what other theoretical tools could be used to describe it.[3] This is due not just to plain force of habit, but also to a fundamental assumption about how signs relate to things. In poststructuralism explicitly and postmodernism implicitly, signs are thought to be tacked onto things belatedly, whether through custom, agreement, or happenstance. To achieve an understanding of things you can only go through signs; hence the sign (or, more precisely, the free-floating signifier) is the starting point for acquiring knowledge, not the thing itself. This basic notion, enormously amplified and elaborated in poststructuralist theory, is very difficult to get rid of once you have it. For the alternative to "going through the signifier" from this point of view is to assume either a mystical union of signs and things – which no one in our secular world does anymore – or to be subject to a partial, usually unconscious failure to recognize that "there is nothing outside the text," as Derrida puts it. And indeed, the force of this particular argument is hard to refute both in theoretical and practical terms. No one wants to get caught practicing "metaphysics" – tacitly basing your entire argument on something that is hidden behind or beyond our semiotic frame of reference and that only you are privy to. The result has been a partly hypercritical, partly defensive discourse that tries above all else to minimize its own participation in "metaphysics" while maximizing everyone else's. Needless to say, this sort of discourse must write off all unified concepts of the sign as old-fashioned, metaphysical bunk.

The broad, practically universal consensus on the untenability of monism has caused us to forget the historic instability of dominant, seemingly unshakeable concepts of sign. A glance at the history of culture shows that there have always been marked alternations between split concepts of sign and monist ones.[4] The prime reason for this seems to be that both sign types have inversely related strengths and weaknesses. Dualist concepts are strong on interpreting signs and weak on describing how things affect us through signs; monist sign concepts do precisely the opposite. At some point the one type begins to exhaust its descriptive and creative possibilities and the opposite one kicks in. Even if you're not a firm believer in neatly marked literary epochs, switches from Romanticism to Realism or from Symbolism to the era of the modernist avant-garde suggest that basic concepts of sign do change, and that it makes a very big difference when they do. Given this historical experience it seems a bit premature to assume that the concept of belatedness is the Last Word in this back-and-forth contest. For to do so you have to assume that the postmodern notion of the sign will be fine-tuned on into posthistorical infinity, but will never, ever again be superseded by a sign that is monist and unified.

As I see it, we are now leaving the postmodern era with its essentially dualist notions of textuality, virtuality, belatedness, endless irony, and metaphysical skepticism and entering an era in which specifically monist virtues are again coming to the fore. For the most part, this process has been taking place directly in living culture, around and outside the purview of academic theory. Although the earliest theoretical expressions of the radical new monism – Eric Gans's *Origin of Language* and Walter Benn Michaels and Steven Knapp's essay "Against Theory" – came out in the early 1980s, they never made much headway against the prevailing dualist mindset. As far as I've been able to tell, identifiably monist works of literature, film, art, and architecture began to appear with some regularity in the late 1990s; this trend has intensified noticeably since the turn of the century. The development has been most conspicuous in architecture – almost nothing built today resembles Jencks's or Ventura's exemplary structures – as well as in art movies, which are more inclined to innovation than mainstream cinema. In the art world, performatism is ascendant but not yet dominant; in recent years major individual artists have begun to stress unity, beauty, and closure rather than the endless ironies of concept art and anti-art. In literature, the new aesthetic is spreading slowly, as many authors still seem to have post-structuralist narrative theory in the back of their heads while writing. The one area, of course, where a consciousness of the new monism is lacking entirely is in the field of literary theory itself. Aware that the times are a changin', but unable to part with the split concepts of sign developed by master thinkers like Derrida, Lacan, Foucault, and Deleuze, academic critics have widened their perspective to include cultural studies, historicism, gender studies, and postcolonialism. Depending on your standpoint, this has resulted either in an enrichment of the original theories or their degeneration into what one partisan of deconstruction calls "the theory mess."[5] However you look at it, though, the concept of sign remains the same. It is split, belated, and devoted to pursuing an endless, irrefutable otherness that is largely of its own making.

The aim of this book is to close the widening gap between theory and the intensifying aesthetic trend towards monism – towards strategies emphasizing unity, identification, closure, hierarchy, and theist or authorial modes of narration. The name I've chosen for the new aesthetic is, for better or worse, "performatism." The term refers to a *strong* performance, which is to say a successful, convincing, or moving attempt by an opaque subject to transcend what I call a double frame.[6] Performatism as I understand it can be defined in terms of four basic categories: ostensivity (a specific type of monist semiotics); double framing (a specific way of creating aesthetic closure); opaque or dense subjectivity; and a theist or authorial mode of organizing temporal and spatial relations. These concepts will be developed systematically in Chapter One as well as by way of example throughout the rest of the book.

In terms of semiotic theory, I don't pretend to originality. The concept of what I call performatism draws heavily on Eric Gans's notion of the ostensive, which he developed in the early 1980s.[7] While Gans and I are in basic agreement about the need to boost monism, there are differences about how we go about it. Gans, for example, treats the ostensive – his elegantly parsimonious concept of the monist sign – as a universal; I treat it as a specific expression of the new zeitgeist, as the semiotic key to explaining the coming epoch. Whereas I limit myself mainly to things aesthetic, Gans has his own, more expansive notion of post-postmodernism, which he calls "post-millennialism" and links closely to a neoconservative worldview that I don't happen to agree with. However, the basic question he poses – how to cope with a world economically unified under global capitalism – is a valid one for left-wing politics too. Works like Arundhati Roy's *God of Small Things* – treated in detail in Chapter Two – suggest a radical path of resistance to capitalism based on a monistically conceived concept of beauty rather than one of the victimary, eccentric otherness still common in most postcolonialist theory.

The book is divided into six parts. After establishing the basic idea of performatism using the well-known movie *American Beauty* as a running example, I'll turn to literature, film, architecture, theory, and art, in that order. In regard to literature I've whittled my analyses down to six case studies taken from contemporary German, Indian, Polish, Czech, and Canadian literature: Bernhard Schlink's *The Reader*, Ingo Schulze's *Simple Stories*, Arundhati Roy's *The God of Small Things*, Olga Tokarczuk's "The Hotel Capital," Miloš Urban's *Sevenchurch*, and Yann Martel's *Life of Pi*. The film section is more inclusive, ranging everywhere from the Danish Dogma 95 films to mainstream movies like *About Schmidt* and *Panic Room*. Special attention is paid to *The Man Who Wasn't There*, the *Russian Ark*, and *Memento*. The chapter on architecture focuses on new buildings in Berlin designed by such leading contemporary architects as Sir Norman Foster, Renzo Piano, Helmut Jahn, and Axel Schultes. The

section on the "new monism" treats theoreticians such as Walter
Benn Michaels and Jean-Luc Marion who are already well known
in America. However, I'll also discuss the work of two provocative
monist thinkers who write mainly in German, Boris Groys and
Peter Sloterdijk, and show how the new monism can work together
with performatism to describe the epochal changes now taking
place in world culture. The section on art treats three types of
media (performance art, photography, and painting) in the work
of the well-known contemporary artists Vanessa Beecroft, Andreas
Gursky, Thomas Demand, Tim Eitel, and Neo Rauch.

In developing my notion of a new monism I've avoided long
polemics with poststructuralism. In fact, it's often helpful to run the
works discussed through a quick poststructuralist analysis to show
the aesthetic advantages of a performatist reading. Having made
the crude – but absolutely necessary – move of opposing monist to
dualist signs, I am well aware that the aesthetic shift now taking
place doesn't break down into neat black-and-white oppositions. All
performatist works feed in some way on postmodernism; some break
with it markedly, while others retain typical devices but use them
with an entirely different aim. Still other works develop seemingly
ironclad monist positions only to fall back into postmodern irony.
Nonetheless, cases of true fence-straddling are rare: the logic of
either one or the other sign type tends to prevail in the end.

A special note is also in order regarding my scholarly background.
As a Slavist by training, I'm tempted to draw on works in not easily
accessible languages like Russian, Czech, or Polish. Living and
working in Germany results in a bias toward that language, too.
For the purposes of this book, though, I've tried to favor literary
works that are available in English or – in the case of movies – are
on the market as subtitled videos or DVDs. Nonetheless, non-Slavist
readers will have to bear with more talk of Slavic films and literature
than they are used to in comparative discussions, and Slavists will
have to do without in-depth treatments of individual authors within
their national traditions. All in all, the book is intended less as a
comprehensive map of post-postmodernism than as a kind of do-it-
yourself manual for budding postmetaphysical monists. Given the

guidelines provided in the following pages anyone with an open mind should be able to construct a performatist map of their own.

This book would not have been possible without Eric Gans and his theory of the ostensive; Eric was also kind enough to publish portions of this work in his internet journal *Anthropoetics*. I have tried to repay that debt performatively, as it were, by demonstrating throughout the book the crucial importance of Eric's generative anthropology for defining the new epoch. Special thanks also go to Erika Greber for giving me the chance to work out the fine points of performatism while teaching Comparative Literature at the Ludwig Maximilian University in Munich. My colleagues in the Slavic Department in Munich, Aage Hansen-Löve, Ulrich Schweier, Miloš Sedmidubský, and Renate Döring, were kind enough to offer me a job that enabled me to continue writing. Students in Berlin, Munich, and Regensburg aided me with their comments, movie and book tips, e-mails, and performatist term papers. Finally, for their friendship and moral support while I was working on this project I would like to thank Franziska Havemann, Marco Klüh, and Galina Vondraček.

Raoul Eshelman
Hausmehring (Upper Bavaria)
November 2007

Chapter 1

Performatism, or the End of Postmodernism
(*American Beauty*)

Performatism may be defined most simply as an epoch in which a unified concept of sign and strategies of closure have begun to compete directly with – and displace – the split concept of sign and the strategies of boundary transgression typical of postmodernism. In postmodernism – as hardly needs to be explained in great detail any more – the formal closure of the art work is continually being undermined by narrative or visual devices that create an immanent, inescapable state of undecidability regarding the truth status of some part of that work. Hence a postmodern building might create its own peculiar architectonic effect by placing an art nouveau swirl next to a modernist right angle, ironically suggesting that it is obligated to both styles and to neither. And, a postmodern novel or movie might present two equally plausible, parallel plot lines that remain undecidable within the confines of the work. Turning to a higher authorial position to solve this quandary is of little help. For the authorial intent behind the work is what is responsible for this inner undecidability in the first place: it simply sends us back to our point of departure. To escape this conundrum, we are forced to turn outside it – to an open, uncontrollable context. Author, work, and reader all tumble into an endless regress of referral that has no particular fix point, goal, or center.

This strategy has a direct theoretical counterpart in Derrida's deconstruction of Kant's ergon, the presumed center or essence of the work.[1] Derrida shows that any talk of intrinsic aesthetic value depends on that value being set off from the "extraneous" context around it by means of a frame. The frame, which at first seems an ornamental afterthought to the painting, reveals itself as its crucial, undecidable precondition; it is that place which is both inside and out, where text and context meet in a way that is both absolutely crucial to the work's makeup and impossible to determine in advance. Any claim that a painting, text, or building is unified and closed can easily be shown to fall into this same trap. Through the frame, the presumed closure of the work is always already dependent on the context around it, which is itself everything other than a coherent whole. Thus even if the work's creator did somehow manage to create a unified effect, it would, through the frame, already be dependent on some aspect of the context around it. Any way you look at it, the prospects for creating a new, autonomous monist aesthetic are nil – at least from the standpoint of the dominant postmodern and poststructuralist mindset.

Performatist Framing

Given this basic – and epistemologically well-founded – suspicion of concepts like intrinsic inner space, closure, and unity, how do performatist works go about establishing a new oneness without falling into old metaphysical traps? The answer lies in a new, radical empowerment of the frame using a blend of aesthetic and archaic, forcible devices. Performatist works are set up in such a way that the reader or viewer at first has no choice but to opt for a single, compulsory solution to the problems raised within the work at hand. The author, in other words, imposes a certain solution on us using dogmatic, ritual, or some other coercive means. This has two immediate effects. The coercive frame cuts us off, at least temporarily, from the context around it and forces us back into the work. Once we are inside, we are made to identify with some person, act or situation in a way that is plausible only within the confines of the work as a whole. In this way performatism gets to have its postmetaphysical cake and eat it too. On the one hand, you're practically forced to identify with something implausible or unbelievable within the frame – to *believe* in spite of yourself – but on the other, you still *feel* the coercive force causing this identification to take place, and intellectually you remain aware of the particularity of the argument at hand. Metaphysical skepticism and irony aren't eliminated, but are held in check by the frame. At the same time, the reader must always negotiate some kind of trade-off between the positive aesthetic identification and the dogmatic, coercive means used to achieve it.[2]

The forced, artificial unification of a work takes place using what I call *double framing*. This in turn breaks down into two interlocking devices that I call the *outer frame* (or *work frame*) and the *inner frame* (or *originary scene*). The outer frame imposes some sort of unequivocal resolution to the problems raised in the work on the reader or viewer. A good example of this is the conclusion of *American Beauty*, which is probably the first popular mainstream movie in a rigorously monist mode. At the end of the movie, the hero, Lester Burnham, is murdered and in effect becomes one with nature. Floating over his old neighborhood as an invisible voice, he extols the beauty of his past life and suggests that we, too, will someday come to the same conclusion after we've also died. You don't have to have studied rocket science – or deconstruction – to figure out what's fishy about this kind of argument. The film's director has arbitrarily endowed an ordinary character with supernatural powers and asked us to accept his literal and figurative point of view as the film's authoritative happy ending. As secular viewers we will be disinclined to believe that Lester can really speak to us when he's dead; as critical thinkers we will be skeptical of his claim that the petty world of middle-class America portrayed in the film is really beautiful. However, if you are at all serious about analyzing the movie as it stands, you have little choice but to accept this authorially certified argument as an indispensable part of the film as a whole.

The dogmatic implausibility of the film's outer frame or denouement does two things. It cuts us off – at least temporarily – from the endlessly open, uncontrollable context around it, and it forces us back *into* the work in order to confirm or deny Lester's odd, authoritative assertion about the beauty of life. In such a case we will encounter two basic possibilities. Either some sort of irony will undercut the outer frame from within and break up the artificially framed unity, or we will find a crucial scene (or inner frame) confirming the outer frame's coercive logic. Whether or not a "lock" or "fit" develops between outer and inner frame will determine whether we experience a work as a total object of closed identification or as an exercise in endless, ironic regress. Obviously, this opposition between the locked frame and ironic decentering is not a cut-and-dried affair. There is always a certain amount of tension between the fit between the frames and our legitimate metaphysical and ideological skepticism. However, we are now being offered a specific *choice* as to the outcome of a reading or viewing rather than being condemned from the start to a misreading or misprision.

Whereas the outer frame has an arbitrary or dogmatic quality and seems to be imposed from above, the inner frame is grounded in an *originary scene*: it reduces human behavior to what seems to be a very basic or elementary circle of unity with nature and/or with other people. Although this reduction can take place under very different external conditions, I have found that it almost invariably involves some element of what Eric Gans calls *ostensivity*. Since Gans's notion is the most elegant semiotic expression of the new monism, it's worth looking at it in more detail.[3]

Gans posits the existence of an originary scene in which two proto-humans, who up to now have no language, become involved in a po-tentially violent, uncontrollable conflict over some object – something that René Girard calls mimetic rivalry.[4] Under normal circumstances a violent struggle would result, with one protohuman asserting him-self over the other by means of physical force. In this particular case, however, one of the potential combatants emits a sound intended to represent the desired object. If the second protohuman in turn accepts this sound as a representation or substitute for the desired object, the sound becomes a sign and the conflict may be temporarily deferred. The two antagonists have transcended their animal status by agree-ing on a sign representing and temporarily replacing a bone of con-tention; through their act of spontaneous agreement they also lay the foundations for all future acts of semiosis, and hence for all culture and ritual. At the same time, because of its violence-deferring power, the ostensive sign acquires a supernatural valence. Its co-creators, who are unable to reflect on their own role in its creation, ascribe it a tran-scendent origin, or what Gans calls the name-of-God. The point is not whether the sign is *really* of divine origin; it's that the sign *could be*; it marks not only the boundary line between the human and the animal but also between the immanent, real world and an outside, possibly transcendent one. Although empirically unprovable one way or another, the transcendent explanation of the sign remains an originary fact that we, too, as secular individuals have no choice but to take seriously.[5] Finally, in his hypothetical scenario Gans suggests that the originary sign is also perceived as beautiful because it allows us to oscillate between contemplating the sign standing for the thing and the thing as it is represented by the sign. We imagine through the sign that we might possess the thing but at the same time recognize the thing's inaccessibility to us, its mediated or semiotic quality.[6]

The diagram below shows how the originary scene arises as a double frame – the inner frame of the sign makes possible the outer frame of the human, which in turn makes it possible to generate still more signs or inner frames.

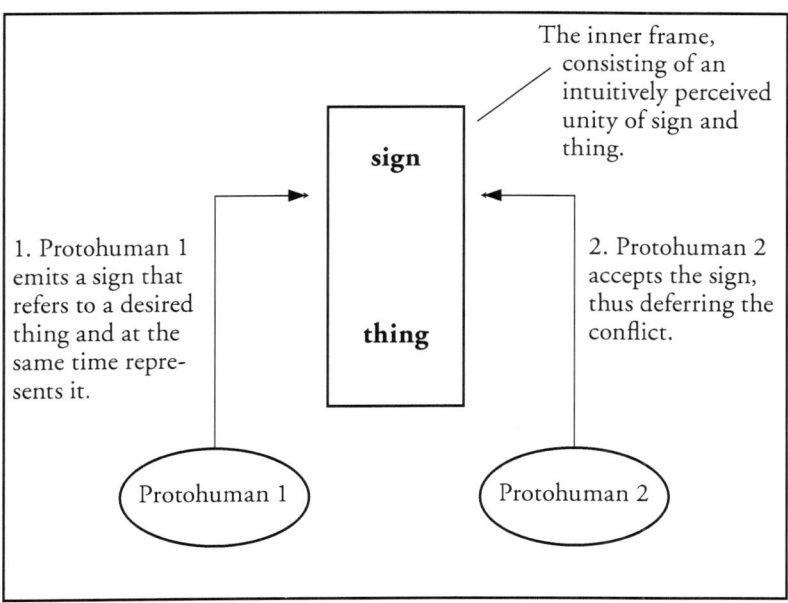

The inner frame, consisting of an intuitively perceived unity of sign and thing.

sign

thing

1. Protohuman 1 emits a sign that refers to a desired thing and at the same time represents it.

2. Protohuman 2 accepts the sign, thus deferring the conflict.

Protohuman 1

Protohuman 2

The outer frame, consisting of the newly created human collective and bounded by an unknowable transcendent outside.

It is revealing to compare the originary monist sign with the notion of double origin common to poststructuralism. A salient feature of the originary, ostensive sign is that it is has no meaning. Rather than automatically presupposing a relation with a binary opposite, as deconstructive theory requires,[7] it is a name referring first and foremost back to its own successful performance – the deferral of the imminent, potentially deadly conflict and the founding of language, cult, culture, and beauty. The ostensive sign is a *performative tautology*, a simultaneous, spontaneously generated linguistic projection that works in spite of the obvious conflicts and contradictions contained within it. Thus you could argue with a certain justification that the struggle for the desired object is only deferred, and that the multiple projection marked by the originary sign is ultimately one of mutual self-deceit. And, you could also object that the real work of culture begins only after more complex, semantic signs have been added on to the simple, originary one. All these assertions would be true. However, you would still have to concede that a synthetic, unified, object-focused projection – and not an epistemological aporia – stands at the beginning of all culture and continues to condition each individual act of language.

Although it's possible to muster both paleo-anthropological as well as ethnological evidence for Gans's hypothesis,[8] neither is crucial to my own argumentation. From my specifically aesthetic and historical point of view, the ostensive is quite simply the most elegant and parsimonious monist answer that we have to the notion of dual origin marked by différance and its many terminological cousins. The ostensive sign and the originary scene provide the minimal tool that can help us describe other monist strategies as they cut through the endless regress and irony of postmodern culture and play out new, constructed narratives of origin in contemporary narrative and thematic guises. The ostensive promises to be to the new epoch what différance was to the old one: a minimal formulation of the dominant concept of sign that manifests itself in everything from lowly pop culture to high-flown literary theory.

In the case of *American Beauty*, this originary scene centers around the white plastic bag which is filmed by Ricky Fitts and which later floats through the air during Lester's farewell address. As Ricky's utterances make clear, he sees in the bag nothing less than an embodiment of the divine:

> It was one of those days when it's a minute away from snowing. And there's this electricity in the air, you can almost hear it, right? And this bag was just... dancing with me. Like a little kid begging me to play with it. For fifteen minutes. That's the day I realized that there was this entire life behind things, and this incredibly benevolent force that wanted me to know there was no reason to be afraid. Ever.[9]

It's also important to remember that Ricky shares Lester's complete tranquility of mind as well as his specific way of partaking of the world's beauty in all its plenitude (Ricky: "Sometimes there's so much beauty in the world I feel like I can't take it... and my heart is going to cave in"; Lester: "[...] it's hard to stay mad, when there's so much beauty in the world. Sometimes I feel like I'm seeing it all at once, and it's too much, my heart fills up like a balloon that's about to burst..."[10]). Obviously, the scene with the white plastic bag doesn't display literally all the features of the ostensive as described by Gans. Ricky and Jane are lovers and not antagonists, and the plastic bag is only the filmed reproduction of the original which Ricky plays again because he "needs to remember."[11] However, the scene still embodies a basic unifying, thing-oriented projection shared by Ricky, Jane and, ultimately, Lester (in fact, you could maintain that Lester actually *is* the plastic bag, since he becomes one with that animate, divine principle of which Ricky has spoken earlier).

Now, you *could* argue that the plastic bag is nothing more than a cheap token of the consumer culture that is satirized elsewhere in the film and that Ricky is simply projecting his own wishful thinking onto it. In terms of a purely epistemological critique you would even be *right*. The problem remains, however, that within the total frame of the work this wishful thinking is confirmed on a higher, authorial level in Lester's farewell speech as well as in terms of plot, when he passes into an animate, beautiful, and comforting nature. If you insist on rejecting the basic premise contained in both the inner and outer frame, you'll find yourself in an unpleasant bind. You'll have "exposed" the work on a dispassionate epistemological level but you'll have missed out on the aesthetic mixture of pleasure and anguish derived from identifying with central characters and scenes.

Even the tragic denouement – Lester's murder by Colonel Fitts – doesn't suffice to break up the movie's immanent argumentation. In effect, Colonel Fitts murders Lester because he follows his liberating example – and is then disappointed to discover that Lester isn't a closet homosexual like himself. The problem is not that Colonels Fitts is evil; it's that he doesn't find the right "fit" within the frame of the movie's world (his violent "fit" is the flip side of this disappointment). *American Beauty*, like all performatist works I'll be discussing in the following pages, is set towards metaphysical optimism. Even though crucial events in it may be violent or have an annihilating effect on individual characters, both perpetrators and victims have the chance of fitting into a greater, redemptive whole, even if the time and point of entry may be deferred for certain characters.

Performatist Subjectivity

Because of its focus on unity, performatism also allows for a new, positively conceived – but not unproblematic – type of subjectivity. As a reaction to the plight of the postmodern subject, who is constantly being pulled apart and misled by signs in the surrounding context, the performatist subject is constructed in such a way that it is dense or opaque relative to its milieu. This opacity is, admittedly, ambivalent, since it achieves a closed unity at the expense of participation in a viable social environment of some kind. Moreover, the closed, opaque subject runs the risk of incurring the enmity of its surroundings by virtue of its very singularity and inscrutability. In some cases, this can be resolved – as in the originary scene – by spontaneously arriving at a common projection together with a potential opponent. This may be expressed as a *reconciliatory, amatory,* or *erotic scene,* depending on the circumstances. However, if the milieu turns violently against the singular subject, we will have a *sacrificial scene* that results not

only in the subject's elimination from the frame but also in its deification, in its being made a focal point of identification and imitation for
other characters or the reader/viewer after it has been expelled from
the scene.[12] Essentially, this is what happens to Lester. His "senseless" hedonist behavior is successfully imitated by Colonel Fitts – who
then makes Lester the scapegoat for their lack of sexual compatibility.
Shortly before his death, Lester himself transcends his original hedo-
nism by not seducing Angela; in death he becomes a narrating deity at
one with the outer frame of the movie as a whole.

I can't emphasize enough that in performatism the subject's newly won opacity or denseness is constructed and doesn't represent a
natural, pre-existing essence. Sometimes this constructedness is intentional – as in the case of Lester, who deliberately sets out to act
like a teenager. However, it can also be completely involuntary, as in
the Russian movie *The Cuckoo* (*Kukushka*),[13] where circumstances
throw together three people who speak three different languages. As
a result, they are unable to communicate with one another except
through ostensive signs, which is to say by pointing at present objects
and trying to arrive at a common projection or meaning beneath the
threshold of conventional, semantically organized language. In these
and other cases the constructed singularity is fairly trivial or even accidental – acting like a teenager or not happening to speak someone
else's language are not positive traits in themselves. Performatism,
while reinstituting the subject as a *construct*, doesn't ascribe it any
particular idealized or essential features before the fact. If the conditions are however right – and the metaphysical optimism of the
new aesthetic tacitly ensures that they are – such subjects can become
figures of identification. This identification can appear in a multitude of guises, but the structure of the ostensive scene suggests two
basic possibilities: the subject can be involved in a sacrificial act that
transcends the narrow frame of the self and invites emulation by others, or the subject can transcend itself and enter into a reconciliatory,
amatory, or erotic relationship with another subject who reciprocates
that move in some way. This singular, identificatory performance, in
turn, invites others to emulate it at a later point in time and under
different circumstances.

It is also worth noting that the notion of constructed subjectivity is not just reserved for fictional schemes. It has a very real counterpart in Erving Goffman's "frame analysis" which studies ritualized micro-situations in everyday life.[14] Like Derrida, Goffman proceeds from an ironic and sometimes rather cynical metaposition from which he demonstrates the unpredictable and ultimately uncontrollable shifts of reference between different codes or frames (what he calls "key-ing"[15]). However, unlike Derrida, Goffman also makes very clear that everyday human interaction is rooted in what one observer called a "common focus on a physical scene of action"[16] prior to language. For Goffman, language is always anchored in some way in such scenes by means of indexical or deictic signs ("that there," "this here" etc.) not immediately applicable to other situations. And, unlike the Der-ridean approach, which begins and ends with a notion of frame-as-paradox, Goffman's is generative and originary: he suggests the ex-istence of "primary frameworks" out of which develop still further, more complex frames or modulations of those frames. These primary frameworks are especially interesting for performatism because they allow us to make an initial decision about events in reality and ren-der "what would otherwise be a meaningless aspect of the scene into something that is meaningful."[17] The frameworks include an explicit sacral dimension, the "astounding complex," which suggests that the first question we ask about any unusual action or event is whether it might have a supernatural origin.[18] Other primary frameworks re-late to "stunts" (whether an action is a well-executed performance or trick) "flubs" (whether an action is a mistake) "fortuitousness" (whether an action is a matter of luck) and what Goffman calls "ten-sion" (whether an action involving the body has an officially con-doned social character or a sexual, proscribed one).[19] The frameworks help us decide, for example, whether the quick upward movement of someone's right arm is a religious blessing, a move in sport, an ac-cident, or a natural reflex.

As Goffman emphasizes, however, several frameworks can come into consideration at any one time, and the transformations of the basic frames or codes – their "keying" – makes it virtually impossible to limit any action to a fixed, one-to-one relation. Goffman's frames, although not stable points of reference are, however, more than just the accidental, transient incisions in the stream of human discourse envisioned by Derrida. In fact, you could say that they are anchored in reality in a way comparable to Eric Gans's notion of the originary scene, which is based on a spontaneous agreement to defer mimetic rivalry through the emission of an ostensive sign (also a kind of index sign pointing to a concrete, present thing and surrounded by a minimal frame of social consensus). Taken this way, the ostensive scene would provide the originary ground missing from Goffman's theory, which does not try to explain how the "astounding complex" came about in the first place, or why it is even a *primus inter pares* within its own category.[20] Conversely, Goffman's theory and observations serve to remind us that ritual and sacrality continue to play a key role in everyday life.

Goffman's notion of frames is also useful in thinking about performatist subjectivity and plot development. At first, Goffman's subject might appear to be purely postmodern – the mere effect of a multitude of overlapping and shifting frames not reducible to one single kernel or core. However, the "Goffperson" is never so consumed by the discourse it uses so much as to lose all sense of orientation or decorum.[21] As Goffman dryly remarks at the beginning of *Frame Analysis*, "all the world is not a stage."[22] Just because we slip in and out of complex sets of overlapping roles doesn't mean that we get hopelessly lost in them, or that fact and fiction are *really* equivalent, or that the *possibility* that something can be fabricated means that our everyday faith in it must be vitiated. Our ability to find a firm "footing" or "anchoring" (Goffman's terms) in social interaction is possible because, unlike the poststructuralists, Goffman also sees social frames in a ritual, sacral dimension.[23] This is rather different from a commonsense, namby-pamby trust in convention which a poststructuralist would have no problem confirming as a fact of social life. Indeed, Goffman, following Durkheim, goes so far as to say that social interaction hinges on a tacit agreement in everyday interactions to deify individual subjects: "Many gods have been done away with, but the individual himself stubbornly remains as a deity of considerable importance."[24] Society, in other words, is held together by individual subjects using frames in a way that both enhance their own "divine" status and uphold the decorum necessary to allow others to do the same. This Durkheimian theme, which suggests that originary or archaic religion has a social, rather than a cognitive, function, and that secular society's functional underpinnings are ultimately religious, can be found explicitly in monist thinkers like Gans and Sloterdijk and implicitly in many performatist narratives.[25]

By citing Goffman I don't want to suggest that performatist plots are more realistic or sociologically true to life than postmodern ones. Performatist plots are however very often centered on breaches of a frame that lead to a subject's being deified either in the transcendent, literal sense – as in *American Beauty* – or in a more figurative, social one. One interesting example of the latter is Thomas Vinterberg's Dogma 95 movie *The Celebration*, in which the main protagonist disrupts the frame of a family gathering to accuse his father of having molested him as a child. By sacrificing himself – by placing himself at the center of attention and repeatedly causing himself to be expelled from the family celebration – he eventually brings the other family members over to his side; the father, by now himself demonized, is forced permanently out of the family circle.[26] These cases demonstrate what I call a *narrative performance*: it marks the ability of a subject to transcend a frame in some way, usually by breaking through it at some point and/or reversing its basic parameters (in *The Celebration* the son doesn't replace the father at the center of power; having forced out the patriarch, he opts to remain on the periphery of the family group). A good formal definition of the "performance" in performatism is that it *demonstrates with aesthetic means the possibility of transcending the conditions of a given frame* (whether in a "realistic," social or psychological mode or in a fantastic, preternatural one).

At this point, a good deconstructionist would interject that if this is so, then the ultimate proof of a performatist work would be its ability to transcend itself, i.e., to become something entirely different from what it was to begin with. In purely epistemological terms this objection is irrefutable. However, it misses the point. For the new epoch works first and foremost on an aesthetic, identificatory level, to create an attitude of beautiful belief, and not on a cognitive, critical one. If the performance is successful, then the reader too will identify with it more or less involuntarily – even if he or she still remains incredulous about its basic premises. The reader is "framed" in such a way that belief trumps cognition.

Theist Plots

Because of its emphasis on transcending coercive frames rather than continually transgressing porous, constantly shifting boundaries (as is the case in postmodernism), performatism acquires a distinctly *theist* cast. The basic plot common to all theist theologies is that a personified male creator sets up a frame (the world) into which he plunks inferior beings made in his own image; their task is in turn is to transcend the frame and return to unify with the creator by imitating his perfection in some particular way. Deism, by contrast, suggests that there is a breakdown of some kind in a unified origin which in turn generates signs whose traces human beings must follow back to their source; the basic plot structure is one of tracking signs in their feminine formlessness and not imitating a transcendent father-figure or phallus. I don't wish to launch once more into the frequently made comparison between postmodernism/poststructuralism and gnosticism or the Cabbala. Rather, I would like to focus on how the new monist aesthetic revives theist myths and reworks them in contemporary settings. Like other such performatist appropriations these are obligated first to the logic of an aesthetic, authorial imperative and only secondarily (if at all) to a dogmatic source. Performatism is an aesthetic reaction to postmodernism's one-sidedly deist bias and not an old time camp meeting.

Since there are countless variants on the main theist plot I'll restrict my remarks to five patterns that have been appearing regularly in the last few years: *playing God; escaping from a frame; returning to the father; transcending through self-sacrifice;* and *perfecting the self.* These plot constructs are almost invariably ironic in the sense that they couple an archaic theist myth with contemporary, secular twists that don't jive well with received dogma. Performatism, in other words, creates a secondary, aesthetically motivated dogma and makes it into the outer frame of a particular work. Although the irony of this dogma is always apparent – its dogmatism is invariably a created, artificial one running counter to tradition – it doesn't vitiate itself or "cross itself out" by virtue of this contradiction. Rather, as indicated earlier, it points the viewer or reader back into the work itself to inner scenes which in turn create a tautological lock or bind with the fixed outer premise. The difference between postmodern and performatist works is not that one is ironic and the other is not. Rather, it's that performatist irony is internal, circular, or scenic: it keeps you focused on a set, "dogmatically" defined discrepancy rather than casting you out into an infinite regress of belated misjudgments of what is going on in and around the work.

In terms of plot, *playing God* is perhaps the most direct way of emulating a transcendent, personified source. A fine example of this is the movie *Amelie*, in which the eponymous heroine sets up little, contrived situations that help unhappy people change their lives for the better (or, in one case, to punish a despotic bully). In contrast to what one might expect from religious tradition, this doesn't lead to acts of hubris and abuse of power on the part of Amelie. Quite the contrary: although she is successfully able to help others with her little traps, she isn't able to find true love herself. Only after her friends and co-workers conspire to apply her tactics to her herself is she able to get together with a monist Mr. Right (whose hobby consists of making ripped-up representations whole – he pastes together pictures torn up and discarded by people using automatic photo machines in train stations). Playing God, in other words, only works after a group has imitated the theist creatrix and projected her own strategy back onto herself. The theist, active role is dependent on its acceptance and reapplication by a social collective.

This basic problem of playing God – that even as a self-appointed creator you can't create happiness for yourself and others by fiat – is treated at length in Lars von Trier's Dogma 95 movie *Idiots*. There, a group of young Danes living together in a commune go about their town pretending to be social workers taking care of mentally retarded patients. At first the group's excursions serve little more than to expose the vanity and insecurity of bourgeois existence by transgressing against basic social decorum – a plot device that is still entirely in keeping with postmodernism's favoring of critical simulation over smug projections about what is "real." As the movie moves on, though, it becomes clear that the real aim of the group is a kind of radical self-therapy. The ultimate goal proclaimed by the group's messianistic leader is not to shock total strangers by simulating mental retardation at the most embarrassing possible moment – and thus simply to confirm your own otherness – but to do so in your *own* familial and social sphere. Ultimately, the only member of the group who succeeds in doing this is a shy, insecure young woman who has just lost her baby. By drooling and slobbering like a retarded child at her stiff, unfeeling family's coffee hour she creates an ostensive sign of solidarity with the dead infant while at the same time breaking with the emotional indifference of her insufferable bourgeois family. This transcendent narrative performance aimed at establishing a sense of self – and not the theist imperative per se – is what makes the work performative.

Another well-established theist plot device is *escaping from a frame*, analogous to the task that a monotheist God places before people trapped in the world of His making. The work of art closest to this archetype is undoubtedly the Canadian cult movie *Cube*, in which seven people find themselves placed for no apparent reason in a gigantic labyrinth of cubes which they have to get out of before they starve to death. The only person who succeeds is, significantly, autistic; he is someone who is socially dysfunctional while having the surest sense of his own self. (The positive reduction of subjectivity to a minimal, invulnerable core of selfhood is impossible in postmodernism, where the subject can experience itself only in terms of *other* signs set by an infinitely receding symbolic Other.) This ubiquitous plot device linking transcendence and the overcoming of closed space can be found in a whole slew of works that will be treated in more detail later in the book; these include the movies *Panic Room* and *Russian Ark* (Chapter Three) as well as Yann Martel's *Life of Pi* and Olga Tokarczuk's short story "Hotel Capital" (Chapter Two).

A more personified, gender-specific variant of the same myth is the plot involving a *return to the Father* (or the *Mother*, as the case may be[27]). As a rule, in performatism we find highly constructed fa-ther-son relationships involving a parity or reversal of strength rather than the oppressive, phallic rule of the Father assumed by Lacan and his feminist interpreters. The most notable example of a constructed return is the movie version of *Cider House Rules*, in which the father-figure, Dr. Larch, uses his position as director of an orphanage to set up one of his charges, Homer Wells, as an ersatz-son. Both part ways over a typical theist dilemma – the son thinks that Dr. Larch's practice of performing abortions means playing God in a negative sense. However, both are reconciled after Homer is himself forced to play God and choose between performing an abortion and delivering an incestuously conceived child. Armed with a phony CV concocted by Dr. Larch, who has in the meantime died, Homer completes the cycle and returns to head the orphanage as a new, benevolent theist creator/destroyer.

A positive transfer of power between fathers and sons is also evi-dent in Ingo Schulze's *Simple Stories* (see Chapter Two) as well as in movies like *The Celebration* and *American Beauty*. In the latter, the true father-figure of the movie turns out to be Ricky Fitts, whom both Lester and Colonel Fitts imitate (Lester takes dope-dealing Ricky as his hedonist idol and the Colonel tries to imitate his son's presumed affair with Lester). In the fictional world of the movie, both these projections are psychologically false but have a metaphysically true focus: Ricky, in spite of his cynical hobbies, is a kind of living portal to God and beauty. As he himself says regarding his video of a dead homeless woman: "When you see something like that, it's like God is looking right at you, just for a second. And if you're careful, you can look right back." And what he sees when he looks right back is "beauty."[28] Evidently, a basic metaphysical optimism is at work here suggesting that it is always possible for sons to reverse positions of rela-tive weakness vis-à-vis their fathers or Father. Ricky's ability to look back at God would be impossible in a Lacanian or Foucauldian world where the Gaze or panoptical vision can never be returned in any sort of adequate, let alone aesthetically satisfying way.[29]

Another important performatist plot motif is that of *transcend-ing through self-sacrifice*. In postmodernism, the victim is always the peripheralized other of a hegemonial, oppressive center; the victim more or less automatically acquires moral and epistemological superiority by virtue of its decentered, peripatetic status as the near helpless target of whatever force the center exerts on it.[30] In performatism, victims are once more *centered*; that is, we are made to focus on them as objects of positive identification rather than as markers of endlessly receding alterity and resistance. Here as elsewhere in the new monism, this recentering is itself an eccentric move that is markedly at odds with religious tradition.

Two of the most radical exponents of sacrificial centering are the Dogma 95 directors Lars von Trier and Thomas Vinterberg. In Vinterberg's *The Celebration* it is the suicide of the hero's sister that motivates his own less drastic act of exposing himself to public embarrassment; in this way the absent, absolute victim is once more recentered in a way that makes her sacrifice negotiable with the collective – and allows the expulsion of the morally debased patriarch from its midst. Thus the traditional mediating role of Christ – the hero's name is Christian, in case anyone has missed the point – is expanded to include a unity of male and female working towards the common goal of evacuating a corrupt, exploitative center. Similarly, almost every movie made by Lars von Trier centers around acts of female self-sacrifice. The most drastic example is his auteur tearjerker *Dancer in the Dark*, where we are set up in a deliberately heavy-handed way to identify with the final sacrificial transaction of the heroine – trading off her own life to save the sight of her son. A complete reversal in terms of plot construction is von Trier's no-less dogmatic *Dogville*, where a female victim is able to return to a fatherly center of criminal power – and responds by promptly wiping out her tormentors down to the last man, woman, and child.

As is the case with the father-son relationship, performatism suggests a *reversibility* of center-periphery or victim-perpetrator positions that isn't possible in postmodernism, where alterity leads to victimization and victimization to still more alterity (and where nobody in his or her right mind would even bother to identify with the "hegemonial" center). Generally speaking, performatism is no less critical of abuses of power in the center than is postmodernism. However, it recognizes the *identificatory* value of sacrificial centering that is completely alien to the ethos of postmodernism, which can only conceive of viable moral positions being established on the run and on the periphery of the social order. Performatism, by contrast, allows for a centering that establishes a proximity between victims and perpetrators – and allows perpetrators, too, to become the object of reader or viewer identification. In Chapter Two I will treat a typical postmodern victimary scenario, Ali Smith's *Hotel World* and its performatist antipode, Olga Tokarczuk's "The Hotel Capital," and examine the moral problems involved in a framed erotic relationship between victim and perpetrator in my discussion of Bernhard Schlink's *The Reader*.

Performatist plots don't necessarily have to tap into Western, monotheist myths. A plot pattern in works drawing on Easter philosophy and religion is that of *perfecting the self*, usually in the sense of communing with an animate nature or entering or approaching Nirvana. This takes place most explicitly in Jim Jarmusch's movie *Ghost Dog* and Viktor Pelevin's novel *Buddha's Little Finger*,[31] which is arguably the most important work of post-Soviet fiction in Russia to date. In *Ghost Dog* the eponymous hero, a black ghetto dweller, adheres rigidly to the Samurai code of the *Hagakure* requiring absolute obeisance to a "master"; in this case, circumstances have obligated him to serve a low-level Mafia family member as a hired killer. Even after he has been betrayed by his mafia employers (whom he then systematically eliminates), his strict code of honor doesn't allow him to betray his "master," who in the end shoots him without the hero offering any resistance. Before deliberately sacrificing himself, Ghost Dog however manages to pass on his code of honor to a small girl who will presumably continue to develop it in a less violent way. Ghost Dog can only develop so far within the confines of a rigidly framed self, which the hero voluntarily gives up after its possibilities have been expended; his conscious self-sacrifice serves to further the perfection of the world as a whole.[32] At the end of Pelevin's novel, by contrast, the hero and his sidekick leave a burlesque, dually constructed world and enter directly into Nirvana (a plot resolution repeated in many other of his works). Many readers choose to ignore these authoritative monist resolutions and treat his novels and stories as exercises in undecidable postmodern irony. However, it would seem that he is entirely serious in his desire to force readers to adopt a Buddhist mindset – if only within an aesthetic frame that flirts with the possibility of converting the reader in real life.

Theist Narrative

Because of their dogmatic posture performatist narratives create certain odd configurations that stand out against the background of both traditional and postmodern story-telling techniques. One of the most curious such devices is first-person authorial narration, an "impossible" device in which a narrator equipped with powers similar to those of an all-powerful, omniscient author forces his or her own authoritative point of view upon us in what is usually a circular or tautological way. [33] A prime example of this can be found in the narrative structure of *American Beauty*. At the film's beginning we see the bird's-eye view of a small town and hear a detached, almost meditative voice saying: "My name is Lester Burnham. This is my neighborhood. This is my street. This... is my life. I'm forty-two years old. In less than a year I'll be dead." As the first scene of the film appears, Lester's voice adds: "Of course, I don't know that yet."[34] Lester's tranquility is made possible by the holism of the narrative framework, which is oblivious to the difference between implicit author and character – and hence to death itself.

In this way even the evacuation or destruction of characters serves to strengthen the whole; after his murder by Colonel Fitts Lester dissolves into the authorial frame, from which he reemerges to introduce the story from a personal perspective in which he is again murdered. The act of narrating itself becomes a circular, enclosed act of belief that cannot be made the object of a metaphysical critique or deconstruction without destroying the substance of the work itself (*Life of Pi*, which is treated at length in Chapter Two, has a similar structure, as does Ian McEwan's *Atonement*[35]). The narrative is constructed in such a way that the viewer has no choice but to transcend his or her own disbelief and accept the performance represented by the film as a kind of aesthetically mediated apriori. This transformation of the viewing or reading process into an involuntary act of belief stands in direct contrast to the postmodern mode of the virtual, where the observer can't believe *anything* because ontological parameters like author, narrator, and character have been dissolved in an impenetrable web of paradoxical assignations and cross-references (as happens to the hapless private detective Quinn in Paul Auster's *City of Glass*).

In terms of reader response, performatist narratives must create an ironclad construct whose inner lock or fit cannot be broken by the reader without destroying the work as a whole. The performatist narrative, in other words, *makes you decide* for a certain posture vis-à-vis the text, whereas the no less manipulative postmodern device of undecidability *keeps you from deciding* what posture to take. The master of this "idiot-proof" narrative form in performatism is Viktor Pelevin, who revels in tricking readers into assuming positions that turn out to be Buddhist ones forcing them to transcend their everyday secular mindset. Of these, the most insidious is perhaps the (as of now untranslated) short story "Tambourine of the Lower World."[36] There the reader, in the course of a rambling monologue on Brezhnev, light rays, mirrors, and death, is encouraged to memorize the curious phrase contained in the title. At the end of the story the narrator reveals that he has constructed a prismatic device activated precisely by this phrase and focusing a mental death ray on the reader; the ray may however be deactivated by sending 1,000 dollars to a dubious-sounding address. Those who treat this threat as a joke are encouraged to "divide up your time into hours and try not to think of the phrase 'tambourine of the lower world' for exactly sixty seconds."[37] As in most of his other short stories, Pelevin forces the reader to enter involuntarily into the Buddhist project of transcending the material world entirely; in addition, the story demonstrates the impossibility of forgetting a mental image or projection after it has been framed within a short span of time.

Many readers still consider Pelevin to be postmodern because of his narrative playfulness and satirical jabs at post-Soviet society; they also distrust the motives of the real-life author, who undeniably indulges in self-mystification. However, a wealth of stories – including "serious" ones likes his "Ontology of Childhood"[38] – makes clear that his focus remains consistently on the Buddhist goal of self-annihilation and not on the eternal regress of the subject common to postmodernism. Thus in the short story "Hermit and Six-Toes"[39] we are party to a series of mystical dialogues pertaining to life in what seems to be a dismal prison camp. Towards the end of the story we discover however that the two protagonists are chickens who are eventually able to "transcend" by training themselves to fly out of their pen. Here, as in many other cases in performatism, we are forced to occupy a superior, theist perspective towards "lower" characters. The manifest ability of these lower characters to transcend is then reflected back onto us as a performative imperative: as a challenge to become something completely different from what we are now. (This device can be found in *American Beauty* as well as the Coen Brothers' *The Man Who Wasn't There*, which I'll examine in greater detail in Chapter Three.)

Obviously, not all performatist narratives depend on these kind of one-shot tricks ascribing impossible acts of transcendence to narrators, characters, and texts. However, even in "realistic" works we can observe that first-person narrators and central, weak characters tend to become invested with more and more authorial authority as the work progresses – a development that is directly at odds with the tendency of postmodern heroes and heroines to unravel, split up, or dissolve in outside contexts (and with the tendency of the authorial positions accompanying them to do the same). Because the analysis of psychologically motivated narrative in performatism requires a careful consideration of character development as a whole, I'll return to the problem of authorial empowerment of "weak" characters in more detail in my treatments of individual literary works, most notably Ingo Schulze's *Simple Stories* and Bernhard Schlink's *The Reader* as well as Olga Tokarczuk's "The Hotel Capital" (Chapter Two).

Theist Creation in Architecture and the Visual Arts

The theist mode is not only active in narrative, but manifests itself strikingly in architectonic structures suggesting that the omnipotent hand of a higher being is at work – an architect playing God rather than playing hard to get, as is the case in postmodernism. As in performatist narrative, the basic aim of this new kind of architecture is to evoke a constructed or artificial experience of transcendence in the viewer; you are supposed to feel the powerful, preterhuman hand of the architect rather than reflect on the interplay of ornamentally familiar forms, as in postmodernism, or be transformed by a compelling functional principle, as in modernism. I have isolated at least nine different devices that the new architecture uses to impress this sublime feeling of transcendence upon the viewer; they'll be discussed in more detail in Chapter Four. For the time being it will suffice to note that most can be subsumed under the concept of what might be called "transcendent functionalism" or "transcendent ornamentalism." Performatist architecture takes individual spatial features or forms that are already familiar from architectural history and uses them in a way that accentuates the possibility of the impossible rather than ironic knowledge of the undecidable. Hence in the new architectures building parts may move (static becomes dynamic), triangular structures are tilted (stable becomes unstable), a glass, purely ornamental facade is placed in front of the real facade (a solid plane dematerializes), or egg or oval shapes are employed (suggesting imperfect originary wholeness rather than rigid geometric functionality). Large chunks may also be sliced out of a building (suggesting the hand of a theist creator); empty frames may imply the act of theist construction as such while transcending the opposition between inside and out. Instead of irony and play we are confronted with a "saturated," paradoxical experience of sublimity and beauty that forces us to change our intuitive perception of seemingly quotidian "givens."[40] Buildings of this kind may seem to point at, topple on, aim at, or otherwise threaten their users even as they suggest the possibility of a transcendent, incomprehensible force at work. Simple, but no longer rigidly geometric forms like ovals or lemon shapes suggest originary harmony and beauty rather than functional, mathematically dictated rigor. These structures can be said to *perform* in the sense that they induce us to experience these sublime feelings using obviously constructed, artificial means. This sublimity is in turn *postmetaphysical*; it is the result of specifically aesthetic, artificial strategies and need not have any specific theological pretensions.

In the visual arts, performatism has developed in reaction to concept art and what is often called anti-art, both of which one-sidedly dominated the art scene from the 1970s well into the 1990s. In a way comparable to that of narrative performatism, performatist art and photography visually bracket off concept and context and force viewers to accept the inner givens of the work at hand. Unlike modernism, where certain qualities such as flatness, abstraction, or reduction were considered essential expressions of beauty, in performatism these inner givens are constructs that are not reducible to any essential qualities. In turn, these constructs are forced on the viewer in such a way that he or she has no choice but to accept their autonomy from a context – which is to say their aestheticity. Vanessa Beecroft's closed, obsessive-compulsive nude performances, Thomas Demand's photographs of evocative cardboard interiors, and the action-packed, but weirdly incomprehensible paintings of Neo Rauch all share this same basic set towards reality. The inner space of the painting/photo/performance creates a new way of seeing or experiencing the world that can at first only be experienced in terms of a constructed aesthetic interior. If accepted by the viewer, this interiority may then be projected back onto the outside contexts around it. Interiority, then, determines context and not the other way around. Just how this works in visual, rather than narrative, terms will be discussed in greater detail in Chapter Six.

Performatist Sex

In performatism there is a markedly different approach to sex and gender than is the case in postmodernism and poststructuralism. Poststructuralist theory, of course, emphasizes the primacy of belated, constructed, heterogeneous sexual role-playing (gender) over preexisting, binarily defined corporeal identity (sex). And, as usual, poststructuralism confronts us with an epistemological critique of essentialism or naturalization that at first glance seems hard to beat. Here we would appear to have two choices. The first is to dissolve sexuality and corporeality into an endless, unstable regress of discursive assignations – the happy hunting grounds of deconstruction and postfeminism. The second is to stipulate exactly what the natural, preexisting features of sexuality would be in every case – an impossible task considering that the very signs we need to do this continually contaminate the presumably natural essence of sexuality with our own belatedly acquired cultural biases. The question arises as to how a monist concept of sexuality is possible that doesn't achieve unity by positing a neat fit between the stable, heterosexually founded binary opposition between male and female.

The key to performatist sexuality lies once more in double framing, in creating an artificial unity that forces us to accept temporarily the validity of peculiar sexual or erotic constructs while making them the focus of our involuntary identification. Here as elsewhere it's useful to take a quick look at postmodern theory and practice before turning to the alternative offered by performatism. In postfeminist theory (as exemplified by Judith Butler), a dominant, heterosexual field of power is thought to project its unified, hegemonic imperative onto subjects presenting heterogeneous substrates not reducible to a simple binary scheme of male/female. Due to the sheer force exerted by the hegemonic matrix resistance to this compartmentalization can take place only in weak, by definition unsuccessful performances that manage to turn some of the dominant system's coercive energy against itself without really placing it in doubt. The real discursive achievement is located less in the performance itself (which is a function of the dominant power matrix) than in a melancholy, metaphysically pessimistic metaposition that unflinchingly records the insufficiency of simulatory resistance while at the same time touting it as the only possible means of undermining the "heterosexual matrix." Ali Smith's *Hotel World*, which I use as a foil for a discussion of performatism in Chapter Two, has made this postfeminist metaposition into its main narrative premise.

Performatism as I understand it is less an ideological reaction to postfeminism than a strategic one. The point of performatism is not to roll back multifarious gender constellations into good old binary sex, but rather to frame or construct them in such a way that they stand out positively within the framework of the "heterosexual matrix" (or whatever other dominant power structure happens to be at hand). The main strategy involved in this is *centering the other*. Instead of automatically equating the other with the marginal and the weak, performatism takes otherness and plops it directly into the middle of the interlocked frames I've already discussed above. Thus at the social center of *American Beauty* we find the "two Jims" – a hearty, healthy, happy gay pair who because of their unified, but plural, gendering can be all things to all characters (they chat about cultivating roses with Caroline and give tips on physical fitness to Lester). Many critics have noted how this positive portrayal of a gay partnership amidst manifestly unhappy heterosexual marriages parodies middle-class suburban values. However, from a performatist perspective it's even more important to emphasize that the two Jims also overcome the violent tension inherent in what Girard calls mimetic rivalry. As doubles in both name and sexual orientation, one would normally expect the two Jims at some point to incur the wrath of the collective (in Girardian thinking, twins and doubles embody the mimetic, contagious violence which society must constantly seek to assuage by victimizing scapegoats). In this case, though, exactly the opposite is true: the two Jims serve as a model not just for characters like Lester and Caroline but also, it would seem, for Colonel Fitts; the success of their relationship holds forth the promise of a successful "partnership" between the Colonel and Lester.

American Beauty takes the sameness contained in homosexual otherness and makes it the unified center of its metaphysical universe; mimesis becomes a positive, reconciliatory mechanism and not a dangerous, competitive one. Colonel Fitts doesn't murder Lester because of mimetic rivalry with someone else; he murders him because he is a disappointed lover – the most believable extenuating circumstance you can have in a metaphysically optimistic universe. By framing and centering homosexual relationships in this way – by giving them a "divine," privileged position vis-à-vis heterosexual ones – *American Beauty* suggests a world in which gender and sex can be transcended entirely. Whether or not this will ever take place in the real world is entirely another matter. However, the performance marking it is centered for all to see, and its aesthetic mediation can make it palatable even to those who find the union of two same-sexed individuals distasteful in real life.

This centering of otherness in performatism applies not only to role-playing and gender, but also to genitalia and genetics. The standard argument advanced in this regard by Butler and other postfeminists is to freely acknowledge the existence of genetic and corporeal influence on discursively determined gender. However, close on the heels of this concession follows a clause effectively rendering it void. For if genetics and the body do act upon discourse, it is then our solemn epistemological duty to determine the exact point where this influence sets in – and that is something we can only do with the help of more heaping portions of non-natural discourse. Arguments supporting a corporeal or genetic privileging of nature over culture can then be neatly disposed of by pointing out the impossibility of ever being able to conceive of corporeality entirely outside of a continually proliferating, uncontrollable discourse that you yourself have been busy piling up in the first place.

Performatism doesn't "correct" this privileging of discourse by flatly propagating nature over nurture or calling for a return to good old binary heterosexuality. What it *does* do, though, is to frame corporeality – and in particular genitally defined corporeality – in such a way that genetic and genital issues are moved to the center of narrative frames and made into vehicles for a transcendent event. A prime example of this can be found once more in the basic plot structure of *American Beauty*. Lester sets up a hedonist frame around himself designed to culminate in the seduction of Angela Hays, who at first appears to be a little more than a slutty version of her homonymic cousin Lolita Haze. Upon realizing that Angela is a virgin (and a very insecure one, at that), Lester however retracts his phallic desire, transcending as he does so his own libidinal self to become something higher and more moral (indeed, you could say, he becomes an adult again). The fact that he is murdered immediately after that by Colonel Fitts doesn't diminish his feat. It simply means he can't be all things to all people at once – in a different context the very same act of chasteness exhibited vis-à-vis Angela turns out to be a mortal insult. In a postmodernist work, this sort of contextualization would vitiate Lester's attempt to establish himself as an autonomous subject. In performatism, however, this contextual paradoxality is explicitly *transcended*. Lester is deified at the movie's end and enters into a higher, beautiful realm for which his multi-sexual chasteness seems an entirely appropriate rite of preparation.

Another quick way of highlighting the differences between postmodernism and performatism regarding sex is to key in on the topic of hermaphroditism. While not exactly a pressing social issue in itself, hermaphroditism has attracted the attention of such prominent theoreticians as Foucault and Butler because it seems to embody the main empirical premise behind postmodernism's concept of gender: namely, that our natural sexuality is a toss-up that a sinister set of encultured norms consistently causes to land on the heterosexual side of the coin. Foucault and Butler, to be sure, disagree on whether Herculine Barbin's hermaphroditism is the "happy limbo of non-identity"[41] (Foucault) or just another example of one-sided sexuality being forced on a hapless victim (Butler).[42] However, the root idea remains the same: the hermaphrodite is about as close as anyone can get to a state of reified otherness exposing the arbitrariness of prevailing heterosexual norms.[43]

The most programmatic performatist reaction to the postmodern concept of hermaphroditism has up to now been Jeffrey Eugenides' widely acclaimed novel *Middlesex*.[44] Eugenides, who is familiar with Foucault's arguments (and probably also Butler's), switches the frame of reference from one of undecidable, irreducible alterity to one of decidable, albeit defective unity. Eugenides' underage heroine makes a conscious decision to become a male, basing this choice on scientifically founded anatomical data that has been concealed from her by a typically postmodern doctor. Like Lester Burnham, she deliberately becomes a male with a (this time permanently) retracted penis, a man who by the end of the book is capable of loving without penetrating the object of his desire. Additionally, the hero proves to be a person capable of ethnic reconciliation. Of Greek ancestry, he eventually moves to Berlin where he lives amicably among the Turks who had once slaughtered his ancestors and indirectly set off the incestuous relation between his grandparents that led to his anatomical – but not intellectual – dualism.

Rather than appealing to genetically encoded heterosexuality, performatism seeks to transcend sexual difference by resorting to strategies ranging everywhere from chastity to genetic engineering to divine intervention. Instead of acting as a place of liminal undecidability and boundary transgression the body becomes a scene of potential unity, irrespective of the "input" involved. Thus in Olga Tokarczuk's heavily Jungian novel *House of Day, House of Night*[45] we encounter the figure of Saint Kummernis, who is miraculously endowed with a girl's body and Jesus's head and who dies a martyr's death because of it; in Michel Houellebecq's *The Elementary Particles*[46] the main character succeeds in cloning a unisexed person who overcomes the sexual tension involved in conventional male-female relations. In one of the most absurd performatist plays with sexual identity, in the movie *Being John Malkovich*, a woman who is inhabiting John Malkovich's "portal" manages to impregnate her girlfriend through the actor and have a child (who can in turn be used as a kind of vessel in which fortunate people can live forever once they have entrance to it). These are not mere gender shifts or weak, refractory "performances" creating small swirls in the power flow of a mighty heterosexual matrix, but whole, albeit incredible constructions of sexuality aimed at overcoming sexuality's most frustrating and perplexing aspects. These transcendency-breeding frames are, in effect, a logical consequence of the radical dualist constructivism propagated by Butler. For once you kiss the corporeal world goodbye – once you start constructing gender relations willy-nilly without regard for their genetic or material substrate – there's no reason why you shouldn't go one step further and *reconstruct* these relations as monist ones that once more include the body within them. As long as your unified new construct focuses on transcending sexuality as we know it – and not simply on reinstalling the old binary, heterosexual opposition between male and female – you will be a sexual performatist. Because these monist constructs by definition allow for a secondary pluralism – each whole construct is different in its own way – there is no dearth of possibilities to construct sexuality anew without one-sidedly tipping the scales in favor of homosexuality by default (as does Butler's postfeminism) or heterosexuality by decree (as does traditional Judeo-Christian culture). Performatism holds out the promise of a plurality of sexual preference in which body and soul *both* turn out to matter.

Performatist Time and History

Most scholars and critics today will readily admit that writing, film-making, art, and architecture are different today than they were back in, say, 1990, not to speak of 1985 or 1980. None of these observers, however, would dream of suggesting that these differences are epochal in nature – part of a massive paradigm shift fundamentally changing the way we regard and represent the world around us. Instead, in discussions of cultural trends we invariably encounter a kind of one-step-forward, one-step-back attitude towards anything laying a claim to innovation. Since in postmodern thinking everything New is by definition always already implicated in the Old, it's easy to dispose of performatism – or anything else promising novelty, for that matter – by dragging its individual concepts back into the good old briar patch of citations, traces, and uncontrollable filiations that make up postmodernism. This posthistorical "yes,-but" attitude is so entrenched in present-day criticism that even such vociferous monist opponents of posthistoricism as Walter Benn Michaels in America and Boris Groys in Germany haven't been able to counter it with positive programs of their own. After introducing a promising monist concept of the new in 2000, for example, Groys has not developed it further.[47] Michaels, for his part, ends a recent polemical book on a note of complete resignation, stating that "history, as of this writing, is still over."[48]

Needless to say, I believe that history is nowhere close to being over. At the moment, history is being energetically pump-primed by writers, architects, artists and filmmakers who have – consciously or unconsciously – switched to a monist mindset and are working with frames and ostensivity to inaugurate a new, manifestly unpostmodern aesthetic of temporality. This performatist switch is generating new concepts of time in two crucial areas: in literary history itself and in cinematography, where temporal experience is aesthetically most palpable.

History

Of the varied postmodern concepts of time and history that may be extracted from the writings of Derrida, Foucault, Deleuze, Jameson and others, the most fundamental undoubtedly remains that of *différance* – the state of temporal and spatial undecidability in which, as Derrida cagily puts it, "one loses and wins on every turn."[49] In *différance*, as hardly needs to be repeated at length any more, space and time are perceived as mutually conditioning one another from the very moment of their appearance as intelligible concepts in language. Mark a move in time and you'll have created a new spatial position; create a new spatial position and you'll have needed an increment of time to do it. Deconstruction intervenes to disrupt the "metaphysical" tendency to privilege one over the other and, of course, to destabilize any historical "ism" that would try to treat a discrete block of time as a "static and taxonomic tabularization,"[50] as Derrida calls it. The net effect, as we know, is a concept of history that is radically posthistorical and radically incremental, since the only thing that can really "happen" – the only true transcendent event – is the destruction of discourse itself. In the Derridean scenario even the buildup to nuclear war follows the pattern of *différance*, since it's all just discourse – up to the point, at least, where the bombs actually go off.[51] Because there's nothing outside of deconstructive discourse except death, being inside that discourse is, conversely, a kind of key to cultural immortality. And, because that discourse can never be superseded by anything short of death, using any *other* discourse that might come after it would presumably be like *being* dead. The difference between postmodern discourse of this kind and everything else isn't just a matter of how you use signs to convey reality in a certain way: it's a matter of intellectual life and death.

The monist notion of history I am suggesting here is not as deadly serious about its own truth claims as is current theory. Adopting a monist set towards the sign instead of a dualist one doesn't mean that we're going back to a naïve metaphysics deferring to God, History, Truth, Beauty, or some other comforting notion residing outside the purview of our discourse. The belief that material reality should be incorporated into the sign instead of being excluded from it is a re-curring feature of human thought that can be observed in Western culture since Antiquity; it is "true" only inasmuch as large groups of people adopt it for certain periods of time and stick to it until they get tired of it again.

At the same time, the epochal concept of history I would like to develop here is also not as arbitrarily personal as someone like Stanley Fish makes it out to be. People adopt a set towards signs "with" or "without" things well before they make the kind of free-wheeling, wildly diverging interpretations that led Fish to pose his famous query "is their a text in this class?"[52] At some point, everyone decides – usu-ally intuitively – on whether to be a semiotic monist or a semiotic dualist. And, having done so, everyone also tends to stay that way for considerable lengths of time – whether due to a desire for internal consistency or due to sheer intellectual inertia. The issue at hand is not that a few scholars here and there have decided to adopt a monist mindset and apply it for their own personal or institutional ends; it's that writers, moviemakers, and architects *all over* have adopted this mindset and are implementing it in works of art. The changes now oc-curring in culture are epochal in nature: they represent a fundamental shift in the way we approach the world. However, because of their obligation to postmodern norms, very few critics are in a position to accept that shift as something desirable, and still less to define it as an historical event, rather than as a mere set of incremental changes. This applies no less to those affecting a critical stance towards post-modernism. Although it has by now become fashionable to dismiss postmodernism as exhausted or obsolete, this attitude means nothing if it is not accompanied by a positive alternative position. If you can't define the Other of postmodernism and write, think, and act in terms of that Other then you are – sorry to say – still a postmodernist.

In discussions of epochs it is always tempting to link normative shifts from dualism to monism (and back again) with larger trends in socio-political reality. In the case of postmodernism, the main repre-sentative of this materialist line of thought has been Fredric Jameson, who sought to escape the poststructuralist "prison-house of language" by welding a lucid, highly convincing account of postmodernism onto the *Unterbau* of what he called late capitalism. Unfortunately for Jameson's thesis, late capitalism – its ominous name notwithstanding – has been looking increasingly robust with each passing year. The fact that postmodernism is petering out while global capitalism continues to boom suggests that Jameson's Marxist reading of cultural history is not much more prescient than the deconstructive one: it simply installs never-ending posthistory in the material realm outside the sign.

Given the collapse of socialism and the present lack of any viable alternative to the capitalist mode of production, it is tempting to suggest that the turn towards globalization and the turn towards a monist culture are two sides of the same coin (this is, in fact, the position taken by Eric Gans with his ambitious notion of post-millennialism[53]). Since performatism is a theory of aesthetics – a theory of why we like certain things for no good practical reason – I don't find it necessary to make such far-reaching claims. It is true, of course, that many performatist works treated in this book feed off of problems arising through globalization and/or the collapse of socialism in Middle and Eastern Europe. However, it is also important to remember that there is no urgent *practical* reason why artists should not keep on thumbing their noses at capitalism using the tried-and-true strategies developed in postmodernism (Ali Smith's *Hotel World*, discussed in Chapter Two, is a good example of a "classic," politically correct postmodern approach to the subject).

In my view, the main reason for the switch to monism is that creative artists have become tired of recycling increasingly predictable postmodernist devices and have turned to its monist Other to construct alternatives – a move that ultimately knows no ideological boundaries. Hence, in the new monism we find a whole gamut of political positions, ranging from Eric Gans's strident neoconservatism to Arundhati Roy's Chomskian critique of American power politics. The criterion for performatism is ultimately not *whether* you are for or against global capitalism, but *how* you go about formulating your position within it. In Chapter Two, I'll discuss in more detail some literary works with historiographic and political implications. Roughly speaking, though, you can make out three positions here:

an accommodationist one that seeks to create warmed air pockets of spirituality within the glacial impassivity of global capitalism (Tokarczuk's "The Hotel Capital," Schulze's *Simple Stories*); a postcolonial one that focuses on creating beautiful unities amidst the moral and political ugliness of the capitalist system (Arundhati Roy's *The God of Small Things*, Jim Jarmusch's *Ghost Dog*); and a terrorist or sublime one, which toys on a fictional level with the possibility of doing away with capitalism altogether (Miloš Urban's *Sevenchurch* and Viktor Pelevin's *Buddha's Little Finger*). Finally, in the discussion of Bernhard Schlink's *The Reader*, I'll show how Schlink tries to overcome the victimary politics arising out of the Holocaust and open up the possibility of individual subjects advancing in history frame by frame.

Cinematographic Time

In aesthetic terms we experience time most intensely in the cinema. Here, too, performatism is changing the way time, space, and the medium of film interact. Up until now, sophisticated viewers have felt most comfortable with the deist notion of dispersed or disjointed time used by postmodernism. Because in deist thinking the spatial markers of divine origin – its signs or traces – are believed to proliferate incrementally and uncontrollably in every which way, the time in which that proliferation unfolds never has much of a chance to develop epic, drawn-out proportions.[54] In (post-)modern deist systems time is either being constantly sliced and diced by space, as in Derrida's *différance*, or removed from chronology and interiorized, as in Bergson's *durée* (which he links with the ability to engage in creative imagination per se). The most ingenious and productive postmodern theory of cinematic time, the one developed by Deleuze in his two "cinema" books, is more gracious in its attitude towards chronological time – he regards the epic "movement-image" of pre-war cinema and the "time-image" of postmodern cinema as different but equal.[55] However, it is obvious that Deleuze's sympathies lie with the neo-Bergsonian "time-image" that shatters the sensory-motor scheme "from the inside"[56] and causes time to go "out of joint."[57] Deleuze's opposition, which is grounded in an exacting and exhaustive treatment of 80 years of cinematic innovation, would also seem to leave us in a typical posthistorical bind. Either cinema can continue to produce the out-of-kilter time-images typical of the 1970s and '80s or it can fall back into the old sensory-motor patterns of pre-war film – or, even worse, recur to the pedestrian, merely chronological use of cinematic time that has always been a mainstay of popular movies. How can filmmakers create a cinematic time not based on the serial montage of sensory motor images or disjointed, temporal ones?

The answer, once more, lies in framing time in a way that is alien to postmodernism and poststructuralism. The focus is on *creating presence* – which is to say on doing something that the Derridean, epistemological critique of time considers impossible and the normative, Bergsonian-Deleuzian concept of time considers insipid.

Just how does this work? For a start, we are not dealing with a naive attempt to create a *primary* presence. There is no way that modern-day cinema-goers are going to be shocked, fooled, or cajoled into mixing up reality and its filmic representation. Performatist film does not try to convince us that it is representing reality in a more "real" or "authentic" way than any previous cinematic school or direction. Rather, performatist film functions by framing and contrasting two types of time: personal or human time and theist or authorial time. Put more concretely, the performatist film, using the usual coercive means, forces viewers to accept a certain segment of time as a unity or "chunk" while at the same time providing them with a temporal perspective that *transcends* that temporal unity. The relevant mode here is not epistemological and reflexive, but ontological and intuitive: it is the feeling of being present in a time frame that is qualitatively superior in some way to a previous one.

The most radical example of this is Aleksandr Sokurov's movie *Russian Ark*, which consists of one 87-minute-long, completely uncut shot. While watching the movie, we are made to experience two times. The first is the real time of the cameraman as he slowly moves through the Hermitage museum in St. Petersburg; the second is the "staged" time of the director as he places a whole series of historical figures and scenes from Russia's czarist past in the path of the passing camera. On the one hand, we plunge with the cameraman into an ever-expanding filmic present corresponding exactly to the real time of the filming procedure (there was no editing and hence no way of shortening or scrambling real time). On the other hand, the *mise en scène* confronts us with characters who can only be interpreted as emblems of transcendent, panchronological time: Peter the Great, Catherine the Great, Pushkin, Nicholas II, and a hodge-podge of other figures taken from Russian history all appear within the same 87-minute sequence. The net effect (which I'll discuss in greater detail in Chapter Three) is that of a quotidian, real time allowing us to participate in a transcendent, suprahistorical one. The key to temporal experience here is the *en bloc* juxtaposition of theist and human time rather than the concatenation of countless time- or motion-saturated frames that forms the basis of Deleuzian film language. Also, needless to say, there's very little point in deconstructing this unreal presentation of historical figures in real time, because even the most simple-minded viewer has no trouble understanding that it's a one-time stunt – an artificial, aesthetic device. *Russian Ark* isn't trying to convince us with cognitive *arguments*; it's trying to make us *believe* by confronting us with a temporal *performance* that we have no way of avoiding – short of not going to see the movie at all.

A less radical, but in principle similar use of time is offered by *American Beauty*, which conveys the same basic device used in *Russian Ark* using much more conventional cinematographic means. Thus the bird's-eye-view establishing shot of *American Beauty*, where Lester Burnham introduces us to "my neighborhood…my street…my life," seems at first little more than a hoary Hollywood device. However, it also marks Lester's transtemporal, transcendent perspective that we can only understand after we, like Lester, have left the everyday time frame of the story line at the movie's end. Besides providing us with a frame favoring panchronological over everyday time, the movie also encourages us, along with Lester and Ricky, to bracket and make present certain objects embodying transcendence – most notably Angela (in Lester's slow-motion erotic visions) and the white plastic bag or the dead bird (in Ricky's real-time videos). This bracketing of chronological time might at first seem to be nothing more than a familiar cinematographic device. In performatist terms, though, it marks the unity of static, framed time and the transcendent time in which the deified Lester partakes – thus staking out a basic agreement between the outer and inner frame, between inner vision and supernatural experience. Conversely, quotidian time in *American Beauty* is framed in such a way that characters can transcend that time; the act of transcendence in turn provides an emotional basis for identifying with these characters. In Chapter Three, which treats performatist cinema, I'll go into more detail on the different ways that movies force both characters and ourselves to experience transcendence as a qualitative shift in spatially demarcated, temporal "chunks."

Summary

Since my introductory discussion of performatism has covered a lot of ground, it seems helpful to close this chapter by summarizing what I consider to be the four basic features of performatism.

1. The basic semiotic mode of performatism is *monist*. It requires that things or thingness be integrated into the concept of sign. The most useful monist concept of sign I have been able to find up to now is Eric Gans's notion of the *ostensive*. Ostensivity means that at least two people, in order to defer violence in a situation of mimetic conflict, intuitively agree on a present sign that marks, deifies, and beautifies its own violence-deferring performance. This originary ostensive scene, in which the human, language, religion and aesthetics are all made present at once for the first time, is hypothetical. My own, specifically historical interpretation of the ostensive is that it embodies the semiotic mechanism generating the new epoch better than any other competing monist concept. The ostensive, in other words, marks the becoming-conscious of the new epoch. Accordingly, the job of a performatist aesthetics would be to describe the different manifestations of ostensivity in contemporary works of art and show how they make these works appeal to us in terms of monist, no longer postmodern mindsets. This book is devoted to realizing that project.

2. The aesthetic device specific to performatism is *double framing*. The double frame is based on a lock or fit between an outer frame (the work construct itself) and an inner one (an ostensive scene or scenes

of some kind). The work is constructed in such a way that its main argumentative premise shifts back and forth between these two venues; the logic of one augments the other in a circular, closed way. The result is a performative tautology that allows the endless circulation of cognitively dubious, but formally irrefutable metaphysical figures within its boundaries. These metaphysical figures are in turn valid only within the frame of a particular work; their patent constructedness reinforces the set-apartness or givenness of the work itself and coercively establishes its status as *aesthetic* – as a realm of objective, privileged, and positive experience. Because they are easy to identify and debunk, these metaphysical figures force readers or viewers to make a choice between the untrue beauty of the closed work or the open, banal truth of its endless contextualization. Performatist works of art attempt to make viewers or readers *believe* rather than convince them with cognitive arguments. This, in turn, may enable them to assume moral or ideological positions that they otherwise would not have. In terms of reader reception, a performance is successful when a reader's belief pattern is changed in some particular way, and when he or she begins to project that new belief pattern back onto reality.

3. The human locus of performatism is the *opaque* or *dense subject*. Because the simplest formal requirement of once more becoming a whole subject is tautological – to be a subject the subject must somehow set itself off from its context – performative characters consolidate their position by appearing opaque or dense to the world around them. This opacity is in itself not desirable per se, but rather forms the starting point for possible further development. This development is best measured in terms of whether (or to what degree) a subject transcends the double frame in which it happens to find itself. In narrative genres, this ability of a human subject to transcend a frame is the benchmark of an event or successful performance. In psychological narrative this transcendence is necessarily partial; in fantastic narrative it may be achieved totally. In architectonic and pictorial genres, which are by nature static, we encounter paradoxical states of saturation[58] or impendency[59] that impose the conditions for transcendence on us without actually demonstrating how that transcendence is eventually consummated.

4. The spatial and temporal coordinates of performatism are cast in a *theist* mode. This means that time and space are framed in such a way that subjects have a real chance to orient themselves within them and transcend them in some way. Because of its obvious constructedness and artificiality, this set-up or frame causes us to assume the existence of an implicit author forcing his or her will upon us as a kind of paradox or conundrum whose real meaning is beyond our ken. In terms of plot, we find a basic conflict between the spatial and temporal coerciveness of the theist frame and the human or figural subjects struggling to overcome it. In terms of spatial representation (in architecture), we find a basic tension between the architect's attempt to effect transcendence and the physical limitations imposed by the material he or she is using; the expansive theist gesture is always accompanied by a human, limited one.

Chapter 2

Performatism in Literature

The performatist turn in literature has been gradual and unmarked by spectacular quarrels, manifestoes, or stylistic experimentation. None of the literary works that I have up to now identified as performatist shows striking formal innovation, and none of the authors has come forth with dramatic public counterproposals to postmodernism. Rather, performatism in literature has worked tacitly, by taking crucial devices of postmodernist aesthetics and retooling them in a way that is no longer compatible with prevailing postmodern norms. In literature this can be most readily seen in strategies that produce narrative closure in double frames and ensure obligatory reader identification with the subjects entrapped in those frames – devices that are at loggerheads with prevailing postmodern notions of how texts work. These changes have not been lost on critics. However, those of them who do identify these strategies are usually content to dismiss them as variants of already known patterns or explain them away as yet another hard-to-follow twist of postmodern irony. The real problem is not that critics are unaware of the new devices; the problem is that they are unable to conceive of them as having a dominant, unifying role in the texts at hand, and they are unable to place them in the perspective of a larger epochal shift. The result has been a massive loss of sensibility for the ethical, political and aesthetic concerns of these new works, whose focus lies in creating a particular posture of belief in a closed aesthetic frame rather than generating yet another cycle of open-ended ironic reflection.

To show how the new performatist devices work in literature I have drawn on seven popular, critically acclaimed texts offering a broad spectrum of styles, themes and ideological standpoints. I will begin by discussing a performatist text from Poland that has a direct doppelganger in the world of English postmodernism. Although using exactly the same gimmick – a fancy international hotel as a allegory of global capitalism – Olga Tokarczuk's short story "The Hotel Capital" arrives at completely different results than does Ali Smith in her stereotypically postmodern novel *Hotel World*. More familiar to Western readers will be Yann Martel's popular, Man-Booker prize winning novel *Life of Pi*. What at first glance seems to be an ironic send-up of a naive religious believer turns out to confirm the act of belief more than to refute it. With the next example, a chapter from Ingo Schulze's novel *Simple Stories*, I'll show how an author develops a performatist plot resolution out of a specifically postmodern intertextual source, in this case Raymond Carver's short story "Sacks." To avoid a completely eurocentric bias I have also chosen Arundhati Roy's international bestseller *The God of Small Things*. Roy's novel demonstrates how a performatist, no longer postmodern concept of unified beauty can be put in the service of radical political resistance and the search for cultural and personal identity. To include a historical perspective, I will discuss Bernhard Schlink's internationally acclaimed novel *The Reader*, which treats the aftermath of the Holocaust in a way no longer compatible with the postmodernist victimary mode. And finally, using Miloš Urban's novel *Sevenchurch*, I'll briefly outline how a sublime, "terrorist" critique of capitalism works in the context of Eastern European culture.

Checking out of the Epoch: Hotel World *vs. "The Hotel Capital"*
Hotel World

On the surface, Ali Smith's *Hotel World*[1] is concerned with the accidental death of a young hotel worker named Sara Wilby, whose name (Wilby – "will be") is already resonant with deferred potential. Sara, who has just taken on a job as chambermaid in the chain Global Hotels, bets a co-worker that she can stuff herself into the hotel's dumbwaiter. Immediately after she performs this feat, however, the elevator cable tears, sending her crashing to death at the bottom of the shaft.

The fatal occurrence and its consequences are recounted in six stylistically very different narrative sections. Although in the novel five striking individuals dominate each section – they are, in order of appearance, the victim herself, the hotel's receptionist, a homeless woman, a female journalist, and Sara's sister – our identification with these figures is constantly being disturbed, undermined, or sabotaged entirely. Thus, in her narration, the dead accident victim appears as a ghost who visits first its family, then its own body in the grave. So that no one might get the idea of taking the heroine's existence in the hereafter all too seriously, the ghost occasionally emits a "o-oo-oo" sound – just like in the comics.

This ironic treatment of characters' discourse applies no less to the living. The reader's identification with the younger sister's anger and grief is undermined by the complete lack of punctuation marks in the chapter narrated by her. Her intensively experienced emotional reaction is overwritten, as it were, by a kind of discursive dysfunctionality whose only source can be that of the author (since no teenager, no matter how grief-stricken, would leave out every last single punctuation mark in her own writing). The suffering of the homeless, tubercular Else is similarly marked by defective language: when begging her speech is reduced to almost incomprehensible fragments like "Spr sm chn" ("spare some change").

These and other plays with script and language show the author to be an proficient, remote administrator of that dysfunctionality and defectiveness which otherwise weighs heavily upon her characters. By contrast, the only figure in the novel who is able to write, speak, and act in a conventional way is mercilessly exposed as a fraud. The person in question is a female journalist who befriends the homeless, disoriented Else while staying at the hotel for a night. The character, aptly named Penny, quickly proves herself to be everything promised by her name. Having written out a large check to Else, she has second thoughts about it later in the night and has it cancelled – thus neatly exposing her own magnanimity as an empty, vain projection. The author doesn't want her character (or us) to buy into a cheap identification with Else; she wants to inscribe herself literally and directly in the dysfunctionality, alterity and suffering of her characters – a contact that however never cleaves to one person for all too long. Like the ghost, the bodiless, preternaturally weightless author moves effortlessly through her own book, haunting now one, now the other character.

By contrast, the author's treatment of space and order is easy to pin down ideologically. At times, in fact, the book reads as if the author had cribbed straight out of something by Judith Butler or Michel Foucault. The hotel is a spatial trap, a panoptic surveillance center in which the employees are strictly monitored and punished according to need. Loopholes in this hegemonic matrix arise only by accident – as when the omnipresent surveillance cameras fail to work shortly after Sara's accident. The characters in the novel, who are equipped with a quasi natural, spontaneous ability to resist à la Judith Butler, put these flubs to immediate use. Lise, the mentally disturbed receptionist, takes advantage of the camera failure to sneak homeless Else into a luxury suite. Else, who is traumatized by enclosed spaces to begin with – some Christian missionaries once tried to convert her inside a locked room – soon flees, but forgets to turn off the bathwater, causing a small deluge. The damage is however quickly repaired and the costs fobbed off on an innocent chambermaid.

As this turn of plot suggests, resistance is both pointless and useless. It can occur only in the involuntary playing out of one's own dysfunctionality but not as a goal-oriented, willful act. Instead, we are encouraged to imagine the *possibility* of such resistance from a higher, constantly shifting vantage point. The authorially mediated metaperspective allows us to experience ironic *schadenfreude* over the small flood caused by Else and Lise even as we realize its accidental, inconsequential character.

In view of the close connection between space and power, Sara's accidental death in the innermost, "dumbest" and most confining space of the hotels carries a certain ideological weight after all. Sara's death and the barely concealed spatial violence emanating from the hotel form a contingency relationship suggesting that something like this *must* not take place but very well *can*. Sara's senseless, accidental, death-by-wager – the embodiment of the aleatoric per se – exposes the reified essence of the hotel as a whole: its omnipresent structural violence asserts itself even in the case of pure chance. Later on, Sara's sister will smash a hole in the wall of the hastily bricked up shaft and throw an alarm clock into it so that she may experience the time span between Sara's life and death on her own. By contrast, the hotel tempts its visitors with a false temporality, a false experience of transcendence: in the hotel's brochure indeed promises that "a transcendent time is waiting to be had by all."[2]

That time is not transcendent, but instead depends on spatial restrictions and contractual obligations is demonstrated vividly in the last part of the novel. Sara's unrequited love for the salesgirl in a watch repair shop is answered – but only belatedly and in a mode of permanent deferral. The salesgirl, who had only fleetingly taken note of the pining Sara and who knows nothing of her death, intuitively realizes her affection ex post facto and – disregarding all regulations – puts on the watch Sara had brought in for repair. Love, then, is possible after all: you love without knowing the other, without wanting to do so, and without having to invest your desire in a bothersome interpersonal projection. Although the salesgirl's wearing of the wrist watch marks a double reconciliation – it is a symbolic act both of loving and of remembrance – this moment can ultimately only be enjoyed from the cool, epistemologically remote vantage point of the authorial metaposition – a position that undermines all lasting identifications and does not stay attached to individual figures or positions for any length of time.

At the very beginning of the novel the ghostly Sara begged the reader to "time me" – to measure her time so that she doesn't disappear in *différance*, in the endlessly receding, arbitrary conditionality of language. This "timing" – the translation of fluid temporality into fixed spatiality – is achieved formally as soon as the salesgirl puts on Sara's wristwatch. Yet even this unwitting act of remembrance threatens to go awry. On the book's last page we find once more the lines that the ghost, who is becoming ever more forgetful, uttered in the book's beginning chapter:

> Remember you must live.
> Remember you most love.
> Remainder you mist leaf.[3]

This tossed salad of signifiers is followed by the ghost's howl, which ends and simultaneously opens the book. The voice of the ever fainter growing Other forms the alpha and omega of the novel as a whole: the hereafter appears as the mirror image of a dysfunctional here and now rather than as a transcendent shore of salvation. Indeed, the ghost and the author turn out to be effects of the same persistent mechanism that holds forth the possibility of transcendence while in the final analysis always allowing it to fall flat. In terms of reader response, this mechanism is at the end passed on to the reader, who by way of a semi-comprehensible half-insult ("remainder you mist leaf") is encouraged to take part, albeit belatedly, in an unending ring-around-the-rosy of misdirected resistance and yearning.

As *Hotel World* graphically demonstrates, late postmodernism is caught in a self-made trap. Whoever presents herself as epistemologically invulnerable falls into an empty, indeed ghostly game of hide-and-seek with the reader and with herself; whoever foregoes this sort of epistemological critique in favor of metaphysical ideals becomes a purveyor of simple-minded, if not downright fraudulent projections. Since there is no immanent way out of this endless loop-the-loop, post-structuralist critics have long been in agreement that postmodernism will never end; it will simply refine and multiply self-ironic strategies for acknowledging belatedness and producing deferral. We are fated, it would seem, to shuttle endlessly between the poles of metaphysical wishful thinking and the merciless epistemological critique of the very same.

"The Hotel Capital"

That things can be done entirely differently is demonstrated by Olga Tokarczuk's story "The Hotel Capital."[4] Using motifs very similar to *Hotel World*, Tokarczuk arrives at a specifically monist, no longer postmodern perspective on the sign, space, and the world in general.

At first it could seem as if "Hotel Capital" is even more zealous in its critique of capitalism than is *Hotel World*. In case anyone has missed the transparent symbolism of its name, the hotel is described in the very first line as being "only for the rich."[5] Like Sara Wilby, the heroine and first-person narrator is a lowly chambermaid and, more-over, a nameless foreigner. As in *Hotel World*, the Hotel Capital exerts an omnipresent, deforming force on the main character. In fact, as soon as the heroine puts on her uniform, she foregoes her own subjec-tive sense of self: "I take off my exotic language, my strange name, my sense of humour, my face lines, my taste for food not appreciated here, my memory of small events [...]."[6] In keeping with the fatal event re-lated in *Hotel World*, the heroine is overcome by a feeling of existential angst when riding the cramped service elevator to her work – she is afraid "lest the lift should stop and I should stay here forever, enclosed like a bacterium inside the body of the Hotel Capital."[7] Finally, we even encounter a small flood in one of the rooms which, as in *Ho-tel World*, temporarily disrupts order in the hotel without washing it away entirely.

The postmodern reader now expecting to be initiated into a subal-tern victim's chronicle of alienation and otherness will be sorely disap-pointed. In spite of the superficial similarities with the ambience of *Hotel World*, "Hotel Capital" proposes completely different semiotic and spatial relations aimed at promoting unity, order, and belief. In particular, space appears as the guarantor of a whole, intimate, indeed sacral ambience which can be experienced only within the confines of the otherwise worldly hotel.

This spatially determined sacral experience can be thought of as a *sphere* in the sense used by Peter Sloterdijk.[8] Sloterdijk calls the sphere an "aspirated commune,"[9] a protected interior space that al-lows intimacy, sensuality, and social cohesiveness to develop at all in the first place. As historians of religion like Mircea Eliade confirm, this interior experience is a primal one. Accordingly, the creation of closed, centered spaces must be viewed not as a metaphysical ploy but as an attempt to make space livable to begin with: "*If the world is to be lived in*, it must be *founded* – and no world can come to birth in the chaos of the homogeneity and relativity of profane space."[10] According to Eliade, this is "not a matter of theoretical speculation, but of a primary religious experience that precedes all reflection on the world."[11] Because it is essential to founding life the primal space is always placed in the middle of the world and displays a vertical, hierarchical structure that literally and figuratively opens up to the transcendent world of the gods.[12]

Now, the claim that there once existed an originary, pre-reflexive, hierarchically arranged space with a built-in escape hatch to the heavens doesn't present much of a challenge for a poststructuralist or postmodern appropriation. Inasmuch as this kind of pre-reflexive, originary world is anchored in discourse it can always be conceived of as arising from a double, irreducible act of inclusion and exclusion. In such a situation a poststructuralist would quite properly insist on giving the excluded and chaotic outer world its just due. And, he or she would insist that an originary space can only be experienced again by way of simulation, which is to say in a belated act that simultaneously undermines and outdoes the original.

This act of appropriation will only encounter serious resistance when the sense of spatial intimacy is put on as a *performance* with aesthetic means. In such a case the text will be presented as a closed space, which, by exerting one-sided pressure on the observer, gives him or her an unambiguous choice between an inside (going along with the work) or an outside (going against the work). This kind of *performatist work* is not mere discourse or simulation, *but rather imposes the closed conditions of the sacral, originary space onto the observer with aesthetic means*. What we have here, then, is the fusion of a privileged aesthetic space in the Kantian sense using rather un-Kantian means that you might describe as ritualistic, dogmatic or compulsive.[13]

It goes without saying that this forced aesthetic experience does not suspend the possibility of critical reflection. No one today can actually return to a sacral or ritual experience of interiority, no one can (or wants to) completely shut out the vibrant hurly-burly of exterior space. The possibility of deceit and of fraud thus still lingers in every performative act of framing – but precisely as a possibility, and not as a preordained, epistemologically guaranteed result as in postmodernism. Readers, in other words, now have a real choice. If this kind of aesthetically mediated inner space remains more or less intact we will be dealing with a performatist monism; if it mixes uncontrollably with exterior space we will fall back into the endlessly undecidable convolutions of postmodernism.

But let us return to "Hotel Capital." If the space of the hotel is a sphere in Sloterdijk's sense, then it is by no means an idyllic refuge. The sacrally aspirated hotel room – no less so than in *Hotel World* – is unavoidably exposed to the pressures exerted by globalization and global capitalism. As the narrator herself remarks, the room is a "four-cornered, prostituted space"[14] that gives itself to anyone who is willing to pay for it. The space of the hotel, whose sacral, protective function is constantly being emphasized by the narrator, is in the secularized world itself helpless and exposed. Space requires an agent who would, as it were, clean up the spiritual and metaphysical mess brought into it by the hotel's guests. Precisely this active, theist role is filled out by the narrator/chambermaid, who intervenes in a life-affirming way in the half-public, half-intimate sphere of the guests. Having temporarily laid aside her subjective personality, she settles into the invisible realm that is neither outside nor in and intervenes from there in interior space – a transcendental subject with a theist mission and a human face.

The postmodern reader secretly hoping for the first-person narrator to be ironically dismantled in the course of the story will wait in vain. Indeed, in narratological terms much the opposite takes place: the first-person narrator acquires distinctly authorial characteristics. In lieu of direct antagonists – as a rule the heroine tidies up in empty rooms – the story appears as a series of quasi-philosophical meditations on space and the people in it; in lieu of disruptive hints from the author we are forced to identify with the heroine and her space-friendly value judgments. From the normative postmodern point of view it is of course always possible to reject this authorially supported mindset as blind self-deception. If you do so, though, you will stumble into a narrative trap. For either you enter into the closed space of the work or you remain outside it. The work frame changes from a place of undecidability to a place of decision – quite contrary to the normative precepts of postmodernism. The act of reading reproduces the simultaneously coercive and comforting quality of the fictive inner space.

This experience of spatially mediated pleasure (Kant's *Wohlgefallen*) must be understood performatively, and not discursively or conceptually. Although we may be in disagreement with individual meanings or arguments in the work, we must nonetheless accept it as a whole. The reader is suspended – half voluntarily, half by way of force – in an aesthetically mediated no-man's land which can only be conceived of or experienced under the given conditions of the aesthetic frame. This spatially determined pleasure is accompanied in turn by a practically idiot-proof, compulsory mechanism that arrests the restless, hypercritical spirit of the postmodern reader long enough until she is able to identify with what is going on in the work's interior space. If the obstinate reader balks at this, then she will remain where she belongs: namely on the outside. Thus once more – with a little dogmatic help – we arrive at the restoration of what Kant calls *necessary* aesthetic pleasure [*notwendiges Wohlgefallen*].[15]

In the case of "Hotel Capital," the coercive frame manifests itself in the sacralization and aesthetization of what at first seems to be purely practical terms of employment. When starting work the heroine puts on a quasi-sacral *uni-form* which cloaks a conciliatory, spatially limited monist mindset; as soon as she takes off her work clothes she returns to a personal, "interested" attitude commensurate with the needs of daily life. The heroine's space-friendly attitude is based on a simple contractual agreement: it is not an authentic, natural, or originary state.

The Hotel Capital itself offers a spatially defined metaphysical order that travelers take advantage of in different ways. The metaphysical ideal of the hotel room is approached most closely by a Japanese husband and wife who leave behind practically no traces – those indispensable poststructuralist bearers of alterity. Their room, remarks the narrator, "gives the impression of not being occupied at all."[16] There are no objects left laying around by mistake, no personal traces, not even an odor. And, when the chambermaid cleans up she "create[s] more disorder than they would make in a month."[17] The only communication between the order-loving Japanese and the order-upholding chambermaid takes place through the tip that the couple leaves behind in a neat stack on their pillow. The coins, however, are not for the chambermaid but for the room itself, for "[...] its silent continuance in the world, for its constancy amid the inexplicable inconstancy [...]."[18] The economy of this gift is transcendental and self-confirming: it represents the sacral opposite of the "prostituted" room and makes the room seem like a "small temple."[19] On the other hand, though, the relationship as a whole remains impersonal and cool. The chamber-maid is familiar only with "the immaterial shape of the footprints left in the abandoned sandals";[20] conversely, for the Japanese guests she re-mains without a body and face. Communication and value exchange don't take place through tattered words or marks ("spr sm chn") but through shared attitudes toward space and the objects in it. The scene with the tip simply acknowledges the latent dualism of this dialectical relationship. The more spiritual and complete the relationship to the absent guests, the more the relationship of the individual to material reality is placed in doubt.

The opposite of the Japanese are the "young Americans," the bear-ers of imperial disorder. This disorder has no true metaphysical va-lence of its own but is rather a "thoughtless, stupid mess" (literally *bałagan* – a kind of Slavic Punch and Judy show) in which "there is no rhyme or reason."[21] This lack of order – with greetings from Baudrillard – is circulated by the media and intensified ad infinitum. The absent young Americans leave their TV on to CNN, and CNN assures the chambermaid that the world exists and is full of young Americans. The imperial arrogance of the young Americans and their "inattentiveness to the present"[22] is countered by the chambermaid's apprehension of their common corporeal mortality: "I clean around roughly, as if afraid of destroying these relics of the transitoriness of the people who live here."[23] This isn't ironic *schadenfreude* but rather existential insight into a shared fear of death – a fear that the cham-bermaid in this case doesn't want to assuage entirely. Later, in the room of the dying old Swede whose body absorbs all odors from with-out, the chambermaid will deliberately leave behind a sweaty, vital whiff of her own self. In a way that is "conspiratorial, respiratory and inspirational,"[24] as Sloterdijk suggests, the chambermaid tries to forge a "dyadic union"[25] in interior space that will set both human frailty and human arrogance to rights.

The chambermaid's job differs, however, from Sloterdijk's in one important respect. Whereas Sloterdijk is trying to reconstruct histori-cally the "morpho-immunological" spheres[26] and "foams"[27] that he considers indispensable for the development of human culture per se, the chambermaid faces a much more immediate problem. Her task is namely to restore a state of interior intimacy within the "prostituted" ambience of the Hotel Capital. And that is why the chambermaid proceeds in such a deliberate way, so to speak in accordance with an authorially approved metaphysical work code.[28] If you want to clean up after postmodernism (or even sweep it away entirely) then you must, as the heroine says, do so with deliberation: you must first frame scattered traces of alienation so that modest inspirational measures can at all take hold.

Given the rigid spatial order of "Hotel Capital," it is justified to pose the question of theodicy, which is to say the question of evil and the responsibility that spiritualized space bears for it. (In *Hotel World* the answer is clear: the spatial order is the sufficient, but not necessary condition of evil.) True to the tradition of metaphysical optimism in which Tokarczuk's story follows, evil doesn't appear as a principle *sui generis* but rather as disorder or as a falling away from spirituality.

The first kind of disorder – that of the "young Americans" – is childish. It corresponds to a lack of consciousness and humility in regard to the world that the young Americans dominate. The second kind of disorder, by contrast, is spatial: it resides in the vast expansiveness of the hotel (and, by extension, the world as a whole). The hotel has a mysterious tract called the "squar" which is designed for long-term guests and has a confusing layout; it is labyrinthine, convoluted, spiraled and dark: "Something strange happens to space here. Space does not like spiral stairs, chimneys and wells. It tends to degenerate into labyrinths."[29] The tangled, invaginated layout of the hotel building appears as a flaw offending against the anthropomorphic space's supposedly natural love of order. It's easy enough to deconstruct this simple personification of space, but it's harder to ignore it within the framework of the story itself – unless, of course, you yourself are intent on spreading disorder as a matter of principle.

The third variant of disorder is no less anthropomorphic than the others. Its point of departure is a self-willed, mischievous room bearing the number 229; its "Kabbalistic sum" is said to equal the number thirteen, which "is a number of excess and trickery."[30] This room has an appropriately subversive effect on visitors: "I suspect that one night here is enough to get them trapped, to bring unquiet dreams, to hold them a little longer, to bring out desires and overturn carefully laid plans."[31] The minor inundation mentioned earlier also had its origin in this room, which induces an intensified sense of corporeality and narcissistic self-alienation in the chambermaid: "The room encloses me within itself, cradles me. It is a most tender if non-physical caress, this embrace which only a closed space can give you."[32] And:

> I feel distinctly that my body exists. [...] I am aware of my skin, conscious that it's alive and breathing, that it has its own scent, and I can feel my hair where it touches my ears. I like then to get up and look at myself in the mirror which never spares me a surprise. Is this me? Really me?[33]

Were the narrator not being caressed by the room around her, one could suppose that Lacan and his mirror stage were lurking somewhere in the wings. For the corporeal and narcissistic feeling of insecurity experienced by the chambermaid is further intensified by the gaze of a guest that severs the chambermaid's metaphysical bond with the space around her. Thus "the established [literally: eternal] order is inverted. My cleaning is no longer omnipotent, it becomes emptied of meaning."[34]

It could at first seem that the presence of the unashamedly gazing guest shatters the Apollonian dreamspace of the chambermaid and revives precisely that patriarchic order which in *Hotel World* could only be overcome temporarily by accident and through deceit. Yet here, too, space and the metaphysical service code offer a way out. As soon as the chambermaid leaves the room she is able to recuperate in that very depth of space which was the death of Sara Wilby: "I [...] stop in front of the banister separating a stairwell two or three stories high. I look down and see only the ground floor from here. And – as usual – not a soul about. [...] This is the best relaxation: to look down to where everything becomes progressively smaller and more distant, less clear, more illusory."[35] The spatial haven of the *theist* perspective has been restored – but with a built-in personal or human dimension of self-deception.

If the solidarity among subalterns in *Hotel World* is characterized by a fleeting, Nietzschean love for pure strangers, then in "Hotel Capital" it reveals itself to be genetic, object-oriented, and monist. The justification for this is provided by the Castilian laundryman Pedro, who resembles a bearded missionary and who draws on an originary history of language and etymology to make his point. According to Pedro, when people "in times of old" were wandering across Europe and Asia they carried their languages with them "like banners. They formed great families, although they did not know each other; only the words were permanent."[36] Pedro, says the narrator, "pulls out the roots from words as if stoning cherries," and those listening to his lecture slowly realize that they all "spoke the same language long ago."[37] Although this doesn't quite apply to everyone – the narrator is (unjustifiably) afraid to ask about her own Polish language, and a woman from Nigeria "pretends not to understand," everyone wants to take cover under the "dark swirling cloud of prehistory"[38] that Pedro unfurls over their heads. This emblematic, genetic concept of language has a direct counterpart in the Swedish Bible that the narrator finds in the room of the dying Swede:

> I cannot understand anything and yet all seems so familiar. A red bookmark marks the Book of Ecclesiastes. I run my eye along the page and I have the impression that I am beginning to understand it. First individual words and then whole phrases float out of memory and mix with the print. *"That which hath been is now; and that which is to be hath already been; and God requires that which is past."*[39]

The foreign words act as small hollow enclosures into which human memory breathes spiritual life; through her ritually mediated reading the narrator experiences the possibility of an originary, linguistic and sacral unity in the sense of Mircea Eliade's *illud tempus*. In Eric Gans's terminology, this understanding of language is specifically ostensive. This reading is neither a hermeneutic exegesis nor an act of inscribing oneself in an already always existing network of signs. Rather, it is a ritual making-present of a prehistoric moment in which the sign is experienced as object-related, but also as conflict-resolving and divine: as a *performance*.

Pi's Believe It or Not

Yann Martel's *Life of Pi*[40] presents us with a curious case. We are introduced to a hero who was the sole survivor of a serious accident and had to fight for his life afterwards under adverse conditions. The hero describes his ordeal at great length to two claims adjusters responsible for checking its veracity. At first, his brave, uplifting story seems consistent and true. At the end, however, a host of clues make clear that parts of the tale must either be a fantasy or lie. There is no doubt that certain details contradict well-founded scientific assumptions about our natural world. After the hero has finished, the claims adjusters point out these discrepancies. The hero denies that he is lying but says he will offer a second story. This one is short, brutal, and to the point. It repeats the basic content of the first story, but in a way not contradicting science and all known evidence. When asked about the discrepancy between the two stories, the hero answers by saying essentially this: "I am the sole witness to an accident in which I have lost everything dear to me. I have two stories that tell about it. One is beautiful and one is ugly. You have no way of knowing for sure which one is true. Which story would you prefer?" In the end, the claims adjuster's report on the case is inconclusive. Based on the facts at hand, he says, he cannot determine how the accident happened. In wrapping up his report, however, he chooses to cite a detail from the hero's first, false story rather than the second, more plausible one.

It's instructive to see how this stripped-down tale corresponds to narrative strategies usually associated with postmodernism. As in many postmodernist narratives, it first causes us to identify with a central character and then abruptly undercuts the terms of that identification. One thing about it, however, is odd. Rather than leaving us in an attitude of skeptical undecidability regarding the hero, as postmodernist texts tend to do, it encourages us to revise our skepticism and identify with his story even though we know it to be false. Our response is evidently supposed to follow that of the claims adjuster, who, though unable to reach a final conclusion regarding the facts, decides to cite the beautiful, untrue story. And, if we flesh out the story with more detail, things get odder still. For the hero is not just a witness to a tragic accident, but also an ardent practitioner of Hinduism, Christianity, and Islam (in later years he also studies the Cabbala to boot). When confronted with the contradiction involved in this kind of multiple allegiance, he says simply, "I just want to love God."[41] The point of the book is evidently to make us identify with and believe in a hero who wants to worship a central, unified deity at all costs.

As my summary suggests, this popular and critically acclaimed book presents something of a logical challenge to postmodernism. Where postmodernism revels in skepticism, *Life of Pi* encourages belief; where postmodernism offers competing, equally plausible worlds, *Life of Pi* gives us a choice between what is false and what is most likely true; and where postmodernism favors decentered, deceptive states of knowing, *Life of Pi* focuses on unity, willpower, and love. While it's certainly possible to deconstruct the latter position, it really isn't much of a challenge to do so. The book itself makes clear that Pi's belief is based on willful self-deceit, and it makes sure that knowledge of the true facts behind the accident will remain deferred forever. From a critical postmodern or poststructuralist point of view, the book seems to be pointless or trite. Why, after all, write a book making us identify with a metaphysical attitude that we know is demonstrably false to begin with?

As I have suggested above, this sort of sensibility is not accessible to the set of critical practices associated with poststructuralism. The problem is not so much that *Life of Pi* resolutely resists deconstruction; it's that *Pi* deconstructs its own metaphysical conceit so completely that there is hardly anything left for the canny poststructuralist reader to do. This happens because *Life of Pi* shifts the framework of its argumentation from an epistemological plane to an aesthetic one. The book says, in effect: "given that we can never know for sure what is true, isn't it better to enjoy what is beautiful, good and uplifting rather than dwell on what is ugly, evil and disillusioning?" The book does not however just pose this question as an abstract postulate. Instead, it forces it on us in terms of a concrete choice: we are given a long, beautiful story and a short, brutish one and asked to decide for one or the other. And this choice, of course, is part of a larger aesthetic set-up or trap. Readers opting for the more plausible, ugly tale will tire of it quickly and let the whole thing drop. Readers choosing the beautiful, untrue tale, by contrast, will continue to reflect on it while treating its precepts as something that *might* be true. This type of novel elicits a specific, aesthetically mediated *performance* from readers by forcing them to believe in a character or event within the frame of the fictional text. Indulging in this doubled suspension of belief might at first seem incautious or naive. However, it is a necessary precondition for all future acts of interpretation, which in themselves may be ironic, intricate and subtle.

At the core of *Pi* is an *inner frame*, which is in this case is presented in the form of an originary scene. This scene, by reducing human experience to a few simple givens, seems to bring us closer to the very beginnings of humanness itself. In the case of Pi, the originary scene is, of course, the lifeboat that he shares with a Bengal tiger (or a murderous cook, depending on how you look at it). Please note that these originary scenes are in no way *authentic*; they are neither entirely natural nor are they prior to semiosis. Rather, they expose characters to a radical, restrictive presence which they must transcend in some way (Pi, for example, must overcome the presence of the hungry tiger).

Within the text, the originary scene or inner frame causes readers to identify in a certain set way with a character who is locked into a situation at the center of our attention. Because of their radical fencing-in of presence, originary scenes tend to be marked by the use of what Eric Gans calls ostensive signs.[42] These are simple, name-like signs that are used to designate present objects or states; in Gans's version of the originary scene the first ostensive sign creates belief and beauty by wondrously deferring mimetic violence.[43] In this particular instance, the ostensive sign is a whistle sound that Pi uses to train the tiger not to attack him (the whistle is made to stand for the rocking of the boat, which makes the tiger seasick). In general, there has to be a lock or fit between the inner frame and the text whole or outer frame for the performatist plot to work.

In the case of Pi, the immanent, ostensively mediated act of training the tiger (the inner frame) allows Pi not just to survive, but also to
confirm his love of a transcendent God – the beautiful story which,
taken as a whole, we have almost no choice but to believe (the outer
frame). If, on the other hand, we accept the validity of a sober, disil-
lusioned interpretation (the more plausible story about the cook), it
would destroy the fit between the frames and lead to a deconstructive,
though not very satisfying, reading of the text as a whole. Once more,
though, the choices we have here are very limited. This is not least because the ostensive way Pi that trains the tiger – by confronting him
with something sickening every time he tries to attack – is transferred
directly to the terms of reader response. The skeptic "attacking" the
belief structure of the book gets an ugly story, the believer accepting it a beautiful one. Our doubts about believing something that is
beautiful but probably not true are never eliminated; however, this
self-doubt is now enclosed within the structure of belief itself.

Although there is still a considerable irony involved in the way
we are made to believe Pi's story, this irony doesn't vitiate the way
we identify with him and his tale.[44] The ultimate frame of reference
is performative, and not epistemological: it applies only within the
confines of the particular text at hand. The point of the text is not
to have us grasp a trace of truth by relating something in the text to
something outside of it, but rather to make us believe and experience
beauty within its own closed space. This is the common goal of all
performatist fiction: it forces us, at least for the time being, to take
the beautiful attitude of a believer rather than the skeptical attitude
of a continually frustrated seeker of truth.[45] Hence our willingness to
believe in Pi's way of believing in God applies only within the peculiar
world of the text. Outside its boundaries we can go back to being our
old secular, skeptical selves again – if we so choose. The act of reading,
however, has been turned toward an aesthetically mediated, closed act
of believing rather than one of open-ended knowing.[46]

The kind of framing or forced identification described above
doesn't rule out intertextual citations or critical reflection. These external factors must, however, always be subordinated to the unbend-
ing outer frame of the text. The frame, in other words, fences the text

off from the truth conditions of discourse in general – that endlessly shifting, infinitely open realm in which seemingly singular, unequivocal arguments can always turn into their exact opposites.[47] While it may indeed be possible to be very skeptical about certain aspects of what is going on in the story, we nonetheless accept it because we have been made to find it beautiful. This makes the aesthetic mode – something that has traditionally always been roped off from the conditions of practical everyday judgment – the privileged place of argumentation. The difference between this performatist type of aesthetic and the traditional Kantian one is, however, that this one works by coercion. Instead of adhering to formal, presumably transcendental attributes of beauty, the text forces us to decide for beauty in terms of a relative, very narrowly defined scene or frame. Performatist aesthetics are "Kant with a club": they bring back beauty, good, wholeness, and a whole slew of other metaphysical propositions, but only under very special, singular conditions that a text forces us to accept on its own terms.[48]

The ironies and tensions growing out of this *quid pro quo* are incidentally more than enough to keep performatist reader responses alive and kicking. Readers are always well aware that their not-quite voluntary experiencing of beauty is part of a trade-off, and indeed one of the main aims of performatist literature is to encourage reflection on just what this trade-off entails. As the name "Pi" itself suggests, the problems raised by the hero's story are not reducible to a whole, finite answer. Indeed, the initially closed-off text raises a whole bundle of theological, ethical, and ideological issues whose discussion would exceed the scope of this essay. The point is not that *Life of Pi* resists being drawn into broader, uncontrollable contexts; it's that the book enters into those contexts under its own terms and in a different way than was the case in postmodernism. Most notably, *Life of Pi* demands (and in a certain sense creates) a new type of reader who is willing to enter into the closed frame of the text and, at least for the time being, identify with its artificially rigged center before going off on his or her own. It would be going to far to say that performatist texts like this restore subjectivity in the grand style that humanist critics of postmodernism have always been longing for. However, they do provide readers with a limited experience of identity-building under controlled, rather coercive conditions.

Sad Sacks vs. Smiles: Ingo Schulze's Simple Stories

One way of highlighting the difference between performatism and postmodernism is to take up a clear-cut case of intertextuality, which is to say one in which a narrative text deliberately cites – and modifies – a postmodern one in a way that runs counter to postmodern norms. Because in the logic of postmodernism any attempt to break out of its force field is already implicated in that field from the very beginning as a trace or quote, an explicit case of intertextuality should be a good litmus test of whether postmodernism can be cited and simultaneously turned in a direction that can't be assimilated to postmodernism's own self-fulfilling prophecies about how texts work.

An excellent example of this kind of intertextual turn is the chapter "Lächeln" ("Smiles") from Ingo Schulze's *Simple Stories*,[49] which transplants the plot of Raymond Carver's short story "Sacks"[50] from Sacramento to Munich, Germany. In both stories, a son meets a father who has broken with his family some time before; the father makes an elaborate confession to the son detailing why he left, and he gives the son a trivial gift – in Carver's story a sack of candy (which the son forgets to take with him) and in Schulze's a pair of handmade potholders.

Carver is sometimes considered no longer postmodern because of his "dirty realism" with its seedy milieus and lower-middle-class characters. However, many of his stories still use the basic postmodern strategy of first fostering, and then undermining, reader identification with central figures.[51] These shifts in sympathy are in turn a direct outgrowth of his characters' radical dualism. The folksy, engaging characteristics we observe superficially or hear in his characters' familiar Middle American diction form a kind of outer shell which effectively obscures the powerful, sinister forces roiling within them. Hence when evil, or brutality, or some strong emotion breaks out of Carver's characters, it often seems to have no immediate cause (a good example of this is the story "Tell the Women We're Going" in the collection

What We Talk About When We Talk About Love). Inasmuch as they
resort to violence, Carver's protagonists seem more like alien monsters
than like the K-Mart patrons they outwardly resemble. If we identify
with them at all, it's because we enjoy the sublime thrill of uncovering
some malevolent force lurking beneath the banality of lower middle-
class American existence.[52]

In the case of "Sacks," the father's story, which is presumably meant
to foster understanding in his son, reveals only the man's thoroughgo-
ing lasciviousness. His confession in fact resembles a traveling-salesman joke, with the father and his mistress being caught in bed by the
cuckolded husband and the father jumping half-naked through the
front window. Although in the process he seems to have experienced
some sort of epiphany, as often happens in Carver, we never find out
exactly what it is: the story breaks off before we learn how it affected
the teller.[53] Similarly, the father's gifts – jellybeans and luscious choco-
lates – are hardly more than tokens of his own petty lustfulness. The
son – aptly named Les – comes away from this reunion diminished
rather than enhanced. A traveling salesman himself, his own marriage
is also on the rocks, for reasons he doesn't choose to mention. At the
beginning, though, Les says he "wants to pass along"[54] his father's
story to us – a story that turns out to be as empty and stale as a bad
joke. In the end, the son does exactly to us what his father has done
to him: he leaves us with his own story, which is no less desolate than
that of his father's.

Having been thrust into the role of the narrator's ersatz sons, we as
readers might expect some sort of positive identification to arise from
this. Yet our relationship with Les remains uncannily empty: we get
even less out of his own story than he got out of his father's, just as
we are haunted by our inability to get a handle on exactly what he is
talking about. In spite of its "realism," Carver's story works more on
an epistemological level than a semantic one. Signifiers aren't there
to transmit inner meaning from a storyteller to someone else; they
simply pass their intrinsic emptiness on down the line. And what's
even worse: we can't get rid of them once we've got them, just as Les
can't "forget" the sack of candy he has left behind at the airport bar.
Communication appears not just as a process of endless deferral and

endless diminution of meaning, but also as the accumulation of this emptiness in involuntary acts of recollection and narration – something well in keeping with the epistemological skepticism and metaphysical pessimism peculiar to postmodernism.

At first, Schulze's father-son reunion in *Simple Stories* seems to repeat Carver's fictional setup under even less auspicious conditions. The father left his family not two, but twenty-four years ago; the son isn't just having marital problems, but lost his wife in a traffic accident and has never recovered from it emotionally. To compound things there is also a typically German East-West divide. The father left his family to defect to the West, where he remarried and became a successful doctor. His contact with his son has been limited and condescending: first a card with a 100 mark bill congratulating him on the birth of his son, then a condolence card, also with a 100 mark bill, upon the death of his wife. The son, by contrast, is one of the losers in German reunification. A former student of art history, he was thrown of out the university and is now reduced to doing odd jobs – among other things, he works as a traveling salesman (as recounted in Chapter 4, "Panic"). The son isn't even too sure about why he wanted to look up his long-lost father in the first place. Maybe he was curious, he says, maybe he was expecting to get some money.[55]

At first glance, his father's story hardly seems designed to bring the two closer. As in "Sacks," the father has experienced an epiphany that he wants to pass along to the son. After suffering a sudden stroke ("just a lightning bolt, and you're left paralyzed"[56]) he becomes a fervent believer in Christ and the bearer of a comforting, self-serving Message: "There's a purpose behind it all [...]" intones the father regarding his condition, "even if *we* can't see the purpose, or at least not right off."[57] The son, for his part, is hardly convinced of his father's sincerity: he has the feeling that "he had planned each sentence, had prepared himself for our meeting as if for a lecture."[58] The father's conversion, however, has an intertextual twist to it, for at its core is a scrambled version of the traveling-salesman story out of "Sacks." After the father's stroke, he and his wife are visited regularly by what he in the German original calls a "Holy Angel" – a Bible-thumping preacher from an unnamed Christian sect. The preacher uses the opportunity to secretly court the wife; both then run off together to Portugal. In this case, though, the joke is on the two adulterers, as the father gets religion precisely because he has been betrayed:[59]

> "So that's what they're like, I thought. That's what's behind all the sanctimony. The world's that simple. I was an enthusiastic masochist. But," my father said, squinting again as if laughing ahead of time at some joke, "do you know what, my boy? My life was only beginning. All alone? Anything but! Jesus Christ was never so close to me as in that moment! Who are we to be offended by those who bring us the message?"[60]

The father's experience, it might be added, is social as well as mystical. After his wife leaves him, the "brother and sisters" of the sect help him regain his self-dependence and make the two potholders (embroidered with an eight-pointed star) which he gives to the son. The son, in turn, hangs them right next to his stove, "so that I just have to put out an arm whenever I need them."[61]

Like Carver, Schulze uses a kind of deadpan prose that makes it difficult to separate the banal from the sublime, the ironic from the heartfelt. When Martin, the son, says he realizes his father's story is a real "Saul-to-Paul tale," he's using a common German figure of speech. Similarly, when patrons of the café smile at the son helping the lame father out of the restaurant to his taxi, it's not clear whether this occurs out of embarrassed politeness or as a spontaneous expression of true sympathy. As in Carver, we have to carefully parse all minor details to find out how they work together as a whole. And the sum of these details suggests that, unlike in "Sacks," the father's story does make a positive difference.

This difference isn't a semantic one – the son doesn't convert to Christianity or take his father's homilies to heart literally. What does happen, though, is that he himself goes through a kind of "Saul-to-Paul" conversion in his attitude towards the father. As he discovers later, the father had always sought contact to his family and assumed they would follow him to the West; it was his mother's second husband, a Party functionary, who made her send back all letters and packages from the father.[62] The son notes this changed attitude in the introduction to his narrative, although – once more in the starkly elliptical fashion typical of Carver – he doesn't tell us why:

> It's hard for me to talk about meeting my father, about how it felt at the time, I mean, to give an account of the impression he and his story made on me. Not because my memory's poor – it was barely a year ago – but because I know more now. I might even say I've become a different person.[63]

This insight is not acquired entirely after the fact. After the father has told his Saul-to-Paul story, the son begins to tell how his wife was killed in a bicycle accident. Suddenly, he is moved to confess his own irrational complicity in her fate: "I wanted Andrea to die, and then it happened."[64] Thereupon the father absolves him of his guilt ("You probably never really loved her, or at least not long enough"[65]) and, to make the ritual complete, passes him a cookie – a communion wafer of sorts, which the son places in his mouth and swallows. Once more, the situation in "Sacks" is reversed: instead of a string of self-perpetuating empty confessions, we have two "true confessions" that in spite of their trivial trappings allow a positive, symmetrical relationship between father and son to develop. The ostensive insignia of this relation – the bracket holding together the inner and outer frame – is provided by the two potholders Martin hangs up next to his sink. They stand not only for the human presence of the absent father, but also the transcendent presence of the absent Father, as embodied in the eight-pointed star. Whether we or the hero take advantage of the one or the other – as in *Life of Pi* – is a question of free choice. The posture of *believing*, however, has once more been thrust on us through the imposition of an exterior, authorially determined frame. The posture of disbelief – of thinking that all Martin has gotten out of the reunion are a pair of lousy potholders – turns into a trap that makes it well nigh impossible to read this part of *Simple Stories* in a satisfying or productive way.

Beautiful Otherness: Arundhati Roy's The God of Small Things

At this point, the critically minded reader might be moved to ask whether the experience of being trapped by an author in beautiful, comforting frames of belief is not some insidious plot designed to keep us from interrogating the exploitative mechanisms of global capitalism. Pi, although hailing from India, is not exactly your voiceless, subaltern victim: articulate and precocious in the extreme, he leaves a cozy middle-class existence in the Third World for an even cozier one in the First. And, while *Simple Stories* doesn't exactly present a rosy picture of life after reunification, it tends to reconcile differences between the ex-communist East and the capitalist West by imprinting Christian symbolism and attitudes on the fabric of everyday life. Given these examples, you might conclude that performatism is best suited to preserving liberal bourgeois norms and values.

Performatism, however, works equally well when embedded in a radical critique of ideology and power politics. The most prominent example of this that I've been able to find is Arundhati Roy's *The God of Small Things*.[66] Roy's credentials as a critic of global capitalism are beyond dispute: since writing her acclaimed novel, she has let loose a whole slew of polemical broadsides against such rewarding targets as the Indian Bomb, post-9/11 American foreign policy, and environmentally destructive development projects.[67] Like many postcolonial writers, Roy is, at least in theory, resolutely anti-essentialist: she has, for example, no patience with those of her countrymen who would separate an "authentic" India from a "corrupted" West.

This steadfast rejection of all originary sources leads to a well-known problem of self-definition. For if there is no essential, ultimate, or originary truth, how can you define your own critical position in an affirmative way? Unless you happen to be a convinced Marxist (which Roy isn't) the standard postmodern answer to this question up to now was usually this: you don't have to justify a single position because you have continually changing positions. By taking the essentialist conceits of a hegemonic Center at face value – and continually exposing their untenability as you move along – you leave behind a dynamic trail of discursive otherness that more than compensates for the loss of a hard-and-fast ideological credo. In theory, this sounds good, but in practice almost no one actually wants to live and write in this Nietzschean, peripatetic mode of endless epistemological interrogation. The result has been a repolitization of critical discourse, with explicit ideological agendas (often Marxist) existing uneasily alongside stinging critiques of essentialist truth and master narratives. Gayatri Spivak's term "strategic essentialism,"[68] which was originally supposed to make this sort of thing seem forceful and circumspect, inadvertently exposed the double standard lurking within it: the term sounds like a carte blanche allowing a discrete subject with a hidden agenda (a "strategist") to get away with doing something that he or she would deny to everyone else.[69]

At first, Roy's own solution to this problem follows a rigorously post-ideological pattern. In her essays as well as in her novel, she portrays not only India and the West, but also capitalism and Marxism as equivalent in terms of arrogance, despotic hubris, and destructiveness. A salient case is that of the Indian bomb. By building its own bomb, India has in Roy's view "enter[ed] into a contract with the very people we claim to despise," which is to say the Western societies whose histories are "spongy with the blood of others," and who "virtually invented [...] colonialism, apartheid, slavery, ethnic cleansing, germ warfare, [and] chemical weapons."[70] But just because they're runners-up in the race to acquire weapons of mutual mass destruction doesn't make the Indians any better: "All in all, I think it is fair to say that we're the hypocrites. We're the ones who've abandoned what was arguably a moral position – *i.e.* we have the technology, we can make bombs if we want to, but we won't."[71] This sort of hypocrisy is no less obtrusive on a personal level. In *The God of Small Things* the skirt-chasing Anglophile capitalist Chacko with his Marxist ideology and the wife-abusing Communist nationalist Pillai with his vested interest in a chutney factory represent two sides of the same dismal coin. And, as Roy's novel shows, when confronted by a threat to its hidden interests this sort of categorical thinking can even become lethal – as when Velutha is murdered for transgressing against the tacit "Love Laws" proscribing sexual relations between higher-caste members and untouchables.

Roy's reaction to the falseness of ideology is however radically different from those current in postmodernism and postcolonial studies. Although her positive program is not broadly formulated or very rigorous, it suggests that she regards love and beauty as *the* basic givens of human interaction:

> Railing against the past will not heal us. History has happened. It's over and done with. All we can do is to change its course by encouraging what we love instead of destroying what we don't. There is beauty yet in this brutal, damaged world of ours. Hidden, fierce, immense. Beauty that is uniquely ours and beauty that we have received with grace from others, enhanced, re-invented and made our own. We have to seek it out, nurture it, love it. Making bombs will only destroy us. It doesn't *matter* whether we use them or not. They will destroy us either way.[72]

Roy, in other words, treats mutually shared affection and pleasure in matters of taste – two utterly traditional metaphysical precepts – as an irreducible point of departure and a last defense against the encroachments of a "brutal, damaged world." The result is an intersubjective free space, a minimal scene of love and beauty amidst what is otherwise an oppressive, violent, class-ridden, sexist and generally threatening outer realm. It goes without saying that this free space can no longer be reconciled with postmodernism. For at its center – hidden, fierce, and immense – stand two metaphysical imperatives which, at least in terms of the novel, cannot be assimilated either to ideology or its endless, a posteriori critique. This is, as it were, "Kant with a sari" – Roy has transplanted the basic premises of Kantian aesthetics to the Indian subcontinent and made its focus a supple, ebony-skinned untouchable and a lambent, wide-hipped divorcée.[73]

I can't emphasize enough that Roy's originary scene of love and beauty is not entirely natural or prior to culture. In its most radical form, it is situated on the very cusp between nature and culture, at that place where distinctions between the two seem to blend most:

in incest. When the emotionally ravaged dizygotic twins Rahel and Estha make love at the end of the book after a long, involuntary separation they are doing nothing more than reaffirming the possibility of productive undifferentiation, of returning to an unregulated, discrete unity enabling them, at least in principle, to cancel out the oppressive world of Ideology, Law and History. Their own private, sorrowful scene is not just a union of doubles but is trinitarian: Rahel is sister and mother in one, a genetic and psychological stand-in for the lost, martyred mother ("She moves her mouth. Their beautiful mother's mouth"[74]). The incestuous threesome holds forth the possibility of a transcendence that is, however, not realized in the book: what the twins share "is not happiness, but hideous grief."[75]

Roy could easily have ended her story on this depressing note. As any deconstructionist would be happy to tell you, Rahel and Estha's reinscription of gender relations, although an understandable reaction to the hypocrisy of an overdifferentiated, "ideological" society, can't bring back the mother physically and can't make the twins' psyches whole. And that is why Roy, rather than tarrying in a victimary stance,[76] chooses to place an affirmative performance at the book's end upholding the possibility of a love that is not just beautiful but also productive and sublime.

This love is at its very inception revelatory and transcendent. When Velutha first catches Ammu's gaze "centuries telescoped into one evanescent moment. History was wrong-footed, caught off guard."[77] Love is a *presence*, a scene transpiring between two humans in a singular, personal moment of mutually shared beauty and affection. This scenic conception of love is repeated at the very end of the book in an affirmative way, as a beautiful *and* sublime unity transcending Law and History:

As he rose from the dark river and walked up the stone steps, she saw that the world they stood in was his. That he belonged to it. That it belonged to him. The water. The mud. The trees. The fish. The stars. He moved so easily through it. As she watched him she understood the quality of his beauty. How his labor had shaped him. How the wood he fashioned had fashioned him. Each plank he planed, each nail he drove, each thing he made, had moulded him. Had left its stamp on him. Had given him his strength, his supple grace.[78]

There is even something here that might, at least for a time, reconcile Marxists and Kantians. Unalienated beauty, it would seem, arises on the borderline between nature and human work upon that nature, just as the Kathakali Man – the ritual dancer of Kerala – is "the most beautiful of men" because "his body *is* his soul": it has been "polished and pared down, harnessed wholly to the task of story-telling."[79] Something similar occurs with words, which both the narrator and her child heroes agglutinate so as to dissolve standard grammatical boundaries in a rhythmic, sensual way ("sourmetal smell," "sariflapping," "Orangedrink Lemondrink Man" etc.). Love, language-play, carpentry and Kathakali are all performances erasing the secondary boundary lines of culture, class, and caste and replacing them with a beautiful presence which, under the right conditions, can transcend its world of "small things" and reach up to the stars.[80] The deferral of this dream in "tomorrow," the tragic last word of the book, isn't meant as an ironic put-down, but as a promise: it marks the possibility of projecting love's presentness into the future. The novel's *story* shows that this projection doesn't work (it ends with the act of grievous incest); the novel's *plot* that it does (it ends with an act of sublime love). As always in performatist works, we are given a clear choice as to what direction our attitude can take. If we opt for chronology and the belatedness of the story, we will be left with grief and desolation; if we choose the aesthetically mediated presence of the plot, we have the inspiration of love and a future which we can act on in an affirmative way.

The End of Posthistory: Bernhard Schlink's **The Reader**

The problem of how to make history present and the future palpable is something that fictional works are now also starting to recast in performatist terms. Normally, the postmodern, posthistorical argument about writing history goes something like this: any attempt to construct a unified history will prove illusory, since the historical construct, inasmuch as it pretends to closed totality, will never quite achieve identity with itself. There will always remain what Jean-Luc Nancy calls an "excess" of meaning that is not reducible to the original, central scheme.[81] Rather than shrugging this off as an insoluble hermeneutic bind, postmodernism turns it into a positive program. Historical writing becomes a double strategy, combining critiques of traditional historiography with the representation of marginalized otherness. Instead of the neat furrow of a master narrative, history becomes a sprawling field of overlapping incisions whose goal is to unearth and empower the peripheral sources of historical experience – that of the everyday, the subaltern, the victimary.

Nowhere is the problem of representing victimary experience more acute than in discourse on the Holocaust. As Eric Gans has often pointed out, the mass murder of the Jews in World War II (and, to a lesser extent, the bombing of Hiroshima and Nagasaki) shifted the focus of political thinking from the utopian center to the peripheral victim, whose fatal experience of exclusion from society became the point of departure for progressive political thought and action.[82] The goal of politics, in other words, is no longer to adhere to the right kind of ideology but to continually position yourself anew in opposition to a hegemonic center – in effect, to take on the role of a virtual victim. In the case of Nazi genocide, the lethal relation between center and periphery leaves no room for ambivalence. Between victim and perpetrator there can be no real reciprocity and no underlying, humanizing unity: you're either the murderous One or the victimary Other. The Holocaust experience, in short, has a double potency in postmodernist thought. It not only identifies Western culture as the center and source of unmitigated terror,[83] but also supplies a moral perspective that can be defined spatially and fluidly, as a position vis-à-vis that center, rather than as a rigid set of counter-rules and prescriptions. The result, as Gans suggests, is a kind of soft-hearted Nietzscheanism, with the victim, rather than the *Übermensch*, acting as the jumping-off point for a peripatetic critique of bourgeois mores.[84]

The term "the Holocaust," which came into currency in the 1960s, is itself a belated, postmodern one; it grew out of the need to make victimary experience memorable in cultural, rather than in personal, terms. In recent years, though, an ever widening gap has opened up between these two kinds of experience. Little new has been added to the vast Holocaust literature in terms of personal documentation, and the visual and literary depictions of concentration-camp horrors are so well known that they have either become clichés or diminished greatly in their power to disturb us.

In late postmodernism, this exhaustion of original victimary experience has given rise to works whose means of arguing are ultimately more aesthetic than didactic or documentary. Peter Eisenman's Holocaust Memorial in Berlin, for example, has visitors wander through a maze of huge dark gravestone-like steles reminding them forcefully of the disorientation and vulnerability of the victim, though without any specific thematic reference to the Holocaust;[85] the slashed, jagged architecture and gaping spaces of Daniel Libeskind's Jewish Museum in Berlin do essentially the same thing.[86] In literature, a Swiss gentile named Bruno Doessekker (aka Binjamin Wilkomirski) identified with the victimary plight of Polish Jews so strongly that he in effect became one and wrote a critically well-received survivor's memoir called *Bruchstücke* [Fragments]. The point is not so much that Wilkomirski/Doessekker was a deliberate fraud – he seems to have serious mental problems – but that a reading public accustomed to horrific descriptions of camp life was readily willing to accept a poetically embellished memoir which, to use Baudrillard's felicitous phrase, was "more real than real." In film, there have been attempts to stray from the well-trodden paths of victimary discourse by depicting concentration camp victims as life-affirming, comic characters (Roberto Benigni's *Life is Beautiful*) or by emphasizing fragmentary, present-day acts of remembrance over a coherent documentary exposition (Claude Lanzman's *Shoah*).

All these examples, although in their own ways successful works of art, take victimary discourse to extremes that are at the same time beginning to exhaust it. The fraudulent effectiveness of Wilkomirski's hyperreal memoir, the thematic emptiness of Eisenman's Holocaust Memorial, Benigni's inappropriate use of a comic genre, and Lanzman's staged recollections of history all suggest a basic need to inflate, exaggerate, and embellish the customary postmodern way of presenting the Holocaust as the non-reciprocal otherness experienced by victims of a relentlessly cruel, monolithic center. The simulatory effort required to renew that victimary experience has begun to compete with the very thing that it seeks to enhance; we are increasingly being confronted with modes of aesthetic excess that distract from the victimary paradigm at least as much as they renew it. In view of the rapidly fading sources of real experience, this increasingly excessive relation between art and victimhood is becoming an unavoidable fixture of all discourse on the Holocaust.

Given this unavoidable reassertion of aesthetics it's justified to ask whether there might be an alternative to victimary discourse that would open up a perspective towards the future without rewriting history to the detriment of its victims. Although the terrain is difficult and dangerous to tread, there are signs that books and movies are now beginning to focus on perpetrators, the ethical choices involved in their actions and, above all, on the possibility of atonement and reconciliation that these choices imply. Of these works, the most prominent English-language examples coming to mind are, in film, Spielberg's *Schindler's List* and, in fiction, Jonathan Safran Foer's *Everything is Illuminated* and Martin Amis's *Time's Arrow*. While I can't go into all the implications of this shift to a perpetrator perspective here, I would like to focus in on an example which treats these questions in a way that is eminently typical of literary performatism. The book I have in mind is Bernhard Schlink's *The Reader*[87] – one of the few recent German novels to become a bestseller in America and unusual in its sympathetic treatment of a former SS prison camp guard.

Although well received by the reading public and many critics both in and out of Germany, *The Reader* was met with icy reserve by those writers who noticed its deviations from the unwritten norms of victimary discourse (the book was sometimes lumped together with Wilkomirski's as an example of "disturbing" holocaust literature).[88] There is, however, a considerable aesthetic difference between the two works. Whereas Wilkomirski's book simply carries virtual identification with the victimary to its logical extreme, *The Reader* breaks with postmodernist norms by framing or artificially uniting victims and a perpetrator in closed, ritualistic scenes.

The first frame, in a Nazi work camp in Poland, is perverse and cruel. In what seems to be an act of childish narcissism, an all-powerful illiterate – Hanna – forces doomed Jewish bearers of written culture to make that culture present by reading to her out loud. Hanna seems to crave *Bildung* but can acquire it only through the application of brute force; in doing so she aids and abets a genocidal system.[89] (You might call this Kant with a cattle prod: a natural disposition towards enlightenment is coupled with pure, murderous power over scapegoated victims.)

In the second frame, Hanna repeats the reading relationship, but now replaces physical power (*Macht*) with a mixture of sexual power (*Kraft*) and maternal solicitude: she becomes a lover and ersatz mother for the underage hero Michael. Unlike the first frame, however, this ritualistic relationship, though still unequal, contains an element of reciprocity. The ritual enables Michael to continually reenact an ideal, incestuous initiation into manhood;[90] Hanna's sexual contact with an innocent allows her to repeat the camp ritual in a purified way (in symbolic terms, this is why the protagonists bathe *before* having sex and reading: they are both trying to preserve and renew what is for them a self-fashioning sacral scene). Although consensual, the affair nonetheless eventually deforms Michael; after Hanna's departure he is unable to enter into long-term relationships with other women.

In the third frame, in prison, the ritual relationship is played out again in a desexualized and depersonalized way. Hanna becomes, at least outwardly, a morally autonomous, enlightened individual: she not only learns to read on her own, but also demonstrates civil courage (she engages in a sit-down protest when funds for the prison library are to be cut off). Eventually, she levies the severest possible judgment on herself by committing suicide at the very moment where she would have been allowed to reenter society in a well-organized and comfortable way. In effect, she resists resocialization by entering into a symbolic frame of a higher order – that of the dead victims, who, as she says, are the only ones who really understand her.[91]

Michael, by contrast, manages to rid himself of the frame in a symbolic act of reduction and restitution. Although the Jewish survivor of Hanna's crime is unwilling to accept the money Hanna has saved up, she does take the tin it was kept in (replacing a similar one stolen from her in the camps and suggesting the symbolic undoing of a past injustice). This ending suggests that two autonomous subjects – a victim and a stand-in for a perpetrator – are larger than the frames that seem to enclose them. The frame, however, remains a real, indispensable means of symbolic communication between the two: even if they can't agree on the content of the frame – the survivor rejects the money inside it – they can tacitly agree on its mediating and consolatory power. This transaction, though without intrinsic value, confirms the originary mechanism of the ostensive and hence the possibility of a future, as yet deferred rapprochement.

Reviewing *The Reader*'s main features we can discern without difficulty two major fault lines running between it and the usual postmodern treatment of the Holocaust. The first such break is marked by the book's metaphysical optimism. Schlink appears to see the world, or, more precisely, the frame at hand, as something that is always open to betterment, albeit in an incremental or incomplete way. *The Reader* doesn't necessarily present us with a less damning picture of German complicity in genocide than postmodernism did – the book makes no attempt to excuse Hanna's crime or deny the suffering of her victims. *The Reader* does however suggest that people – and in particular perpetrators – are enclosed in ritualized frames at least partially of their own making, and that these frames can change (or be changed) for the better over time. This contrasts starkly with the metaphysical pessimism of postmodernism, which would condemn us to simulate endlessly a victimary condition now lying three full generations behind us. Using a fictional scenario, *The Reader* demonstrates the possibility of framed, individually constructed historical change rather than the Eternal Return of the Slightly Different.

The second radical break with postmodern norms is *The Reader*'s insistence on framed identification with a perpetrator as well as on the common origin (not the common moral status) of perpetrator and victim. *The Reader*'s postmodern and/or psychoanalytic critics were quick to point out that the book maneuvers us into identifying with a perpetrator and her lover, who is in a sense both her accomplice and victim.[92] From a postmodernist perspective, which allows no commonality or reciprocity between victim and perpetrator, this forced identification with a perpetrator is accompanied by a fatal *quid pro quo*. According to this view, Schlink causes Michael to usurp the victimary position usually occupied by the Jews, but only at the cost of encasing him in an obsessive, sexually charged shell that effectively shuts out all moral reflection.[93] In this interpretation, Michael is burdened by the "inability to mourn," which is to say by the inability to rid himself of his obsession with his narcissistic love-object Hanna. Michael, it would seem, is condemned to repeat the experience of the entire German people, who, in the sweeping vision of the psychoanalysts Alexander and Margarete Mitscherlich, redirected their libidinal energy after the war into "derealizing" or repressing the memory of Nazi crimes and their own self-serving love of Hitler.[94] The cure recommended by the Mitscherlichs in 1967 was, incidentally, precisely that drastic confrontation with images of heaped-up corpses that has since grown into a visual cliché.[95] This remedy is repeated in one form or another by *The Reader*'s postmodern critics, who urge us to reflect once more on "the incommensurability of the victimary perspective and the experience of the perpetrator collective"[96] or, in a more resolute Nietzschean mode, to grapple with the possibility that the defining feature of humanity is its ability to inflict an infinite amount pain on others for no particular reason.[97]

As such, it is no surprise that postmodern and psychoanalytically minded critics reject out of hand a book that shows how a perpetrator develops morally in terms of closed, ritualized frames. In themselves, these frames – the work camp, the secret affair with a minor, the prison – are at worst cruel and at best ambivalent. However, they help create inner scenes of self-fashioning which, though flawed and constricted, allow Hanna to transcend the previous frame that she happened to be caught up in. This sort of ritualized, spatially staggered individuation fits in well with the sociological concept of framing developed by Erving Goffman in the tradition of Emile Durkheim.[98] Goffman sees patterns of everyday behavior as transpiring within social frames or codes that enable individuals to maintain a modicum of dignity and selfhood under trying or embarrassing circumstances (these frames are in turn thought to represent the secularized remnants of what was once a universally binding religious experience[99]). This closed, face-to-face mode of individuation stands directly opposed to the Nietzschean-Freudian one, which demands that subjects forthrightly bare their psyches in a virtual, open-ended confrontation with the overwhelming terror of the Holocaust – a confrontation in which the subject can by definition never win. *The Reader*, it would seem, argues implicitly against the kind of over-intellectualized, self-accusatory type of discourse that has long characterized the Holocaust discussion in Germany.

The ultimate scandal associated with *The Reader* is however its "confusion" of victimary and perpetrator roles. Once more, *The Reader* never conflates these issues in a moral or legal sense. There is never any doubt about Hanna's guilt, and in spite of Michael's identification with her (which we share in a vicarious, but guarded way) she never becomes the object of false, unmediated sentiment.[100] The true scandal from a postmodern perspective is that the illiterate Hanna's actions are motivated by a fear of being socially stigmatized and scapegoated – precisely that fate that is visited upon the Jewish victims of Nazi genocide. Hanna is subject along with the Jews to what René Girard would call the victimage mechanism, an originary event in which societies seek to distract from the mimetic rivalry within them by lynching innocent victims.[101] The crimes perpetrated by Hanna (whose Germanic name is homonymous with the Hebrew Hannah) arise from her own private fear of that potential victimage; in fact, that fear is so powerful that it later causes her to incriminate herself in court in a wholly irrational, self-defeating way. In the same way, Hanna's grotesque misuse of Jewish prisoners to acquire *Bildung* suggests that she is has no fear whatsoever of being contaminated by their racially defined otherness. Hanna's ritualized, narcissistic framing of her own self – her basic state of opacity – makes her immune to pressure from the victimizing community, but also to abstract legal reasoning and racist ideology. In the end, as Bill Niven has pointed out, Hanna doesn't even really become a morally autonomous individual, in spite of her immersion in Holocaust literature and the classics of bourgeois culture.[102] Rather, by sacrificing herself through suicide, she remains true to the victimage mechanism. In a final act of sacrificial hubris she expels herself from society, in effect preferring to deify herself as a victim rather than reenter society as an autonomous, morally responsible individual.

The Reader doesn't try to justify Hanna's obvious moral deficits or her complicity in mass murder. It does, however, recast the problem of reckoning with the Holocaust in terms of frames in which a combination of love, enlightenment, and coercion enable the slow, albeit incomplete restitution of an autonomous moral conscience. The book encourages us, along with Michael, to *believe* in Hanna's step-by-step redemption; although this belief is only partially fulfilled, it also enables us, along with Michael, to break with a cycle of endless mourning over a traumatic past. In spite of Schlink's metaphysical optimism – marked by his implanting an unquenchable desire for culture in an unlikely heroine – *The Reader* doesn't enthrone that desire as the linear, progressive accumulation of sweetness and light. This is because the frame is both a haven and a burden. While creating a ritualized free space in which a subject may develop more or less on his or her own terms, the frame at the same times cuts the subject off from the public domain in which that development could achieve general acceptance.

In the long run it is neither the frame itself nor its content taken alone that are essential for progress, but rather a positive *performance* that transcends both. This performance is, I think, embodied in the symbolic transaction between Michael and the Jewish survivor. The frame – the tin – is not discarded or denied, but instead becomes a concrete, unified (ostensive) sign of a perpetrator's desire for redemption and a victim's desire to undo the horrific experience of the victimary past. Projected onto a common object, these two mutually exclusive perspectives allow us to *believe* that we can transcend the past, for without this belief we are condemned to repeat it endlessly. The deconstruction of this double projection – which is once more not terribly hard to do – throws us back into a cycle of virtual mourning; its acceptance creates a framed, minimal moment of presence that would allow us to move forward into the future. The danger is not so much that we are going to succumb uncritically to old illusions, as the posthistorical critique insinuates,[103] but that we are going to miss out on the future by endlessly simulating an increasingly hazy, emotionally distant past. The performatist projection doesn't seek to blot out that past and plunge blindly into the future; instead, it offers a frame grounded in presence that mediates between the two. Given the rapid waning of real historical experience and the aesthetic excesses that inevitably accompany the simulation of that experience, the performatist projection offers a very real perspective for moving, frame by frame, out of the seemingly endless expanse of posthistory.

Conclusion

The examples discussed here suggest that the switch to a radical monist, post-millennial, or performatist kind of consciousness is not going to cause writers to burst out in hosannas to global capitalism. What it does mean, though, is that the ironic act of displaying your political impotence on the one hand and flaunting your epistemological superiority on the other is becoming increasingly obsolete as a literary device. By contrast, the rise of radical monism – and here one must emphasize the word "radical" – appears to meet a real cultural need to create spatially discrete identities or performances within global capitalism that would enable whole, beautiful, or spiritualized pockets of resistance to arise within it.

Using the examples I have discussed here as a rough guide, you could speak of a "right" and "left" path to this goal. The "right" method is not uncritical of capitalism. However, it tries to work within it by creating inspirational projections in its inner space (by aspiring what Sloterdijk calls spheres or foams – whole bubbles of belief, faith, truth etc.). The "left" strategy corresponds roughly to the attempt to amalgamate variegated otherness into an appealing, tasteful object of cultural identity (a nice hot chutney, so to speak). This strategy seems particularly appropriate to postcolonial writers, as it would allow them to reify attributes from their own cultures that are at the same time universally binding or "necessary" for others to enjoy in the Kantian sense.

Finally, there is also a "terrorist" alternative suggesting the possibility of a *total* critique of capitalism that takes place in the mode of "as if." The terrorist aesthete plays *va banque* with the sublime possibility of a radical monist alternative to capitalism, postmodern society or Western culture per se – all, of course, within the ostensive confines of a fictional frame. This perspective is, interestingly enough, indigenous to Eastern Europe, where the annihilation of capitalism is treated as a metaphysical rather than as a real possibility. In Russia the main proponent of this line is Viktor Pelevin, whose work has been touched on in Chapter One.[104] A recent Czech example is Miloš Urban's *Sevenchurch. A Gothic Novel of Prague*,[105] whose basic plot motif is the struggle for control over post-postmodern space and form. Echoing an old theme of Czech culture, the book sets the Gothic style of the Czech high Middle Ages against the Baroque of the Counterreformation, whose onset coincided with the long-term loss of Czech national sovereignty. The main protagonists of *Sevenchurch* are all enthusiastic, if not to say fanatical, admirers of the Gothic and detractors of the Baroque, whose ornamental bombast and playful superficiality are clearly reminiscent of postmodernism. The Gothic, by contrast, is declared to be the only epoch at all capable of realizing architectonic transcendence, "it realized the victory of spirit over matter in human dwellings. In all preceding and following epochs exactly the opposite was the case."[106]

The hero and narrator of the novel, a failed history student and ex-policeman named Švach, is gradually initiated into the plans of a mysterious sect that seeks to roll back democracy in favor of a medieval regime. The novel takes the form of a detective story emphasizing the sublime, "gothic" side of the narrator-hero's perspective as he uncovers ever new atrocities and eavesdrops on ominous sexual practices (part of which, incidentally, takes place in the corridors of a dark, labyrinthine hotel). After the zenith of sublime terror has been achieved – the hero is subjected to a fake execution – we find out that the sect has already achieved its goal. Švach, who has now become a faithful disciple of the group, informs us that the center of Prague has been cut off from the surrounding world and is being ruled according to the cruel dictates of the "wonderful, beatific 14th century."[107]

As in "Hotel Capital," *Sevenchurch* forces a spatially defined monist order upon the reader. However, this odd novelistic performance is neither ideological in nature – the real-life Urban is not a closet monarchist – nor can it be explained as an exercise in infinite post-modern regress. Rather, we are confronted with a setup or frame similar to that in "Hotel Capital." The point is not that we actually identify with the sect's claims about Gothic style, but that we more or less involuntarily assume a position of terrified awe vis-à-vis the text. Upon finishing the book, we are transfixed and stunned by its representation of the victory of a whole, monist order without necessarily agreeing with its actual content.[108]

All in all, *Sevenchurch* allows us to assume the cognitive position of a *terrorist* without having to share his or her practical interests. This sublime or terrorist monism comprises a *necessary* counterpart to the monolithic capitalist world order, whose metaphysical destruction must take place all at once in order to be truly gratifying (we will recall: in the Butlerian ambience of *Hotel World* the unshakeable hegemony of global capitalism is expressly *confirmed*: resistance takes place only partially, in a mode of murky, haphazard solidarity among victims). Rather than basking in a victimary mode *Sevenchurch* employs a high aesthetic that allows you to shoot off your resentment all at once in the framework of a sublime projection. All this, needless to say, takes place in a atmosphere of self-irony suggesting that totally transcending capitalism is a possible, but not a viable option. For better or worse, we are stuck *inside* the whole of capitalism, and these and similar works suggest that authors in the new epoch are starting to deal with this situation on their own terms.

Chapter 3

Performatism in the Movies

Had I set out to write an aesthetic assessment of artistically ambitious movies fifteen years ago, my discussion would have been heavily skewed towards such topics as otherness, undecidability, belatedness, and ironic regress – in short, towards the devices and ways of knowing normally associated with postmodernism. As examples, I might have singled out movies like David Lynch's *Blue Velvet* (1986), Jim Jarmusch's *Mystery Train* (1989), Lars von Trier's *Europa* (1990), Jonathan Demme's *Something Wild* (1987), or the Coen brothers' *Barton Fink* (1991). And, had I ventured a glance into the future, I would almost certainly have predicted that the ironic perspective, deferred identifications, and metaphysical pessimism of these films would continue on seamlessly into an endless posthistorical future. Beginning sometime in the mid-to-late 1990's, however, a massive sea change in the subject matter and focus of independently made movies began to take place. These movies, which all bore the imprint of sophisticated *auteur* sensibility, began to do curious things. They starting treating themes of identity, reconciliation, and belief. They forced viewers to identify with single-minded characters and their sacrificial, redemptive acts. And, as if all this were not enough, they began to set up dramatically staged, emotionally moving denouements. As milestones in this development you could cite productions like Lars von Trier's *Idiots* (1997) and Thomas Vinterberg's *The Celebration* (1998); Jim Jarmusch's *Ghost Dog* (1999); Tom Tykwer's *Run Lola Run* (1999); and, in mainstream cinema, the Oscar-winning *American Beauty* (1999). Before the year 2000, it might still have been possible to write off this sort of movie as a sentimental aberration. Since then, however, dozens of important and striking films have appeared that follow this same threefold pattern. Indeed, it has become increasingly hard to find serious movies wholly committed to postmodernist

themes and strategies, and it is becoming increasingly hard to apply
poststructuralist theory in a productive way to the new type of film.

In the following discussion, I wish to apply the notion of performatism developed in the previous chapters to film. In terms of
plot, this requires no great adjustments. The basic rule of the double
frame applies the same way to movies as it does to narrative literature.
Inner frames (or originary scenes) have to "lock" with outer ones,
otherwise no performance – no move by an opaque subject towards
transcendence – is possible. Movies, however, also employ specific
audio-visual means requiring a theoretical frame of reference of their
own. Using Gilles Deleuze's deist theory of cinema as a foil, I have
constructed a theist, performatist alternative that I think is better
suited to explaining the current innovations now taking place in contemporary cinema.

When talking about movies systematically in any way, you are
usually faced at some point with the choice between mainstream
Hollywood productions or so-called art movies. As it turned out,
the nature of my topic – epochal innovation – didn't allow for too
much leeway. Hollywood does turn out innovative movies, but for
the most part tends to sugarcoat the themes and devices I'm interested in (Tom Hanks movies like *Forrest Gump*, *Cast Away*, and *The
Green Mile* are a case in point). The main problem with art movies, by contrast, is accessibility. Not being a festival-hopping professional critic, I decided to concentrate on European movies and
North American independent productions that are readily available
on video or DVD. For comparison's sake, though, I have included in
my collection several bona fide mainstream Hollywood movies such
as David Fincher's *Panic Room* or the Jack Nicholson vehicle *About
Schmidt*. Needless to say, it would have been possible to expand
greatly the selection of movies to which performatism can be said to
apply. To make the discussion manageable I've restricted myself to
about fifteen striking examples; towards the end of the chapter I've
devoted a separate discussion to three movies that are particularly
interesting in cinematographic terms: The Coen Brothers' *The Man
Who Wasn't There*, Aleksandr Sokurov's *The Russian Ark*, and Christopher Nolan's *Memento*.

Framing in Performatist Film

As in narrative genres in literature, performatist movie plots are centered around inner or ostensive frames. These frames, although very different in their individual details, resemble the originary ostensive scene in the sense that they create a constructed or artificial proximity between things, people, and simple physical acts. As is the case with originary ostensivity, they have both an immanent (human) and a transcendent side to them. These two sides – the immanent and the putatively transcendent – interact in peculiar ways to generate performatist plot patterns.

In their anthropological, "psychological" guise these scenes form by more-or-less spontaneous agreement among characters, tend to be unstable, and are marked by an element of deceit. When the two lovers in Patrice Chéreau's *Intimacy* meet to copulate without exchanging words, they create precisely this kind of scene in an erotic, human mode. When Amélie (in the eponymous movie) "plays God" by returning a small box of toys to the lonely man who as a child once hid them away, she creates a revelatory scene which is accepted by the man as an everyday miracle. When the seven unfortunate characters in the science-fiction thriller *Cube* wake up for no good reason in a very large and extremely dangerous labyrinth of interconnected boxes, the scene challenges them to act in an ethically coherent way to get out. Although the movie suggests that the frame is man-made, we never learn exactly who made it or why. The frame itself remains an ineffable origin, as if God-given; the characters in it show their humanity – or lack of it – in trying to overcome its lethal traps.

The thing-related closure experienced in such primary scenes acts as a *ground* for the rest of the plot. To work, the constructed ur-scene must be confirmed somewhere else on the higher, authorial level of the outer frame. If this occurs, it enables the protagonists and ourselves us to experience such scenes as part of a greater, transcendent frame, and thus as *ethical, beautiful,* or *sublime.* Beauty and sublimity are constructed, for example, when Ricky Fitts deifies a white plastic bag in *American Beauty,* and a kind of ethical beauty is generated when

Amélie sets up her little traps in which people "discover" small objects that bring happiness to them. One of the most poignant such ethical moments, in Lars von Trier's *Idiots*, involves two Hell's Angels, an exposed penis, and an act of urination – you have to see it to believe it.[1] Depending on theme and plot, however, many other variations are possible, including suspense and comedy. In David Fincher's slick Hollywood production *Panic Room*, for example, the primary frame is a trap, with the designer of the safe room trying to break back into his own creation. In Spike Jonze's brilliant, bizarre comedy *Being John Malkovich* the primary frame – John Malkovich himself – is patently absurd, as are the magical principles governing its usage.

Inner frames in themselves do not necessarily lead to greater realism, and certainly not to any sort of authenticity. The sex practiced by the breathless, physically rather ordinary couple in *Intimacy* may appear "realistic" to us against the background of dreamily filmed Hollywood sex scenes. However, there is nothing particularly authentic or natural about their trysts, which are based on a kind of contractual agreement (which dissolves anyway as the movie goes on). Similarly, there is nothing intrinsically authentic about the digitalized movie of a plastic bag whipping around in the wind in *American Beauty* or about Amélie's little pranks, which take place in an idealized Montmarte and are based on well-meant deceit. Artistic ostensivity involves a performance that creates ethical beauty or sublimity and occludes meaning. However, this is possible only because of a fit between an inner scene and a higher, authorial will that causes that ethical beauty or sublimity to occur, or that meaning to be shut out. There is nothing at all authentic about this spontaneous agreement, and indeed it is always accompanied by resentful suspicion – intrinsic to the ostensive sign – that someone is benefiting from it more than he or she should. Performatist art tries to frame and contain this resentment, to create scenes or constructs in which viewers or peripheral characters can identify with a central, often sacrificial experience to the point where they can benefit from it themselves. The point of performatism is not to restore the dogmatic authority of the center, but rather to return, if only temporarily, to the originary scene as way of reviving the ostensive experience of love, beauty, and reconciliation.

I cannot emphasize enough that this "return" to originary scenes is an artificially arranged journey subject to ironic twists and turns of its own. One of the most effective and moving attempts to portray a lengthy sojourn in ostensivity is the Russian movie *Kukushka* (The Cuckoo), which, unfortunately, has not been widely distributed in the West. In *Kukushka*, the circumstances of the Russo-Finnish war in 1944 throw together three people who don't understand one another's language: a young Lapp woman whose husband is lost in the war, a Russian officer who was betrayed to the secret police by a trusted underling, and a Finnish sniper fighting for the Germans (who have in turn betrayed him). Unable to explain the nuances of their political and personal plight to the others, all have to make do with purely ostensive means of communication (dubbed-in oral translations allow us to understand what the Finnish and Lapp characters are actually saying). Trying to demonstrate to the Russian that he is a former student and not a Nazi, for example, the Finn helplessly yells at him using the only Russian words that he knows: "Tolstoy – *War and Peace*! Dostoevsky – *The Idiot*!" Not surprisingly, this sort of ostensive communication doesn't lead to any natural sort of rapprochement. In fact, just before he learns the war is over the Russian grievously wounds the Finn, whom he thinks is a convinced Nazi.

Kukushka vividly demonstrates the multiple ironies that arise when we, as creatures of semiotic complexity and nuance, are forced to return to direct, non-narrative modes of communication. The movie could have chosen to make a shambles out of this irony: instead, it presents us with a happy end based on feeling and being rather than on knowing. At the movie's conclusion, the young Lapp woman tells her two twin sons (who could have been fathered by either the Finn or the Russian) an idealized – and false – version of who their fathers were and how they got along. This falsification isn't intentional: the Lapp woman simply never did understand the things that happened out of her immediate line of sight and that were "explained" to her in Finnish or Russian. None of the three characters, in fact, will ever understand exactly what happened to them in the ostensive situation; all, however, are able to overcome the resentment and rivalry inherent to it. As viewers, we know that the characters lack this understanding, but we identify with their ability to transcend all the same. The post-modern moment of knowing is contained in the aesthetic gesture of the movie; it is simply not intended to be the last word.

Just how the resentment arising out of a primary or ostensive scene is dealt with in narrative is a problem of *intermediate frames*. These frames "compete" in a certain sense with the primary frames established by or around key characters. Examples of a fatal competition would be that between the Samurai frame of Ghost Dog in the eponymous movie and the Mafia frame of his "master" Louie. Through Ghost Dog's self-sacrifice at the end of the film, however, it is clear that the competition is one-sided. Although the Mafia code triumphs in a purely physical sense, Ghost Dog's samurai ethos is successfully carried over to a little girl, who will presumably continue the struggle in a non-violent, more spiritualized way. This sort of struggle is even more intense in *Cube*, where seven differently "framed" characters – an architect, an escape artist, a policeman, an autist etc. – help and hinder one another trying to get out of an enormous, inexplicable labyrinth. The beneficiary of this process is the person with the simplest frame, the autist Kazan, who at the same time represents a new, minimal origin. Once more, it is absolutely imperative that the inner frame lock into the outer one, creating a coherent event or denouement within the work in question.

When postmodernists misinterpret performatist works it is almost always because they think that there is only kind of legitimate frame: the intermediate one. This corresponds, in effect, to the Derridean notion of the parergon: it is that which mediates between inside and out while being reducible to neither.[2] The irreducible frame (a.k.a. différance, pharmakon, hymen, trace, gramme etc.) becomes the focal point of interest, even though (or, more likely, exactly because) it itself does not represent anything in particular and fails to bring about the closure it seems to promise. Performatist works of art, of course, also allow contradictory and/or deceptive intermediate frames to develop. However, if the work is to remain performatist, such frames must always be locked into a kind of full nelson between the primary and the outer frame, which *do* stake out binding positions within the world of the narrative. The existence of such a basic narrative lock or fit between outside and in is *the* crucial element defining a performatist work, and, from a postmodernist point of view, its most disturbing and unacceptable feature. [3]

Outer frames (or work frames) give performatist works their peculiar unpostmodern fit or feel. The outer frame deliberately creates a monolithic point of view forcing the viewer back "into" the work (in this sense you could say that the movie itself becomes one giant ostensive sign which the viewer must accept or reject in one fell swoop). Instead of constantly intertwining the inner space of the work with the endless outer space of the context, as Derrida prescribes, the outer frame drives a wedge between the work and its context. It forces us, at least temporarily, to perceive the outer space as a blank, transcendent Beyond, and it forces us to focus back in on and privilege certain objects, acts or persons in the work. The outer frame, in short, creates the temporarily binding conditions that cause mundane objects, acts or people to become beautiful or ethical, sanctified or sublime. For example, the famous white plastic bag in *American Beauty* that Ricky Fitts thinks is beautiful would not appear so to us if it did not turn up again in the outer frame of the movie narrated by the now deified Lester Burnham. Similarly, in Lars von Trier's *Dancer in the Dark* you would not give a hoot about a half-blind Czech factory worker, her money troubles, or her passion for schmaltzy musicals if she did not sacrifice herself in such an ostentatious and "fitting" way at the end of the movie (she foregoes the money needed for her defense so that it may be used for her son's eye operation).

Postmodernists, by contrast, tend to think of outer frames either as instruments of hegemonial repression or as supplemental frippery that can be ignored at will. This applies to anyone, for example, who thinks *American Beauty* is nothing more than a scathing deconstruction of American middle-class life. If you believe this, you will also believe that the frame represented by the deified narrator is little more than an odd device that helps wrap up the social criticism practiced within the movie (interestingly enough, if do so, you will be taking the position Derrida ascribed to Kant in *The Truth in Painting*, i.e., you will write off the sacralizing frame as a mere ornament). Performatist outer frames always *do* something to a viewer, so that he or she – at least temporarily – resists being sucked up in the infinite regress of discourse so dear to postmodernism. In keeping with Goffman and Gans, you could say that the outer frame (in its "lock" with the inner one) makes the work itself into a scene to which the viewer or reader reacts in a cult-like, ritualistic way. Additionally, the frame of the performatist work "buys time" for viewers to plunge back into the scene and be affected by it once more, rather than leading them out into an endless tangle of spatial and temporal traces from which there is no return.

Ultimately, of course, the performatist outer frame is not impermeable or inviolable. Performatist works, in fact, are probably no less rich in citations and allusions than any others (a notable example is *The Man Who Wasn't There*, which draws heavily and obviously on noir classics like *Murder, My Lovely* and *Double Indemnity*). Also, the rigid outer frame cannot and should not be exempted from ideological and metaphysical critiques. As a general rule of thumb, though, the more closed and restrictive the narrative outer frame, the more performatist it will "feel" to the viewer, and the greater will be its aesthetic-ritualistic impact. In this sense performatist movies tend towards the "closed" type of film described by Leo Braudy.[4] In such movies, as Braudy suggests, "plot and pattern seem imposed from above,"[5] and the viewer has the feeling of being entrapped and manipulated. However, unlike the malevolent atmosphere projected in the movies of Braudy's "closed" directors like Hitchcock and Lang, performatist films use rigid outer frames to suggest the existence of a redeeming transcendency, of a purifying Beyond outside the film. When the exposed and humiliated child-abusing patriarch in Vinterberg's *The Celebration* voluntarily leaves the family gathering to exit forever into the blinding glare of the morning sun, then this is just such a redemptive ending. The toppled patriarch has now become the scapegoat of the family collective; his expulsion from the group is not just an act of belated justice, but also one of sacralization in the sense used by René Girard.[6] The evil patriarch will become a Danish family deity; he will be transported into a realm of "white" myth from which the regrouped collective will continue to derive solace and inner strength from having defeating him.

Here, a poststructuralist might object that the collective is simply whitewashing a trauma in order to preserve the paternal, phallic order. And, indeed, as Derrida likes to say, there is no way of preventing anyone from taking this kind of stance. However, such a viewer will have missed the point of the movie, which is to make us identify with the ability of a lifelong victim to transcend his victimary status in a way that is also productive for the community around him. The performatist work shows how it *feels* to be a victim of incest, and it shows how a corrupted social frame can be rejuvenated in order to accommodate what evidently remains a very basic problem of human interaction. This rejuvenation, in turn, can only be done by framing – by artificially focusing in on – the victim's debasement, which is revealed and ritually reenacted before the eyes of all. In *The Celebration*, Christian's revelation of his own victimization causes him to be temporarily expelled from the group, thus offering himself as a scapegoat – but also as a medium of redemption for the family, who tacitly aided and abetted the father.

By contrast, in Derrida's way of thinking, which transforms everything from defloration to the threat of nuclear war into an endless skein of discursive paradoxes, the victim's psychological and physical plight is never made the focus of a centered identification. Instead, victims are compensated with a privileged, elusive position allowing them to act as the critical, incontrovertible Other of whatever hegemonic force happens to be weighing down on them. In a Derridean world, Christian's victimary experience would have been intellectualized and sublimated in a network of decentered sign relations rather than played out again in a simplistic and rather obvious ritual; the Derridean dynamic allows no performance or scene that you could identify with directly.

Performatism also has "open" films. However, these are constructed differently than postmodern conundrums or the sort of cinematic waltzes through reality described by Siegfried Kracauer. Examples of fairly open performatist films would be the Norwegian comedy *Elling*, Spike Jonze's *Being John Malkovich*, and Tom Tykwer's *The Princess and the Warrior*. *Elling*'s hero, a self-proclaimed "mother's son," must be pulled out of a closet by the police after his dominating mother dies.

Cast out of a mental institution into the world, he gradually acquires the ability to overcome the spatial and social frames confining him. In the end, he walks the city streets at night – still a "mother's son," as he says, but now also an unknown urban poet (he publishes by placing his poetry in miniature frames – boxes of sauerkraut that he buys and returns to the supermarket). Elling has transcended the series of closed institutional spaces confining him, yet still remains true to the kernel of his own closed-in self, which is the result of an imposed matriarchal order and not an authentic state of being or knowledge.

In *Being John Malkovich* the openness is rooted in the absurd outer frame of the movie, which suggests that human "vessels" can be occupied by other people, thus allowing them to live forever. At the end, a new vessel – a little girl – is ogled by the old vessel – John Malkovich – and the film gives us to understand that the framing process will be continued ad infinitum. And, in Tykwer's *The Princess and the Warrior*, the two main characters, having successfully fled from a sanatorium where the "Princess" works, escape to a cottage facing out onto the vast, sublime expanse of an open, unmarked body of water – itself a larger incarnation of the live-saving pond into which the two lovers leapt from the hospital rooftop. This kind of leap into transcendence is even more pronounced (or overdone, as the case may be) in Tykwer's *Heaven*, in which the two fleeing protagonists hijack a police helicopter and literally disappear into the sky. Openness in Tykwer's movies is practically identical with the experience of sublimity, of a transcendent, unfathomable limit.

Openness can also result from ambivalence in the outer frame (not to be confused with undecidability, which as an aesthetic device rubs your nose in the fact that you can never definitively know what is going on in a movie's plot). *Intimacy* doesn't really end happily – the two lovers Claire and Jay part forever – but it seems clear that Jay, whose jealousy and curiosity destroyed the silent relationship, has actually fallen in love with Claire. Their last meeting is "consecrated," as it were, by the near presence of the gay French bartender Ian, who is the only person in the movie with a positive attitude toward human relationships (earlier on, when Jay cynically "confesses" that he meets a woman just to copulate with her in silence,

Ian earnestly replies that "it's not often you come across somebody who wants the same thing" – a perfect formulation of the ostensive scene in an erotic mode). It's not clear what will happen to the protagonists – hence the openness – but the movie does suggest that it is possible to love, even if the realization comes belatedly.

Something comparable also happens in *About Schmidt*, in which the widowed, retired hero is forced into conflicts with practically all the conventional social frames surrounding him. Although he doesn't succeed in transcending these frames in a satisfying way, it would seem that he nonetheless experiences a kind of epiphany at the very end of the movie (Schmidt bursts into tears upon receiving a drawing from his African foster child that shows two stick figures next to one another holding hands). We're not sure what will happen to Schmidt after this, but it seems certain that this confrontation with an originary, scenic affirmation of human love has moved him in some fundamental way. The ostensive implication of the drawing – which Schmidt appears to understand – is that a loving relationship is still possible between humans anywhere, under any social circumstances, and in spite of all conventional trappings.

From Deism to Theism

One way of thinking of the shift from postmodernism to performatism is to conceive of it as shift from a radically deist notion of the world to a radically theist one. Regarding film, this theological subtext must be taken quite literally. This is because the most incisive and comprehensive postmodern theory of film, that of Gilles Deleuze,[7] is based on an entirely conscious use of the deist metaphysics developed by Leibniz and continued later by Bergson. In this tradition, the notion of a personal God is replaced by a dynamic, constantly shifting relation between parts and a whole. By definition, the whole represents a virtual field of possibility that the parts actualize in their own dynamic, individual ways. Leibniz, whose frame of reference is mainly metaphysical, calls the virtual whole "God" and the parts "monads." For Bergson the virtual whole becomes Time; for Deleuze, "cinema" or "meta-cinema." Unlike his predecessors, Deleuze considers the parts to be fairly arbitrary; they can be just about anything that is physically set off from the never-ending flow of energy coursing through the world. Deleuze, for example, treats what he calls "frames" (*mise en scène*), "shots," "images," and even "faces" in pretty much the same way that Leibniz speaks of monads. Each part actualizes the virtual whole of the movie (or the virtual whole of all movies); at the same time, the virtual whole is constituted by the specific inner dynamic of the image unfolding within it. The part, which represents a certain segment of movement through the whole, is defined by the whole, while the whole, in its virtual plenitude, eludes anything but partial, constantly shifting perceptions of what it might be in toto. Deleuzian concepts reverberate with this radically relational, decentered logic, which is meant to cut through our spatially fixed concepts and tap into the virtual, open Whole of relations around them – much in the same way that Bergson wants us to cut through our spatially fixed concepts in the *durée* and tap into a rather static, diffuse kind of virtual Time (in reality the simultaneity of all dynamic, immanent relations, or the deist God).

The point here is not to belittle Deleuze's theory, which is a brilliantly conceived work of applied philosophy and a useful tool for thinking about movies. Film *is* a fluid and temporal medium, and certainly no theorist today – let alone director – would want to return to an aesthetic based on still photography or the ironclad type of montage practiced by Eisenstein. However, I think it is time we realized that the flowing, endlessly open, deist world of postmodern film effectively described by Deleuze is now being exposed to strategies of framing, centering, and ordering that are comparable to those found in theist cosmologies.[8] In short, filmmakers are beginning to impose closed, monistically organized narrative frames on what is by nature a moving, fluid medium. Rather than being based on abstract or impersonal part/whole relationships, fictional worlds are now shown to be set in a world that appears to have been "framed" or formed by a personal creator, who may appear explicitly or implicitly in the film.

Within this framed world, characters tend to act like personal creators in their relations with other people. Worlds constructed in this way become ethical by definition (whether subjects really *act* ethically in that world is another matter – deceit is always possible). What is important, however, is no longer the relation of a part to a whole, but rather of one discrete, creative subject to another within the greater frame of the narrative world – a situation that is specifically ethical and aesthetic in the way used by Kant, and specifically anthropological in the way used by Gans.[9] Performatism, you could say, seeks to restore a space where transcendence, goodness, and beauty can be experienced vicariously, by identifying with fictional ostensive scenes (inner frames) and with the possibility of transcendence as such (outer frames). In this kind of "framed" art, we can all appreciate and be moved by incredible events even if we "know better" – i.e., even if we know they don't apply in the practical world.

This ethical imperative regarding other individuals can be made into a element of plot, even in rather unconventional, violent situations. In *Panic Room*, for example, the theist creator of the safe room, Burnham, played by Forest Whitaker, is driven by a double dose of resentment. He resents Meg's having a three-story Manhattan townhouse – the loot from a messy divorce – and he needs the millions hidden in the panic room to resolve a nasty custody battle of his own. After successfully getting into the room, however, his respect for the human object of desire (the child in the custody case, equivalent to his own) causes him to aid Meg's daughter, to whom he administers a badly needed insulin shot. Ultimately, Burnham will shoot the evil, faceless Raoul to save both mother and daughter; at the end of the movie, the cornered burglar stands with arms spread, Christ-like, as 22 million dollars in ill-gotten bank deeds flutter away in the wind.

The rather more cynical and complex *Cube* is less sanguine about how human nature reacts in a closed, threatening frame. At the end of the movie, only the resentment-free autist Kazan manages to get out of the Cube, with all the other characters either falling prey to their own hubris or to resentful rivalry. The movie suggests that an act of transcendence – escaping the Cube – can come about only through a transpersonal mixture of rivalry and cooperation, of intentionality and disinterestedness. The movie ends by deifying a new, "simple" origin represented by a cowed, stuttering character who fears the color red – the color of blood – above all else. And, as in *The Celebration* and *The*

Man Who Wasn't There, the hero stumbles out into a blinding white light suggesting the infinite openness and sublimity of experience beyond the outer work frame. The deification of the subject, though hardly noticed any more in everyday life, is now being brought to the fore in narrative arts like the cinema.

The performatist subject, like Goffman's, is a constructed or framed one. Unlike Goffman's facile and highly adaptive social actor, however, performatist heroes and heroines are, at least at the beginning of their development, locked into a tight "fit" with a single, set frame. These fits can be more-or-less self-imposed, as in *Idiots*, *Ghost Dog* and *American Beauty* or, as more usually seems to be the case, involuntary, as in *Amélie, Elling, The Celebration, Being John Malkovich, The Man Who Wasn't There, The Princess and the Warrior, Dancer in the Dark, The Cider House Rules, Panic Room, Cube*, or *About Schmidt*. In these movies it is up to the subject to transcend the constraining frame in some way, often with the aid of "fortuitous" happenings suggesting the handiwork of a theist creator (i.e., an omnipotent, but unreliable author intervening at odd times in the plot). Almost always, the framed subject is forced to become a theist creator itself, though always in a vulnerable, peculiarly human way. Conversely, it is possible for theist creators to "fall" into a personal, vulnerable mode. *Panic Room*, for one, uses these ironic switches very effectively to create suspense. At first, the weak, seemingly powerless mother and daughter reside in the powerful center frame, with the designer of the safe room helplessly trying to get in; the roles of weak and strong switch back and forth as the film progresses. As it turns out, the true objects of identification in the movie aren't the victims – the edgy, vengeful Jodie Foster character Meg and her know-it-all daughter; it's the theist burglar Burnham, who combines the languid spirituality of Forest Whitaker's Ghost Dog persona with the involuntary self-sacrifice carried out by Burnham's namesake in *American Beauty*. By the end of the movie, everyone left alive has been redeemed through the Forest Whitaker character, albeit indirectly. Meg's unfaithful husband gets badly beaten up (by Burnham's unwanted accomplice Raoul) while trying to help her, and Meg and her daughter, seated on a Central Park bench, begin to look for an apartment suited more to their modest living needs than to draining the bank account of her by now redeemed ex.

In my original formulation of performatism, I suggested that the prototypical performatist subject is dense or opaque.[10] The former quality must not be taken too literally – performatist characters don't necessarily have to be fools or play at being them. Performatist heroes and heroines are, however, almost invariably opaque, since their initial identity is the result of a too tight fit between their selves and a primary frame. Amélie, for example, is at first caught up in an isolated personal frame caused by her father's mistaken diagnosis of a dangerous heart condition. Cissy, the "Princess" in Tykwer's movie, practically grows up in the mental institution where her father is incarcerated and has trouble interacting with men in non-institutional settings. Homer Wells, of *The Cider House Rules*, who is reared in an orphanage, is a "creation" of the institute's theistically inclined director, Dr. Larch, who named him and later trains him as a doctor in his own mold. Warren Schmidt in *About Schmidt* is trapped in a web of social conventions that, at least until the end of the movie, prevent him from expressing any open, heartfelt emotion. The simple display of tears at the movie's end is all the more effective because Jack Nicholson, who plays Schmidt, transcends his own Hollywood persona by underplaying it at the most crucial moment. Anyone familiar with Nicholson's characters from *Five Easy Pieces, One Flew over the Cuckoo's Nest*, or *As Good as It Gets* follows the movie expecting either a manic outburst or a cynical twist; Nicholson's contorted facial expressions and barely contained seething at his own impotence feed this expectation throughout the film. In the end, though, Nicholson manages to find an opening in his own screen persona that cannot be reduced to either of these two extremes: he in effect transcends himself as an actor.

As in Goffman's frame analysis, the problems inherent in this "fit" between subject and frame usually become apparent only after something goes wrong with or within the frame – hence the great role played by theistically motivated "accidents," which often have a liberating effect on the subjects inside. In the case of the Princess, it is a traffic accident that allows the Warrior to penetrate and literally breathe life into her by way of a tracheotomy – theist symbolism

doesn't get much more explicit than this.[11] For Amélie it is the death of
Lady Di, which through a series of small coincidences causes Amélie
to step into the role of a bevenolent theist prankster bringing happiness to others. The break can however be brought about willfully.
Homer Wells, for example, leaves the orphanage and Dr. Larch after
a conflict over abortion – an especially drastic and ethically controversial kind of theist intervention. After being faced with an serious
ethical dilemma of his own in the outside world (he carries out an
abortion on behalf of a woman impregnated by her father), Homer
accepts his theist responsibility and returns to take over the role of
the by now deceased Dr. Larch. With credentials faked by the good
doctor, Homer becomes the new director of an institution devoted to
turning out ever more opaque, constructed subjects. You don't have
to have studied poststructuralist rocket science to figure out that the
whole theist, paternalistic order behind the orphanage is a giant, albeit
benevolent scam. In a typical performatist ploy, the movie affirms this
deceit while at the same time forcing us to identify with its two theist
heroes in spite of our better knowledge. In this way deconstruction is
given its due – and at the same time defused for good. The point is not
to *know*, but to *identify* with someone caught up in a frame that will
always be generating intractable ethical problems.

In comedy, there are many ways of playing around with this sort
of opaque character and its theist frame. In *Being John Malkovich*, the
whole idea of a framed personality is carried ad absurdum by making
John Malkovich himself into a "vessel" that can be entered for fifteen
minutes at a time (at one point the hero and heroine charge 200 dollars a shot for this). The point is not that the characters involved experience continually unfolding alterity or multifarious shifts in gender,
as poststructuralist philosophy of self proposes. Instead, they enter
into an artificial, opaque mode of being, a frame which allows them to
transcend their own social positions and/or gender in one fell swoop.
Thus Maxine is able to have Lotte's baby (conceived while the latter was in John Malkovich), and Craig, a talented but unsuccessful
puppeteer, is able to manipulate John Malkovich while inside him,
using Malkovich's renown to make himself into the famous puppeteer
Craig always wanted to be. The point is not that Lotte or Craig are

experiencing otherness in an especially extravagant or subversive way; the point is that otherness can be appropriated by invading the "holy" – and whole – frame of someone else, in this case the hapless John Malkovich. You might call this a cynical version of the performatist or Goffmanian self: being involves role-playing or getting into an opaque frame *in the present*, within a certain time frame, and exploiting that frame to its utmost.

Lotte, Craig and the others who inhabit John Malkovich do not really experience otherness in the way envisioned by someone like Judith Butler, i.e., as a belated, constantly unfolding play with bits and pieces of gender having no natural, preordained configuration. Rather, the characters get to buy into a whole, though temporary, otherness by being John Malkovich for fifteen minutes at a time. The grotesque point of the movie is that people don't revel in otherness for sheer pleasure or to escape some hegemonic dictate of society. Instead, they want to control and inhabit others so that they may live forever *as their own selves*. Ideal selfness, in other words, consists in appropriating otherness (understood as someone else's whole frame) for your own ends. Conversely, as the movie makes clear, you can't achieve ideal selfness through oneness with yourself. When John Malkovich finally gets wind of what is going on and enters his own portal, he is aghast to find a world in which *everyone* is John Malkovich and in which "John Malkovich" is the only word spoken – a nightmarish world of asocial, redundant self-deification.[12]

Being John Malkovich brilliantly parodies a basic, insoluble problem of theism: namely, that as a theist creator, you need someone else in order to be yourself.[13] Fashioning someone in your own likeness inevitably involves creating someone weaker than you and dependent on your own self (it is no accident that the hero is a puppeteer). Conversely, a character striving for deification will also attempt to mold others in his own image and manipulate them as much as possible according to his own needs. Much more reconciliatory, on the other hand, is the movie's wildly dark suggestion that this kind of manipulation can be carried out by a collective (at the end, a group of genteel-looking elderly people enter the actor and proclaim: "*we* are John Malkovich!"). Ultimately, we don't even mind this sort of appropriation, since John

Malkovich, with his vaguely malevolent persona and his postmodern ability to slip into any role whatsoever, is the ideal vehicle for it: we do not mourn the "loss" of a personality that is opaque and infinitely adaptable to begin with.

Performatist Cinematography

It would be premature at this point to make any sweeping claims about performatist cinematography. Its most memorable individual devices – jumpy use of hand-held cameras (the Dogma movies), black-and-white noir-style photography (*The Man Who Wasn't There*), and rhythmic use of fade-outs (*Memento*) etc. – are quite familiar in formal terms and are in themselves not enough to define an epochal shift. What does seem to hold true for most performatist cinematography, however, is a double strategy that is "predicted" by the double nature of the originary frame. Accordingly, performatist movies can be said to *anthropologize* time-space relations on the one hand and *sacralize* them on the other.

Just how this works becomes clearer when considered against the background of Deleuzian, deist cosmology. In the deist tradition everything in the world takes place on a single, immanent plane: psychomechanically defined impulses of energy on the one side are processed by psychomechanically defined consciousness on the other. Deleuze, for example, speaks of cinema as a "spiritual automaton";[14] the brain is for him "nothing but [...] an interval, a gap between an action and a reaction."[15] Our consciousness is a material extension of reality and reality a spiritual extension of our consciousness. The two are different expressions of the same thing, although by definition they are always somewhat out of sync – you are not what you perceive in the world and the world's energy will always have flowed a bit farther down the line by the time your perception of it gels into a fixed concept. Rather than running after reality trying to paste cut-out concepts back onto it, deists try to bring the two disparate types of immanence to meet in the way they think best fits the metaphysical flux of the world, i.e., in terms of time and relationality. Because this happy meeting of mind and world must still take place in the vulgar confines of space, this is easier said than done. Bergson, for example, rejects film as a mechanical deceit because his radical intuitivism rules out any positively defined semiotic mediation between mind and matter; for similar reasons he is unable to make any coherent statements about aesthetics or poetic method.

Deleuze, by contrast, is a good deal more flexible on this point, arguing – quite plausibly – that consciousness and world can be thought of as converging in the medium of film.[16] Because Deleuze thinks of film as either conveying something of the essence of fluid materiality (the "movement-image"[17]) or as the direct apprehension of time caused by the disruption of coherence and teleology (the "time-image"[18]), this leads to two basic types of movie, depending on what kind of image is emphasized. In discussing film's historical development, Deleuze likes to speak of an "action-image" on one hand and a "crystal-image" on the other. Stripped to its barest essentials, the action-image can be thought of as a focal point capturing primary human emotions and the binary conflicts growing out of them; the latter, in turn, can unfold either in large, epic forms (as an integral) or in small, ethical ones (as a differential). The action-image and its many variants form the basis for the practices dominating pre-World War II narrative cinema. The crystal-image, by contrast, breaks away from the chronological, motivated representation of affect and conflict in order to tap into the virtual Whole of the world (Leibniz's God and Bergson's Time). This Whole is an endlessly open Other, the virtual, constantly unfolding totality of all moving relations. The "crystal-image" refracts and reflects, plays with sound and sensuality, causes characters to be "swallowed up" in non-localizable relations.[19] Deleuze relates this convincingly to the techniques of postmodern cinema, beginning with postwar cinema in Italy and the French Nouvelle Vague of the 1960s. There is no doubt that these concepts lead to very subtle and productive insights on film, and there is no doubt about their basic compatibility with postmodern and/or poststructuralist thought.

Unfortunately, Deleuze's concepts have the same effect on cultural history as do all other basic strategies of postmodernism: they choke off any further attempt to describe cultural development above or beyond them. If you force the crystal-image still further, you will plunge even deeper into the depths of postmodernist virtuality; if you fall back on the action-image, you will be doing little more than ironically (or naively) citing tried-and-true techniques of pre-war cinema. As a matter of fact, if you stick with the concept of image as *the* filmic and metaphysical nexus between reality and consciousness, you will be condemned to shuttle back and forth endlessly between part and whole, as is the case in Deleuze's deism. The point is not to rework the concept of image, but to start thinking of cinematography in terms of a human/theist double frame. There are indications that just such a change is occurring right now on the practical level in performatist cinema.

As suggested above, performatist cinema likes to approach the world in terms of fixed, boxed-in spaces and bought or apportioned time. This approach is neither a repetition nor a citation of grandpa's narrative cinema, nor does it mark a return to the cookie-cutter type of montage common to the early days of film. Its focal point is once more the *frame*, which must be understood as a temporal, spatial or ethical limit imposed on someone from without. The frame itself may be thought of as having a *theist* or *sacral* dimension on the one hand and *anthropological* or *human* on the other. The theist side of the frame impinges on, crimps, or temporarily cuts off the continuous passage from one state of affairs to another in an authoritative way. Such frames are imposed from above or without and cannot be easily overcome or placed in doubt. They are, for the most part, onerous givens that – like theist cosmologies everywhere – subject the characters within them to severe tests of faith, courage, or perseverance. The flip, or inner, side of the sacral frames is that their constraining character sets off an impulse to transcend in the human characters locked up inside of them. The "bound" characters, in other words, react to their incarceration by trying to break out of, rework, or somehow overcome the frames confining them.

The force exerted by the theist frame and the intensity of the human reactions to it manifest themselves directly in plot and cinematographic technique. For in film, more so than in any other genre, we are simultaneously confronted with the impassive, fear-evoking authority of theist time-space and the emotional pathos of human time-space trying to overcome it. Perhaps the most effective allegory of this situation is *Cube*, in which the unforgiving theist space makes purely human time – the time before hunger and thirst are going to incapacitate the seven would-be escapees – into the measure of all things. Whereas the deist space-time continuum provides consolation by letting you tap into the infinitely unfolding otherness of the world, theist space puts the heat on you, challenging you to use your own time to become like the higher, ineffable will that is bearing down on you from above.

The Man Who Wasn't There

One of the most striking examples of how temporal framing works in the new cinematography is the Coen Brothers' *The Man Who Wasn't There*. At first, the viewer might be inclined to see the movie as nothing more than a lengthy, ironic citation – the movie fastidiously imitates noir conventions both in its camera work and in its depiction of a criminal case unfolding in a small Californian town of 1949. Although there are admittedly breaks and discrepancies within the movie's period style, they do not interfere with our perception of it as a whole slice of time. (Real noir films, for example, never mixed science fiction and detective plots, as happens here, and the Production Code would not have allowed a young girl to make a sexually explicit pass at an older man, as happens between Birdie Abundas and Ed Crane, the hero. Neither device however represents a break with the paranoid ambience and sexual forthrightness common to noir.) The question remains, however, as to just how this slice of time acts upon us as viewers.

Given the similarities between *The Man Who Wasn't There* and various other films of the Coen Brothers, you could, I suppose, make a case for the movie being a postmodern critique of 1950-ish American mores. The society in which Ed Crane lives is founded on politically incorrect norms clearly tailored to empowering white, male, Anglo-Saxon heterosexuals. Either you're a real man, like Big Dave Brewster (who is killed by Ed), or a "pansy" like Creighton Tolliver (the traveling salesman killed by Big Dave). Sexually mature women like Ed's wife Doris are defined by nylons, lace underwear, perfume, and the like; innocent girls like Birdie Abundas wear bobby sox and v-neck sweaters. In terms of language the white, Anglo-Saxon culture sets the tone: Japanese are "Nips," Germans "heinies," and Italians "wops"; a Jewish lawyer and a fat Frenchman of color don't come off too well either. These two hegemonic orders – the white Anglo-Saxon one and the male, heterosexual one – meet ideally in the form of Big Dave Brewster, a ladies' man who has made his reputation mowing down "Japs" in World War II.

As in their previous movies, the Coen brothers expose the grotesque inconsistencies and flagrant rule-bending peculiar to this order. Big Dave, for example, gladly dons an apron on in order to spend some time washing dishes with his mistress, Ed's wife Doris. Doris, who is herself of impeccable Italian lineage, hates "wops" and tries to assimilate as much as possible. The teenage girl, Birdie Abundas, proves to be anything else but innocent. And, as a hired detective later discovers, Big Dave's heroism in the war is a fabrication designed to further his business career.

If the Coens were really only concerned with exposing the falsity and hypocrisy of 1950s America or exhaustively citing noir norms, the movie would hardly be very memorable. What in fact makes the film remarkable is its focus on transcendence and the hero's – and our – gradual realization that such a transcendence might be possible and desirable.

This can be better understood if you think of the whole movie as a temporal frame. We experience this frame as a homogenous chunk of concrete time, rather than as the diffuse garbling of virtual time peculiar to postmodernism (as an example of this you could take David Lynch's *Blue Velvet*, which deliberately mixes up styles taken from the fifties, sixties, seventies, and eighties to create a Deleuzian, vaguely paranoid feeling of a Time existing outside of space and chronology[20]). In addition to being homogenous, time in *The Man Who Wasn't There* is also depicted as both historical and obsolete: details like the wearing of fedoras and the use of politically incorrect language mark it as irrevocably passé. This historicity creates in us a feeling of distance to the time frame: we, who neither wear fedoras nor verbally abuse minorities, can easily feel superior to it. This is *theist time*, which at first appears well-defined and set: like theist creators or authors we stand outside of it looking in. At first, theist time would seem to stand in simple contrast to Ed's personal or human time, which is measured by the heads of hair he cuts and the inexorable, step-by-set unfolding of the plot. So far, these two types of time – the authorial and the personal – are part of standard narrative procedure and not in themselves noteworthy. What keeps *The Man Who Wasn't There* from being just another remake of a noir "action-image" plot is the way we (and Ed) are made to reverse our apprehension of the two types of time. In the course of the movie, our feeling of temporal superiority to Ed gradually changes to one of identification, whereas Ed's feeling of living incrementally gradually becomes more and more expansive and spiritual, until he disappears completely into the transcendental whiteness of the screen.

This interplay of theist and anthropological time takes place in several ways. Originally, Ed's scheme to blackmail Big Dave in order to co-finance a dry-cleaning franchise (run by a homosexual traveling salesman) seems petty and emotionally almost unmotivated – he and Doris carry on what appears to be a marriage of convenience, and he isn't all that perturbed by being two-timed ("I guess, somewhere, that pinched a little, too"[21]). Gradually, however, we discover that Ed's attempts to escape his time frame are motivated by a vaguely felt kind of spiritual quest. Dry cleaning, which is touted with preacher-like fervor by Creighton Tolliver ("You heard me right, brother, dry cleaning, – wash without water, no suds, no tumble, no stress on the clothes" [12]), appears as the first step in a search for ways to achieve a spiritual cleansing not possible in the cramped social setting of the late 1940s. Here, our theistic superiority to Ed's time frame helps provide a moment of involuntary identification: we know that dry cleaning is not a scam, just as we know that there is a way out of the 1940s-style mindset with its wops and pansies. We know, in other words, that we can transcend.[22] At the same time, the wall-to-wall noir cinematography causes us to experience 1940s-style temporality as an inescapable, intuitive fact. As spectators, we are outside the time frame intellectually but in it emotionally and visually. This makes it possible for us to take Ed's last words before he is executed entirely seriously, as the prophetic expression of a transcendent longing that may also be our own:

> I don't know where I'm being taken. I don't know what waits for me, beyond the earth and sky. But I'm not afraid to go. Maybe the things I don't understand will be clearer there, like when a fog blows away...Maybe Doris will be there...And maybe I can tell her all those things they don't have words for here.[23]

The question posed at the end of the movie is not so much "who is Ed Crane?" but rather "who are *we*?" One, quite plausible answer might be that we are postmodernists. That would mean that we are stuck in an ironic bind of already always possessing partial knowledge about the conditions necessary for achieving transcendence but never quite being able to experience it ourselves. Taking this a step farther, you might argue that Ed Crane died for nothing. Had he lived to transcend his own time frame he would have wound up in *ours*, in which a premium is placed on ironic reflection rather than on the search for "things they don't have words for here." The movie, however, anticipates this argument and counters it using a split appeal to our theist and human ways of identifying with Ed. The crucial scene takes place in Doris's cell (based on circumstantial evidence she has been falsely accused of murdering Big Dave). Her attorney, a cynical, money-hungry, obviously Jewish lawyer named Freddy Riedenschneider, suggests a defense based on his version of the Heisenberg uncertainty principle:

> ...They got this guy, in Germany. Fritz something-or-other. Or is it. Maybe it's Werner. Anyway, he's got this theory, you wanna test something, you know, scientifically – how the planets go round the sun, what sunspots are made of, why the water comes out of the tap – well, you gotta look at it. But sometimes, you look at it, your looking changes it. Ya can't know the reality of what happened, or what would've happened if you hadden a stuck in your own goddamn schnozz. So there is no 'what happened.' Not in any sense that we can grasp with our puny

minds. Because our minds...our minds get in the way. Looking at something changes it. They call it the 'Uncertainty Principle.' Sure, it sounds screwy, but even Einstein says the guy's on to something.[24]

From our theist vantage point this sounds like a parody of postmodern sophistry, as also does Riedenschneider's later defense of Ed ("He told them to look not at the facts but at the meaning of the facts, and then he said the facts *had* no meaning. It was a pretty good speech, and even had me going..."[25]). In terms of noir visual devices, Riedenschneider is deliberately cast in a bad light: as he talks, he moves in and out of sunbeams flooding in starkly from above the cell; in the moment that he ends his speech he turns away from the light, his face utterly black and no longer visible. With Riedenschneider, the Coen brothers use the incarnation of an anti-semitic stereotype to debunk the notion of posthistoire – i.e., the idea that "there is no what happened." However, this kind of ad hominem argumentation remains completely acceptable because we experience it as having been set in a time frame we have transcended – thus proving that "something has happened" after all. Placed in the proper theist frame, any form of ugliness can become ethically good, aesthetically appealing, and sublime.

The noir cinematography in *The Man Who Wasn't There* is quite obviously a gimmick – an effective, though one-time thing.[26] Gimmickry of this sort is not absolutely necessary, but it does seem to crop up frequently as a side-effect of performatist attempts to make transcendence visible and palpable. The most famous such gimmickry is, of course, enshrined in the Dogma 95 manifesto. Widely misunderstood in postmodern circles as a misguided attempt to return to authenticity, the Dogma 95 credo is really nothing more than a theist frame set up so that humans may transcend it or, alternately, so that theist moviemakers may be humbled by having to assume a crudely human perspective. Lars von Trier's *Idiots* takes the latter route: until the very last scene of the movie, which makes everything fall into place, you may have felt yourself in the presence of an "idiotic," literally unfocused director. In truth, of course, the sloppy camera work is a – admittedly tiring – gimmick setting you up for a carefully planned denouement deifying a meek heroine.

The much more artful *Celebration*, by contrast, uses a break with the anthropological, hand-held camera perspective to suggest the possibility of transcendence. In one scene, oddly shot from a bathroom ceiling, we are suddenly shown a perspective that can only be that of Christian's dead sister, whose suicide was the driving force behind the hero's decision to confront his father (appropriately, Vinterberg "broke" the Dogma 95 vow of chastity and used a crane to make the shot). Gimmicks abound, too, in the other movies mentioned—the director of *Amélie* uses digital techniques to show the heroine's heart pounding away in her chest when she falls in love, and the people who climb into the John Malkovich portal view the world through a slit at the top of the screen that represents his seeing-eye view. Taken together, these devices do not, of course, an epoch make. However, it is important to take them seriously as part of the performatist play with immanence and transcendence, with the theist and the human.

The Russian Ark

The most striking cinematographic feature of Aleksandr Sokurov's *The Russian Ark* is its use of a single, 87-minute long shot made possible by the use of a body-mounted video camera. As with the Dogma movies, the point here was not to return to a "simple" or "direct" perspective – the moviemakers spent more money on digital touching-up in postproduction than they did on the actual shoot. Instead, the one-shot sojourn through the Hermitage museum in Petersburg resulted in a new type of movie that cannot be assimilated to existing notions of time and montage.

The notion that *The Russian Ark* might be something entirely new is, of course, unacceptable to critics still caught up in the poststructuralist mode. The Slavist Dragan Kujundzić, for example, writing in the internet journal *Artmargins*,[27] does all he can to make Sokurov's unbroken long shot sound eccentric, unhuman and technologically intimidating. Kujundzić speaks of the "unblinking eye" of the video camera as well as of a spectral "visor effect" associated with an invisible narrator; the camera is said to move in a way that is "not so linear and sequential, and often wavers in an undecided and aporetic temporal and spatial opening." Viewed through a glass darkly, this may all be true. However, it doesn't seem to me to grasp the main, dominating effect of the unified long shot, which is quite simply to make the camera vision and its movements dreamily anthropomorphic. Tilman Büttner's floating, gently panning camera doesn't have the net effect of frightening or chilling us. Instead, it acts, relative to cut film, like the totality of a constructed human gaze. The tone for this is set in the opening scene, where the camera's unnaturally wide, indifferently focused vision is for several minutes rendered almost identical to a human one by having it pass through a crowded, dark corridor (as Natascha Drubek-Meyer, writing in the same internet issue, aptly observes, the scene "emanates warmth and privateness"[28]). Unless you really expect the camera to blink and reproduce saccadic eye movements, this is about as close as you can get in mechanical terms to the human experience of seeing – the catch being that this all depends on a severely inhibiting frame or mise en scène that cannot be upheld for all too long. And, indeed, once you have been drawn into the space of the museum this particular effect recedes. However, as Drubek-Meyer points out, the anthropomorphic effect continues in other ways. The complete lack of montage causes the viewer to pay more attention to the tactile and auditive elements of the *mise en scène*, which we experience in the continuously unfolding, uncut presence of real time. This also explains the occasionally "aporetic" movements of the camera within the film: the cameraman is pretty much on his own within his own real time, and the director has no way of belatedly "cutting back" to a previous position or "cutting forward" to a future one. In this movie, we are all made to feel the cutting edge of presence – even as we realize *later* that it is an epistemological illusion.

It is easier to understand the logic of the long take in *The Russian Ark* if you compare it with Dogma cinematography, which may possibly have influenced it directly. The original Dogma directors – most notably Lars von Trier and Thomas Vinterberg – used grainy film and wobbly, hand-held cameras to convey a specifically personal (human) feeling, even as their movies – *Idiots*, *The Celebration* – turn out to be highly constructed and tightly plotted authorial (theist) constructs centering on emancipatory acts of self-humiliation. The "amateurish," seemingly spontaneous cinematography works in conjunction with a higher, very constructed artificial plot; both converge in an aesthetic totality not reducible to either of its two parts (poststructuralists regularly assume that the shaky Dogma cinematography is aimed at conveying authenticity, which is demonstrably not the case when the movies are considered as a whole). Sokurov's protest regarding the possibility of a prize being awarded to his German cameraman,[29] though disconcerting in terms of its nationalist sentiments, is at least understandable from an aesthetic point of view. The long camera shot and the director's *mise en scène* are not meant to be cut apart anywhere, at any time. (For similar reasons, the Dogma filmmakers' "Vow of Chastity" stipulates that the director must not be credited – what counts is the totality of the film, and, at least in theory, not the individual pretensions of a creative auteur.)

Also helpful for a better understanding of *The Russian Ark* are the Dogma group's "Vows of Chastity" – using only a hand-held camera, shooting only on location, not using optical work or filters etc. These are meant to impose a certain sense of humility upon the nearly omnipotent director, the intent being to create an equilibrium between his or her constructive will and the endlessly passive malleability of the script and *mise en scène* (the Vows are in fact regularly broken by the directors, who then "confess" their breaches publicly on the internet[30]). Measured against the admittedly rather arbitrary rigor of the Vows, *The Russian Ark* can be said overfulfill at least one, namely No. 3 (to use only a hand-held camera). By welding shot and *mise en scène* into an uncut, pristine unity, it achieves something even the radical dogmatist Lars von Trier never dared. This, however, is where the similarities end. The act of extreme visual self-limitation (and, for the cameraman, probably also of self-mortification) is used to record the contents of an unbelievably lush "arkive" encompassing not just major works of representational art but also selected, resuscitated personages plucked from 300 years of Russian history. *The Russian Ark* presents the transcendent from a visually very limited, "human" point of view, while simultaneously ennobling the limited point of view by using it as a portal to the transcendent. The result is a performative work-frame whose total achievement is irreducible to either of its parts. Take away the unified shot, for example, and you have a hard-to-explain montage of unconnected historical scenes; take away the transcendent historical scenes and you have a boring audio-visual tour of a very large museum.

Another source for the one-shot movie is Sokurov's mentor Andrei Tarkovsky. Tarkovsky, who made no bones about his dislike of Soviet montage theory, suggested that the stylization of time in long shots should be the central focus of cinema; he expressly regretted that it was not possible to make a one-shot movie no longer than about 12 minutes (the technical limit at the time he was writing).[31] Given this background it might seem credible to argue that Sokurov simply took Tarkovsky's cinematic last wish and fulfilled it using the latest technical means. A quick visual comparison of Tarkovsky's own long shots and *The Russian Ark*, however, leads to completely opposite results. Tarkovsky's long shots are almost always tracking shots or pans; the excruciating, mechanically controlled slowness with which the camera moves radically distorts and "freezes" our temporal experience of the mise en scène. In *The Russian Ark*, of course, this situation is the exact opposite. The camera in *The Russian Ark* is dynamic in a specifically anthropomorphic way – it literally ambles on foot through the museum. Also, depending on where it is and what it's aimed at, it plays with our subjective perception of time (it's slow when focused on the paintings and speeds up in the ballroom sequence, when the camera almost literally begins to dance). In fact, applying Tarkovsky's static cinematography to *The Russian Ark* would have resulted in a technical and aesthetic fiasco: it would have meant either one long, devastatingly dreary pan or one long, equally monotonous tracking shot. Although the original idea for the one-shot movie may well have come from Tarkovsky, Sokurov's interpretation of it is very much a thing of his own making.

This leads into the question as to just what kind of a technical or aesthetic innovation is really implied by Sokurov's film. In spite of the film's great commercial and critical success, the one-shot movie is almost certainly going to remain a one-shot affair. The reason lies not in the technological prerequisites or artistic skill required, but in the closed performative totality that I noted above. *The Russian Ark* only works aesthetically because the immanent long shot has been made to pass through an even longer transcendent span of time. Sokurov's movie is more like a stunt or a gag that you can only pull off once – rather like Columbus and his famous egg. What is new and what is meant to endure is not the individual device, but rather the fact of its performativity per se, whose success or failure is independent of any epistemological critique. *The Russian Ark*, in other words, doesn't need an epistemological justification for its performance to work; the performance embodies its own goal, which is to jump-start history again, to create a singular event in the open sea of an otherwise eventless posthistorical expanse. In epistemological terms, the stunt involved in *The Russian Ark* is just as derivative and iterable as is everything else – but that's not the point. What counts is the monist, encapsulated performance, which, strictly speaking, cannot be repeated with any real effect. In fact, it can only be superseded by another, differently constructed performance, which in turn forces us to accept or reject it as it stands. If enough of these successful performances accumulate, a new epoch will be formed – a process that I believe is taking place right now. Deconstructionists may gnash their teeth and wail at this reversion to what from their point of view is a mindless monism. However, this is the only way to overcome a posthistorical discourse which reduces all innovation to epistemological questions of filiation, iteration, and citation.

There is yet another unpostmodern side to the long shot. The aspect of a camera being tied to a specifically human perspective for almost ninety minutes leads to a cinematographic treatment of time that is no longer compatible with the Deleuzian (and Bergsonian) concept of time informing poststructuralist film theory. For if you think carefully about what the hand-held camera does in *The Russian Ark*, you can only conclude that it is the exact opposite of what Deleuze and Bergson tell us is "good" time or duration. The reader will recall that Bergson differentiates between psychological time and duration – psychological time being that tendency to chop up time into chronological, spatialized segments of presence easily digestible to the mind. Duration, by contrast, is experienced negatively as the divergence from sequential or chronological time and positively as participation in the totality of Time (a time "out of joint" with space and linear movement[32]). In film, Deleuze tells us, montage creates the image of time, either synthetically (through the net effect of montage) or analytically (by allowing us to extract an apprehension of time from the movement-image in anticipation of the cut).[33] Both operations, however, depend entirely on editing strips of film after the fact.

What happens when you take montage away entirely, as in *The Russian Ark*? The answer, I think, is that we get two times: the camera's (or cameraman's) time and the time conveyed by the *mise en scène*. Both come together in a singular way that does not jive well with Deleuzian, deist notions about how time works.

The first kind of time, the uncut 87-minute time of the shot, is Everyman's time. Taken at face value, it's the same time you would get if you were, say, to film your sister's wedding reception with a camcorder in one continuous sequence. The time of the shot is real time, essentially parallel to the viewer's time; it is completely chronological and linear (the line, it is true, meanders, but it is still essentially a line[34]). In Bergsonian-Deleuzian terms, this is banal, artless time; it's the time you want to get out of by tapping into duration. The second kind of time, the time of the *mise en scène*, would at first seem to meet that urgently felt need. Through characteristic costumes, personages and language we are confronted with a jumble of historically very different times in one place, much as one might expect in a properly postmodern, posthistorical movie. This spatially conveyed experience of different times (i.e., duration) however suffers in Bergsonian terms from several major flaws. First, it is highly conceptualized and hierarchical (the fact that uniforms, a symbol of rank, help convey this historical information is symptomatic). Secondly, it is highly spatialized and compartmentalized, much in the way that the Hermitage offers us rooms with "17th century Flemish masters" and the like. The Bergsonian-Deleuzian aesthetic, which places a premium on gradation, has to cope with what it must feel is a double banality: that of being stuck in chronological time per se and that of conceptually segmented space conveying duration. The real reason that the Berg-

sonian concepts don't quite hit the mark is that in *The Russian Ark* we
are dealing with an entirely different, theist or spatially demarcated
concept of time: it's the time you need to transcend the space confining you (the time of the shot, the time you're in the space of the
museum, of the world). This goes for the narrative situation, too. The
movie recapitulates *the* basic theist plot, which plunks people into an
inhospitable environment to see if they can overcome it while remain-
ing spiritually whole (the basic deist plot, by contrast, is that of the infinite regress and alienation experienced when you search for Sophia,
the durée, epistemological truths, or what have you not).

   The use of theist time in *The Russian Ark* also creates problems for
Kujundzić, who is intent on assimilating it to Deleuze's notion of the
time-image. According to Kujundzić, "what the film represents is the
very moment of keeping of a tradition by means of the 'live' gaze of
the camera. The live gaze sees an entire epoch obliterated and in ruins.
It is precisely this tension between the utmost visibility and the ruin-
ation of representation that creates the most interesting effects..."[35]
Unlike many of Kujundzić's deconstructive moves, which are clever
and instructive, I don't find this especially convincing or even very
precise. The "live" gaze of the unbroken long shot is quantitatively
and qualitatively much more limited than in a normally cut film with
its richness of quickly shifting times and perspectives. Filmic visibility
isn't here at its utmost; its about as restricted as you can get. Also, I
fail to see how the representations involved are "ruined" – if anything,
they've been made to come alive in the most banal sense of the word.
The movie, after all, magically revives Pushkin, Catherine the Great,
Anastasia, and a whole bevy of Russian aristocrats and places them
in front of the camera for us to see. And, if that isn't enough, the
museum is also filled with some of the world's most highly valued
representational paintings, which by all appearances seem to be in
pretty good shape. In some trivial sense, I suppose, you could speak
of a "rupture between the camera and the object of representation,"
as Kujundzić does, but it's hard to imagine how it would get under
anyone's skin – after all, the movie can hardly be mistaken for an
authentic attempt to film the contents of the Hermitage or provide
a comprehensive review of post-Petrine Russian history. What *does*

happen, is that a specifically human, limited apprehension of time is combined with a specifically theist, transcendent apprehension of time in such a way that history is not only recorded, but also made. The film's own aesthetic demonstrates the possibility of the new not just discursively, as an epistemological postulate, but also performatively, as an aesthetic fact.

This raises a larger question as to the movie's basic metaphysical mindset regarding historical time. Kujundzić, in keeping with the metaphysical pessimism of postmodernism, argues that the film is pessimistic, too. At first glance, there seems to be something to this argument, since at the movie's end the ark empties and the Russian aristocracy marches off to its doom. Kujundzić is no doubt justified in equating this scene (and also a few others) with posthistorical melancholy and nostalgia for the Petrine period.[36] However, this relates to only one aspect of the Hermitage, which, apart from being a popular museum, is also a historical location which people have always passed through anyway. In my mind, its other, more fundamental function is *to transport aesthetically valued sacral representations that allow us to renew culture after a devastating political deluge.* The appeal of these representations extends not just to people able to "read" them, as the worldly Custine can, but also to those intuitively captivated by their aesthetic, visual force, which would appear to be coextensive with their spiritual one (most of the paintings discussed or focused on in the movie treat sacral themes). Hence the dialogue between the French aristocrat Custine and the timid museum visitor admiring Van Dyk's *Virgin with Partridges*, in which Custine – unjustly – complains that the young man can't understand the painting without knowing the Gospels. The power of these representations is in fact so fundamental that people don't even have to *see* them – hence the sightless curator who has internalized the Hermitage's representations to the point where she can explain them "blind." As she herself says: "God protects them [the figures in the painting]. There is no doubt about His unseen presence." From off-camera Sokurov's voice sighs: "Sir, leave her, she's an angel."

Sokurov, it is true, seems to be laying it on pretty thick here. As secular observers, however, we aren't obliged to adopt these professions of faith ourselves. What is more to the point is to realize that the sacral – the possibility of transcendence – can be experienced best within a secular, constructed aesthetic frame such as Van Dyk's painting, the institution of the Hermitage, or the unified long shot of Sokurov's *Russian Ark*. Indeed, you could say that the real point of such frames is their specific ability to transcend life-threatening unbelief (the Soviet era) by preserving higher or sacral value in representational aesthetic signs in closed settings. The positive set towards these signs as bearers of future salvation is ultimately more important than their literal religious content, which is open only to "blind," dogmatic believers. The framework enabling belief to be represented in the future, in other words, is more crucial to culture's survival than belief itself – or to knowledge about the conditions of that belief gained ex post facto. That is why I think that the basic attitude of the movie is aimed towards the future and not towards the past. The Russian ark is not the Titanic: it swims on instead of sinking.

While I disagree with Kujundzić's pessimistic and occasionally downright morbid assessment of the movie, I would like to emphasize that the movie itself is not a completely consistent example of what I have identified as the performatist paradigm. One major difference between *The Russian Ark* and "classic" performatist movies like *The Celebration, Amélie, Ghost Dog,* or *Kukushka* is that while *The Russian Ark* contains a striking, no longer postmodern cinematographic performance, it lacks an event, a crucial moment of individual redemption and identification focused on a whole, usually opaque or simple person. The central figure of identification in *The Russian Ark* is in fact almost from the beginning a double one (Custine and the voice-over), and Kujundzić is entirely justified in stressing the tensions between the two; theirs is a dynamic, unstable relationship that gnaws at the heart of the movie, as well as of Russian culture as a whole. Also, as Kujundzić aptly puts it, *The Russian Ark* "leaks": it stuffs so many historical allusions into the *mise en scène* that you can't but help wanting to pursue them further outside the confines of the movie. All this notwithstanding, though, *The Russian Ark* is not just immersed in the past. Rather, through a specific, one-time conflation of shot and *mise en scène*, it catapults itself into a no longer posthistorical future.

Memento

One of the most radical exercises in performatist cinematography can be found in a movie that remains, when viewed as whole, with at least one foot still firmly planted in postmodernism. This is Christopher Nolan's *Memento* (2000), by now something of a cult classic. The main conceit behind the film is that the hero, Leonard Shelby, is suffering from a memory disorder caused by a blow to the head received while he was trying to defend his wife, who he repeatedly states was raped and murdered. As a result, Leonard has only a short-term memory; he can remember his life before the attack, but forgets everything else after about fifteen minutes. The movie presents his basic story as a series of twenty-two slightly overlapping temporal frames or scenes documenting how he tries to seek revenge. To make things even more complicated, *Memento* splits up into two times: Leonard's stunted, framed time, and chronological time, which, in an act of theist willfulness, has been set to run backwards. The movie begins with the end of Leonard's attempts to find and kill the murderer of his wife; as it progresses (backwards), frame by overlapping frame, we learn more and more about how Leonard's final act of vengeance came about. The hero experiences a series of framed presences in terms of a dysfunctional human time, while we experience the accumulation of these presences in terms of both his time and a theist, authorial one.

In the beginning, these two times are practically identical: in the first few scenes we are as confused as Leonard is as to what is going on. This feeling of absolute bewilderment caused by a cruelly limited frame forces the viewer, at least at first, into a close identification with the hero – we, too, experience an odd, frantic kind of need to overcome the frames confining us and to find out what the things around us mean. Gradually, however, a distinct split in intuitive experience and knowledge develops. For, as our theist time accumulates, we begin to realize that Leonard, who knows that he forgets things, has set himself up by writing (not very reliable) notes instructing himself what to do and whom to trust or avoid. The man he kills at the beginning of the movie, a corrupt cop named Teddy, is by all appearances probably not the murderer; he's someone who tried to manipulate Leonard and whom Leonard decided to make the scapegoat for his wife's murder. Leonard, who is stuck in a hellishly limited personal time, becomes the self-appointed executor of an impersonal vengeance that will always be seeking new victims or scapegoats. In a way, Leonard is the prototype of all participants in mimetic rivalry. He embodies a kind of minimal human consciousness programmed to seek revenge over and over again – the acts of vengeance being his performances, his way of transcending what he experiences as one, severely limited time frame or present.

This view of human consciousness, though limited and pessimistic, could at least be considered the ground of a primary, monist frame.[37] Nolan, however, complicates things still further by adding a *second* set of frames to his movie: he intersperses the backtracking color frames recounting the murder story with backtracking black-and-white frames in which Leonard recalls a character named Sammy Jankis, who suffers from the same mental condition as he. Without going into all the details, it will suffice to say that Sammy kills his diabetic wife without being aware of it and then falls apart; we seem him sitting in a mental institution – and for a split second we see in his place Leonard Shelby. What at first seemed to be a neurophysiological, monist origin becomes a psychoanalytical, double one. Just as we think we are about to get the hang of Leonard Shelby's original motive, we are told that he is, psychologically speaking, someone else. Whether or not this basic confusion about who Leonard is makes *Memento* a better movie is a matter of some debate.[38] *Memento*, however, remains interesting as a case study because the dividing line separating postmodernism from performatism runs right through it. As long as the frame has an ontological, anthropological ground it is performatist; as soon as the ground is made into an undecidable double origin the frame becomes postmodern.

Memento reminds us that we are still in a transition period from postmodernism to performatism. There are movies that start off with a seemingly firm performatist premise but then fade back into postmodern murkiness, and there are movies that have a primary, "grounded" frame but hide it in what at first seems to be an undecidable tangle of double attributions. As an example of the first type of movie you could take David Fincher's *Fight Club*, whose yuppie, Caspar-Milquetoast narrator (Edward Norton) teams up with a subversive and willfully cruel character named Tyler Durden (a slumming Brad Pitt). The two begin by founding a "fight club" devoted to bloody, bare-handed fisticuffs; eventually, the Brad Pitt character moves on to organize an urban prankster group called Project Mayhem (this is one movie that could not have been made after 9/11 – it ends with two towers of an unnamed, ostensibly empty financial center collapsing into themselves after a bomb attack by the Project). The fight club and the prankster-like terror group are evidently meant to re-empower the raw-knuckled kind of masculinity that was repressed for so long by effeminate postmodern culture (this is the avowed intention of Chuck Palahniuk, who wrote the book on which the movie is based). Seen in semiotic terms though, the movie is naive: it would like to take us back to *before* the originary scene, to a state of pure, signless mimetic conflict in which resentment is purged through the application of brute force and not through signification (one of the rules of the Fight Club, in fact, is that you're not allowed to talk about it). As in *Memento*, the movie ends by swatting us over the head with a postmodern red herring that it has been dragging through the plot the whole time: Tyler Durden, as it turns out, is the narrator's evil alter ego. Although the narrator believes he has purged himself of Durden by the movie's end, the last frame of the movie suggests that quite the opposite is true – Durden enjoyed splicing snippets of porno movies into family films to disturb viewers subliminally, and this is just what we see (though not quite subliminally) at the movie's very end. The cruel prankster Durden, in other words, is still in control of the frame.

By contrast, movies like David Lynch's *Mulholland Drive* and Alejandro Amenábar's *Open Your Eyes* (the Spanish movie on which *Vanilla Sky* is based) seem at first to offer us nothing more than a spectacular off-and-on between two undecidable, highly confusing perspectives. As Eric Gans has however shown, one perspective in *Mulholland Drive* does turn out to be real – it acts as a psychological ground for the bizarre phantasy sequence with which the movie begins.[39] Lynch's movie, though still exuding postmodern paranoia, turns out to be devoted to a surprisingly unparanoid theme – that of unrequited love. *Open Your Eyes* also confronts us with the interplay of two seemingly undecidable perspectives: it concerns a handsome young Spaniard and his grotesquely disfigured alter ego, who continuously, and seemingly senselessly, replace one another as the film rolls along. Just before the confused hero (and the viewer) are about to give up in despair, the movie provides a watertight, reconciliatory explanation. The hero, it seems, has died, but a futuristic society has developed a process allowing him to dream his own life through again even in death. The disconcerting appearances of his disfigured self can be willed away in the next cycle of the dream, which begins with the hero jumping from a rooftop and landing unscathed below. The character, in other words, has the power to be both theist and human; he can frame his own life-after-death in the transcendent reality of the dream.

I don't pretend to have described the transition from postmodernism to performatism in film in a comprehensive way. There are dozens of other contemporary movies that fit the performatist bill, and there are numerous films that in the early and mid 1990s were already edging away from the postmodern mode – Eric Gans has noted this development in several of his internet *Chronicles*.[40] However, I believe that the broadly drawn borderline of 1997-1999, which in my view marks the beginning of performatism in film, will hold up to further scrutiny. The thematic and cinematographic innovations introduced by the films in this period have not only caught on, but are also being constantly reapplied and renewed. There is little doubt in my mind that the performatist devices and themes just described will continue to develop in exciting new ways in the coming few years, even as the tried-and-true postmodern ones wither and fade. Much less easy to predict is when film critics and theorists will begin to jettison their increasingly unworkable poststructuralist concepts and begin to apply more fitting, monist ones to the new epoch. But that, of course, is where an already well-developed performatist theory can lend a helping hand.

Chapter 4

Performatism in Architecture

My interest in architecture after postmodernism began with an epiphany of sorts. The occasion was a visit to the newly renovated Reichstag in Berlin in the summer of 1999. Having seen – and been in – the building sometime in the late 1970s, my expectations were not especially high. Built at the behest of Wilhelm II, the Reichstag had never been an appealing edifice. Its massive, pseudo-classical frame was, if anything, meant to intimidate parliamentary democracy more than to showcase it, and the interior projected an atmosphere of gloomy pomp. The new Reichstag, though, turned out to be anything but an exercise in spike-helmeted imperial nostalgia. The architect in charge of restoration, Sir Norman Foster, had gutted the building's insides in a way that made it spacious and light. Glass partitions caused the workings of parliament inside the building to become literally transparent. A huge, shiny aluminum needle seemed to plunge from above into the parliament's plenary hall. And, interesting details for a Slavist like myself abounded: graffiti left by victorious Russian soldiers in 1945 had been painstakingly preserved in a way usually reserved for works of high art. The real surprise, though, came in the building's transparent, walk-around glass cupola. On that day the sky was a clear, cloudless blue. Having ascended the gangway that winds around the cupola and paused at the top observation deck, I suddenly felt dizzy (I have a mild fear of heights). For a moment, I had the exhilarating feeling of being suspended between heaven and earth.

The more I thought about these unexpected impressions, the more they started to fit in with the notion of narrative performatism that I was developing at the time. Foster had neither restored the Reichstag's imperial stuffiness nor decked it out with a jumble of posthistorical citations. Instead, he had carried out an "impossible" architectonic performance by dematerializing a massive, gloomy building and dissolving its cupola into thin air. But just how did this particular stunt fit in with the larger picture in architecture? A one-year teaching stint in Berlin three years later gave me the chance to expand my intuitive impressions into a systematic description.

Berlin, I might add, was not just a venue of convenience. Since German reunification in 1990, after which it replaced Bonn as the country's capital, Berlin has gone through a phase of rebuilding unparalleled in any other major city in the world. Practically every important architect has built there, and both commercial and government planners have given them a freer hand than might have been the case elsewhere. Hence Berlin offers the best and boldest of what is going on in the world of architecture today. In the following remarks, using twenty especially striking examples from Berlin, I would like to propose a definition of performatist architecture.

Transcendent Functionalism and the Spatial Representation of Ostensivity

Performatism in architecture arises when minimal spatial relations are arranged in such a way as to suggest the possibility of achieving transcendence. Given the background of modernist architecture, in which there has been no lack of minimalist attempts to stylize or appropriate transcendence, and that of postmodernist architecture, which ironicizes its predecessor's program, this implies several restrictions. Like modernist architecture, performatist architecture stylizes functionality and tends to use simple forms suggesting a single, monist end. However, unlike modernism, performatist architecture is aimed at evoking transcendency through devices that are perceived neither as being motivated by modernist notions of ideal functionality (whose most obvious token is the grid or square) nor as displaying an ornamental plurality in the postmodern sense (citing and mixing received, recognizable codes). Instead, performatist devices call attention to spatially mediated, minimal relations which seem to overcome certain material or physical limitations. One might call this *transcendent functionalism* or, as the case may be, *transcendent ornamentalism.* Both variants of the same principle are opposed to the technical functionalism of modernism and the ludic ornamentalism of postmodernism. Instead of expressing a geometrically founded principle in a consistent, foreseeable way, the performative device suggests the possibility of overcoming some spatial scene with heretofore unrecognized functional means. Since this functional striving for transcendence is necessarily always incomplete, the result is a "useless" architectonic remainder, or ornament – something that modernism rejects out of hand. At the same time, this type of ornamentation is not a playful, ironically presented citation of previously existing styles. Rather, it is the willed, paradoxical by-product of an architectonic act aimed at showing how transcendence might be achieved under particular, auspicious conditions. This turn towards stylizing transcendence is not some sort of mystical escapism, but a logical reaction to the legacies of both modernism and postmodernism. A brief look at these traditions will help show why.

Modernism sought to realize the aesthetic qualities of simplicity and unity in architecture by equating these with an essentialist principle, functionality. The result was a supposedly non-ornamental, rationally founded "ism" that with time revealed itself to be no less ornamental and no less metaphysical than any of its predecessor styles. From the postmodern point of view – as acerbically documented by authors like Charles Jencks or Tom Wolfe – this led to glaring inconsistencies between theory and practice. Modernist architects began using the square frame and the glass box indiscriminately, without regard to their actual functional consequences – leaky roofs or overheated, giddy office workers. And, the blind application of grand utopian plans to inner cities led to the creation of unliveable urban ghettos whose destruction marked the eclipse of modernism with a bang.

Postmodern architects reacted by uncoupling style from any essentialist claims, resulting in a profusion of wittily cited ornaments and an ironic, can't-nail-me-down-to-anything attitude. The result has been a highly context-sensitive, but also stylistically superficial architectural vernacular. Postmodernism also places a premium on *knowing.* It shows us in an aesthetically and intellectually absolutely convincing way that knowledge of anything involves entering an endlessly complicated, uncontrollable regress with no origin, no pre-set goals, and no binding answers. Postmodern buildings embody the contextualization and dissemination that are also the hallmarks of postmodern narrative and play with literary genres.

Performatist architecture reacts against both modernism and postmodernism by returning to an aesthetic of simplicity that is founded not in functionality or in stylistic citation but in the *human* – more specifically, in the semiotically mediated human capacity to believe. Performatism does this by forcing us to focus in on simple, incredible object relations that seem to transcend the material conditions of their own existence and that challenge us to accept them whether we want to or not. It is this specific form of challenge that separates performatism from the postmodern and modern. We already *know* – just as the postmodernists and modernists do – that these architectonic relations are implausible and staged, but that is now beside the point. For these relations force us to focus our attention on an ostensive act of transcendence and to *identify* with that act in a coherent, unified way. The sum of this implausible architectonic act and the involuntary identification with it is a *performance*, a kind of invisible frame around building and observer that exists, if only for a time, in a state of vibrant, unstable unity. As is the case in narrative performatism, this unity comes about partially through coercion and partially through pleasure – and, of course, by blocking off the contextual distractions that are the mainstays of poststructuralism.

Is it possible to evade this unity? As a matter of individual choice, this is no problem at all. Whoever is content to *know* these incredible acts – to "unmask" their obviously staged appeals to belief – can do so to their heart's content. However, such viewers will have missed the point. Although effortlessly maintaining their epistemological superiority vis-à-vis the "naive" performatist work, these critics will remain entrapped forever in the endless loops of a postmodernist mindset that no longer has any direct physical correlate in present-day architecture.

Nine Devices of Performatist Architecture

In the originary ostensive scene, the human arises when two subjects intuitively agree to dematerialize a desired object by replacing it with a sign. At the same time, the reconciliatory power of the ostensive act creates an outer frame separating the human from the transcendent (or, more properly, from the Unknown, to which the reconciliation is ascribed). Conceived in the simplest terms, performatist architecture consists of a spatial scene highlighting a spatial relationship that seems to overcome its own involvement in the material world. This scene, in turn, creates a palpable, visualized tension between the immanent and the transcendent or, alternately, between the human (the observer) and a theist creator (the architect). Based on my perambulations in Berlin I have identified nine basic devices of performatist architecture, arranged roughly in order of importance:

1. Theist creation (addition/subtraction of mass)
2. Transparency (dematerialization)
3. Triangulation (destabilization)
4. Kinesis (moving the immovable)
5. Impendency (sublime threat)
6. Wholeness (closure)
7. Framing (dissociation)
8. Ostensivity (centering)
9. Generativity

Here is a brief rundown of each category.

1. Theistic Creation (addition/subtraction of mass)

A striking and very common architectonic device of performatism is to slice mass out of buildings on a grand scale (less frequently, mass is added to them in peculiar places). The effect of this slicing or adding is *theist* rather than ornamental or functional in the postmodernist or modernist sense. The user or viewer is meant to feel the powerful, preterhuman hand of the architect rather than to perceive some sort of ornamentally familiar form or compelling technical principle. The addition or subtraction of mass suggests a quasi-divine ability to giveth and taketh away; the architect presents himself (or herself) in the manner of a potent, but nonetheless limited manipulator of matter, as an anthropomorphic divinity who intervenes in the world below in an goal-directed, forward, but nonetheless ineffable way.[1] This may be contrasted with the demiurgical architect of modernism, whose striving for rationally guided technical perfection is not open to any sort of self-doubt, or with the gnostic architect of postmodernism, whose seemingly indifferent combining of unrelated, received styles creates an ironic metaposition lacking any fixed point of origin. In general, the performatist act of slicing/adding suggests a decisive, half-human, half-transcendent act of originary architectonic creation. This explains why in performatist structures we often see parts of roofs cut away to reveal the sky. The suggestion is that the architectural object is mediating some higher, celestial frame – the architectonic sign conveying the transcendent message ostentatiously reveals the transcendent through a gaping hole or lack in its own material makeup.[2]

2. Transparency (dematerialization)

Transparency, which strongly implies the transcendent act of dematerialization, is another ubiquitous feature of performatist architecture. Performatist structures constantly evoke the possibility of transcending materiality by presenting it in the form of transparent, seemingly dematerialized planes. Postmodernism, by contrast, likes reflective surfaces because they refer back to a context and away from an origin, and bright colors, because they evoke secondary semantic associations not particular to the materials being used. Modernism, which also employs transparency a great deal, uses it to highlight internal formal or structural essences. The best known example of this is Mies's dictum that a building's glass skin should reveal its structural bones.[3] Rowe and Slutzky, in their well-known essay,[4] suggest that in modernism there is, in addition to this literal transparency, a phenomenal one that creates overlapping, ambiguous planes, as in Le Corbusier's villa at Garches. Performatist transparency, by contrast, is demonstrative and tautological. It reifies, albeit imperfectly, the possibility of transcending materiality per se rather than revealing anything particular about a structure's inner workings or essence. This has a certain analogy in the ostensive scene as described by Gans.[5] The originary sign at first refers transparently to the thing. Upon seeing the thing in this mediated way, however, we discover that it isn't the thing itself we desire, but rather, as Gans puts it, the "center of the scene of representation that the sign brought into existence. The referent vanishes, to be restored through the renewed mediation of the sign."[6] Transparent planes or frames that do not reveal a particular essential content replay this semiotic disappearing act on a grand, sublime scale. In Gans's thought, I might add, this dematerialization also has crucial sacral implications, since it leads to the "discovery" of God, i.e., the principle missing from the center.

3. Triangulation (destabilization)

A key spatial figure of performatist architectonics is triangulation. The triangle is a minimal figure embodying the transition from one- to two-dimensionality (from the horizontal to the vertical). Functionally, in the form of the lean-to, it is the earliest form of man-made shelter. Visually it can be thought of as a figure valorizing the opposition between divergence and convergence. On the one hand, the apex of the triangle acts as an index sign pointing to something particular; on the other, as two lines extending away from the apex, out into infinity. Triangles also render space dynamic by creating slants and inclined planes. Modernism, although striving for geometrical purity and simplicity, traditionally disdains triangular figures, which it associates with folkloristic gables; it prefers squares or blocks connoting infinitely rational functionality (the block acts as the base for still another block, which is the base for still another block etc.). The A-frame house, which is planted firmly on the ground, is not yet performatist. From the postmodernist perspective it might be thought of as citing the primal, triangular lean-to; from the modernist perspective it carries a structural feature – the gable – to a logical, unifying conclusion.

Performatism, by contrast, takes triangularity and makes it into a figure of belief. It tilts triangles and positions them in precarious, unexpected ways suggesting that their normal function of providing shelter and stability has been overcome. A secondary device involved in performative triangulation is the use of acute angles. These "sharpen" the dynamic relationship between the concrete presence (convergence) and ineffable absence (divergence) that is played out in the triangular scene. The acute angle, which constricts space within the building and wastes space without, suggests mathematically mediated precision and rigor without usually having any real functional value.[7]

Finally, triangulation suggests a paradoxical, performative way of overcoming the semantic opposition between verticality and horizontality that normally helps define all architectural epochs. Utopian modernist architecture, for example, foregrounds verticality according to the building-block principle noted above. Postmodern architecture, which is interested in the horizontal relations of context and conditionality, relativizes and sometimes even parodies the utopian rationality of modernism (when Philip Johnson, for example, tops the International Style of his famous A.T.&T. skyscraper with a piece of bric-a-brac, he effectively brings the high-flying utopian aspirations it cites back down to historical earth).

Performatist architecture, by contrast, revitalizes the upward motion by casting it as a dynamic, oblique line or plane. Conversely, this line can also be perceived as a conduit of downward motion (see also the discussion of kinesis further below). Such a line is neither ornamental nor functional, but demonstrative and performative. It draws attention to a symbolic relation located along the axis of the high and the low. As in the original ostensive scene, we are made to perceive architectonic space as a paradoxical unity existing prior to these two semantic opposites. It is also perhaps not entirely coincidental that the triangular constellation is reified in the originary ostensive scene itself, which cannot be reduced to anything less than a triadic relation.[8]

4. Kinesis (moving the immovable)

Kinesis is important to performatist architecture because it is uniquely suited to reifying transcendence with architectonic means. This is done by suggesting that a static object – a building – is doing something that it cannot, which is to say move. Usually, this takes place in the functional context of triangulation. The oblique side of the triangle suggests that a dynamic, "sliding" relationship between up and down is being mediated by the building. Modernist architecture, inasmuch as it follows the building-block principle, tends to promote stasis; postmodern architecture (such as the early Frank Gehry house) often suggests movement, but always in a non-directed way. An intermediate position seems to be occupied by Gehry's recent work, as in the Guggenheim Museum in Bilbao, the Nationale-Nederlanden Building in Prague or the conference room in the DG Bank in Berlin. These structures, which seem to wriggle and squirm in all directions without really going anywhere, might still be thought of as examples of postmodern undecidability. At the same time, however, their undulating folds and bends may also be considered unique, amorphous forms evoking the very origin of form itself.[9] Deconstructivist architecture, such as Daniel Libeskind's Jewish Museum in Berlin, is also very much kinetic. Libeskind, though, emphasizes dysfunctionality and absence; the fractured, oddly arranged floor plan of the Jewish Museum is reminiscent of a shattered Star of David, and the empty inner spaces suggest the void left by the murder of the European Jews rather than sliced-away matter. In principle, at least, the kinetic architecture of performatism would always have to point out where it wants to move to – hence the importance of triangulation.

5. Impendency (sublime threat)

A device related to kinesis and theist creation is what I would call impendency (from *impendere*, to hang over, threaten). Buildings of this kind are architectonically so dynamic that they seem to be on the verge of collapse; they work, as it were, by putting a sublime fear of the Lord and awe of the architect into the viewer at the same time. This device, which I have found in several cases in Berlin, has certain equivalents in modernist architecture, as, for example, in Frank Lloyd Wright's elegantly cantilevered Fallingwater House or Mies van der Rohe's National Gallery in Berlin, whose massive steel-and-concrete roof seems to float on air. The difference between modernism and performatism can be defined most simply as the difference between transcendence mediated by technical rationality and transcendence mediated by simple, wondrous configurations. In impendent modernist structures like the ones named, we are supposed to be aware that technical wizardry such as reinforced concrete or high-tension steel is keeping the precipitously hanging structures in place. In performatist ones, we are deliberately made to experience how a building seems to overcome the drama of imminent collapse that it itself is staging for us. This sublime drama is human, and not technical: it is an expression of the architect's will or wilfulness, rather than a demonstration of technical prowess. Postmodernist, particularly deconstructivist, buildings also thematize collapse and dysfunctionality. However, they do this without the metaphysical optimism of performatism, which plays out the non-rational, faith-based possibility of overcoming materiality, gravity, or functionality *per se*.

6. Wholeness (closure)

Wholeness and closure are frequent themes in performatist architecture, which stylizes them using novel, egg-shaped structures rather than the geometric, rational circles of modernism. Closure is of course anathema to postmodernism's tactics of boundary transgression and delimiting; modernism tends to favor open spaces and the utopian unlimitedness implied by them. The notion of closure is, incidentally, a crucial aspect of the originary scene according to Gans. In his scenario, the protagonists who have just created the first sign must stand back from it to admire its wholeness and closedness: "the creation of a formal object in the sign requires that the criteria for formal closure be imposed by the subject."[10] This ability to impose closure through semiotic mediation is, in turn, the condition marking the "minimal structure of human will."[11] Performatism, one could say, revitalizes this originary moment in an architectonic act.

7. Framing (dissociation)

Intermediate frames are an unreliable, but nonetheless essential part of the performatist scene. They provide the structure enabling dynamic acts of transcendence at all to occur but are themselves necessarily fallible and dependent on an ostensive sign (the "inner frame") or on other, extrinsic frames. As is the case in impendency, performatist architecture often employs frames as tokens of theistic self-revelation. Frames may bend dynamically at odd angles or have missing chunks suggesting a paradoxical confluence of architectonic might and impotence in the face of the Beyond. Very often, the frame seems to dissociate itself radically from its content (or vice versa).

Postmodernist architecture sometimes highlights frames, but, like Derrida, isn't really interested in them as mediators of origin or transcendence. An example of this is the Frank Gehry house, which is an older building framed by a sort of junky-looking new fence that establishes a liminal space between the two (for more on this see Jameson's discussion of the house in his well-known book on postmodernism[12]). The modernist frame, as exemplified by Mies van der Rohe's Banking Pavilion in the Toronto-Dominion Center or the National Gallery in Berlin, creates an autonomous, transparent space for the individual to regard the world anew through a frame connoting technically mediated rationality.[13] The postmodernist frame is a liminal, schizoid one that creates a relationship of spatial undecidability between the solid frame and its voided content. Examples of this can be seen in many buildings of Oswald Mathias Ungers, who likes to cite and stylize the modernist, structural grid, in effect making what was once an essentialist principle into a superficial ornament.

8. Ostensivity (Centering)

Performatist structures like to point at things for reasons outlined above in the discussion of triangulation; sometimes they also like to center them *and* point at them. I have found a few odd examples of this, although it seems a minor, hard-to-implement device. Post-modernism, obviously, eschews all centrification; modernism centers things by way of symmetrical arrangement but does not point at them (modernism does not allow the suggestion of any sort of higher rationality external to its own principles).

9. Generativity

In at least one instance, I have found a building, Mathias Oswald Ungers' Family Court in Berlin, that plays with a single form (a square) in a kinetic, three-dimensional performance suggesting that other forms are being generated out of it in a dynamic, open-ended way. This mixture of rational, radical monism and ludic generativity suggests a synthesis of modernism and postmodernism. Modernism is rigidly monist but doesn't play; postmodernism hates monism but likes to play. Representing generativity in architecture directly is in any case a very ambitious, aesthetically risky move that will probably be limited to a small number of structures.

Performatist Architecture in Berlin

Before I start my visual stroll through Berlin, the reader should be aware that I will be treating these buildings in terms of their place in the performatist code rather than in regard to their urban context, the oeuvre of their planners, and their success or failure as functional and aesthetic objects, i.e., the usual subjects of architectural criticism. Those familiar with German and curious about these and other topics of local concern might want to consult Falk Jaeger's well-informed and richly illustrated *Architektur für das neue Jahrtausend* [Architecture for the new millennium],[14] which provides the most up-to-date critical overview of the architectural scene in Berlin of the 1990s.

The Estrel Hotel (triangulation, framing, impendency, theist creation)

The Estrel Hotel (figure 1.) is performatism at its most exuberant. The hotel's main structure is a gigantic wedge whose apex points down toward a specific spot on earth (you, the observer) while its open angles stretch upwards and outwards toward the infinite bounds of the sky. The upwardly directed push from solid, gleaming mass to nothingness is accentuated by an empty frame above extending the wedge structure below. The sky itself then fills out the emptied earthly construct – a common performatist device suggesting a transcendent goal. The most striking feature of the building is the enormous wopperjawed wedge resting on the inclined plane of the building's forefront. You could think of it as an impendent threat (the proverbial ton of bricks about to slide down onto your head) or as a load on a ramp miraculously defying the laws of gravity. The theist implications are here, I think, self-evident. As Falk Jaeger writes, "you can almost imagine how the architects took a knife and carved the form out of a block of clay."[15] Viewed from the side (not visible in the picture), the Estrel also suggests the intent of a theistically inspired creator to overcome materiality. A large chunk has been carved out of the fore

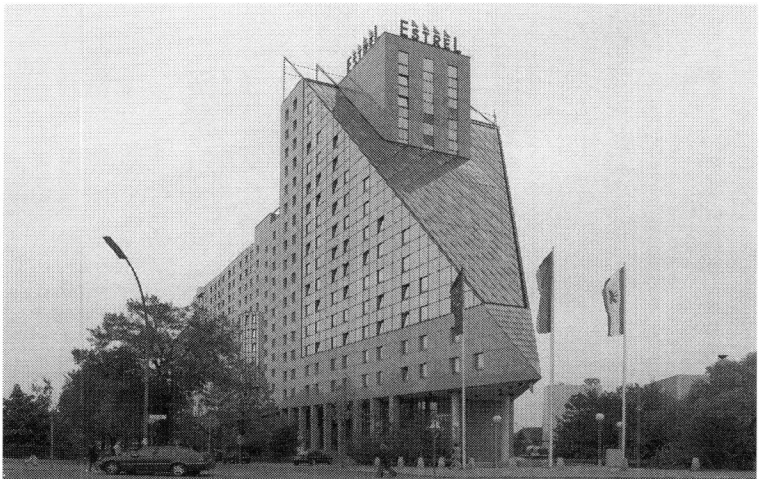

Figure 1. The Estrel Hotel

and aft parts of the building, which are linked only by a catwalk; the jaggedly running juxtaposition of glass (above) and stone (below) along the building suggests a wilful, if uneven, transition from solid earth to immaterial sky.

The Kant Triangle (kinesis, triangulation, impendency)

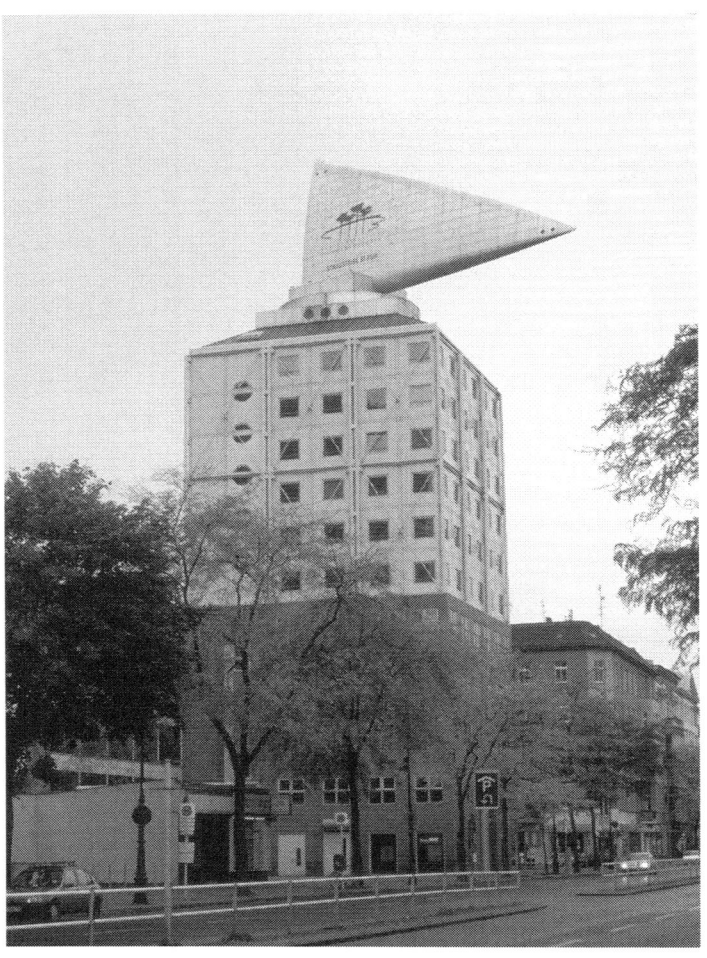

Figure 2. The Kant Triangle

The Kant Triangle (figure 2.), located prominently next to the Bahnhof Zoo train station, is not especially performatist in terms of its basic ornamentation. Indeed, the reflective glass surface on the side, the juxtaposition of quadratic and circular figures as well as the ornamental struts are all typical features of postmodernism. What makes the building extravagantly performatistic is the fact that it really and truly *moves*. The triangular gizmo on top is a kind of gigantic weather vane or sail that actually shifts when the wind gets strong enough (initially unaware of this fact, I made a mental note to stay clear of the thing when the first big gust of wind came along). The oversized weather vane does have a function of sorts – it can be used to clean the building – but there are probably easier and less ostentatious ways to go about doing this. With this kind of building, the context is secondary. Your attention is centered on the giant triangle, which, depending on the way the wind is blowing, decenters itself again by pointing outward towards something in the scene around it. This is a good working example of transcendent functionalism. The "function" of the vane is to attract attention to itself so that it can refocus that attention elsewhere once again; the agency guiding that function (the wind) is part of a bigger, natural, ineffable frame that transcends us all while at the same time leaving a spatial, terrestrial marker incontrovertibly demonstrating the immanent existence of a higher principle.

Neues Kranzler Eck Shopping Mall, Kurfürstendamm (triangulation, transparency, framing, kinesis, theist creation)

Also centrally located near, and visible from, Bahnhof Zoo. The extreme acute angle of the transparent, triangulated facade "wastes" space in an extravagant, visible way incompatible with any quotidian function (figure 3). Paradoxically, this grand display of ornamental excess is derived from the Euclidian axiom that two non-parallel planes in space must converge. The true function of this rationally motivated ornamentation would indeed appear to be to direct the observer's gaze upwards in the most radical possible way (figure 4). As in many other structures, the half-built transparent roofing and the incomplete frames (figure 5.) suggest that the heavens above are the real, ultimate roof of the work of art (designed either by a theist, personal God interested in building a shopping mall, or a theist, incompletely omnipotent architect, in this case Helmut Jahn).

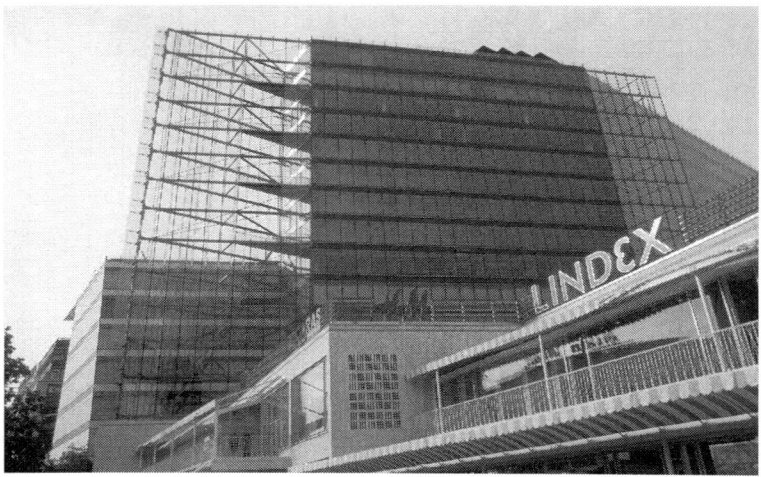

Figure 3. Neues Kranzler Eck

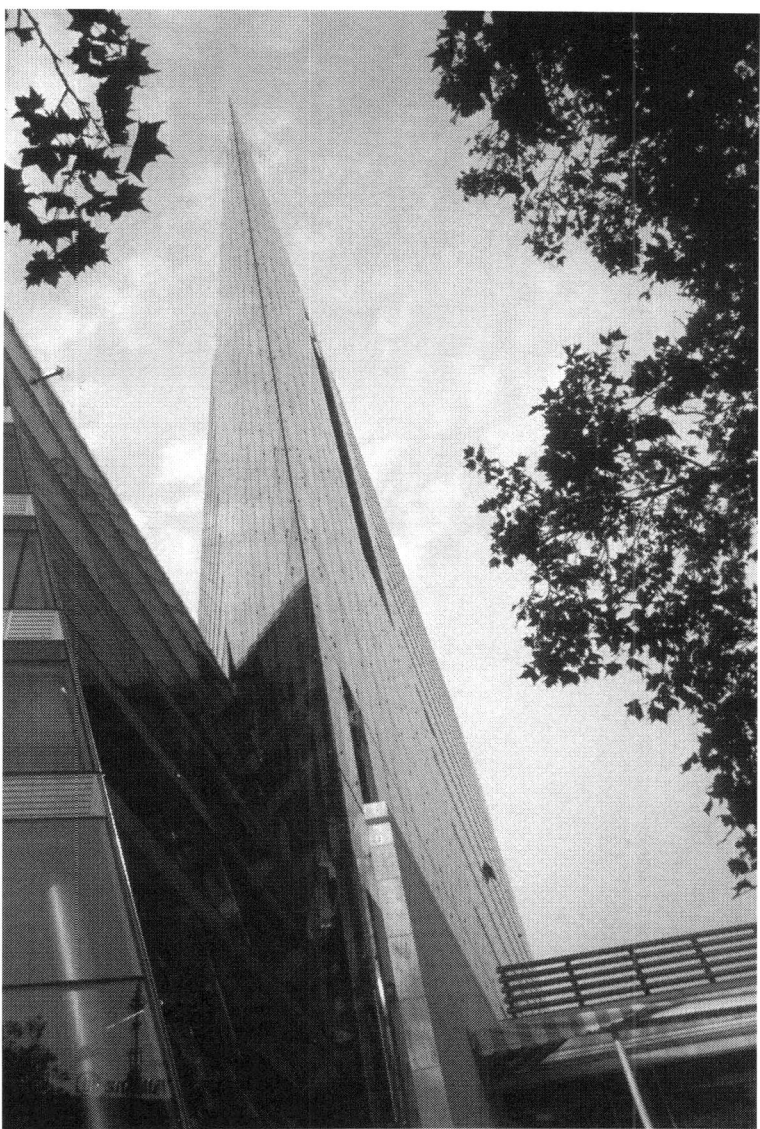

Figure 4. Neues Kranzler Eck

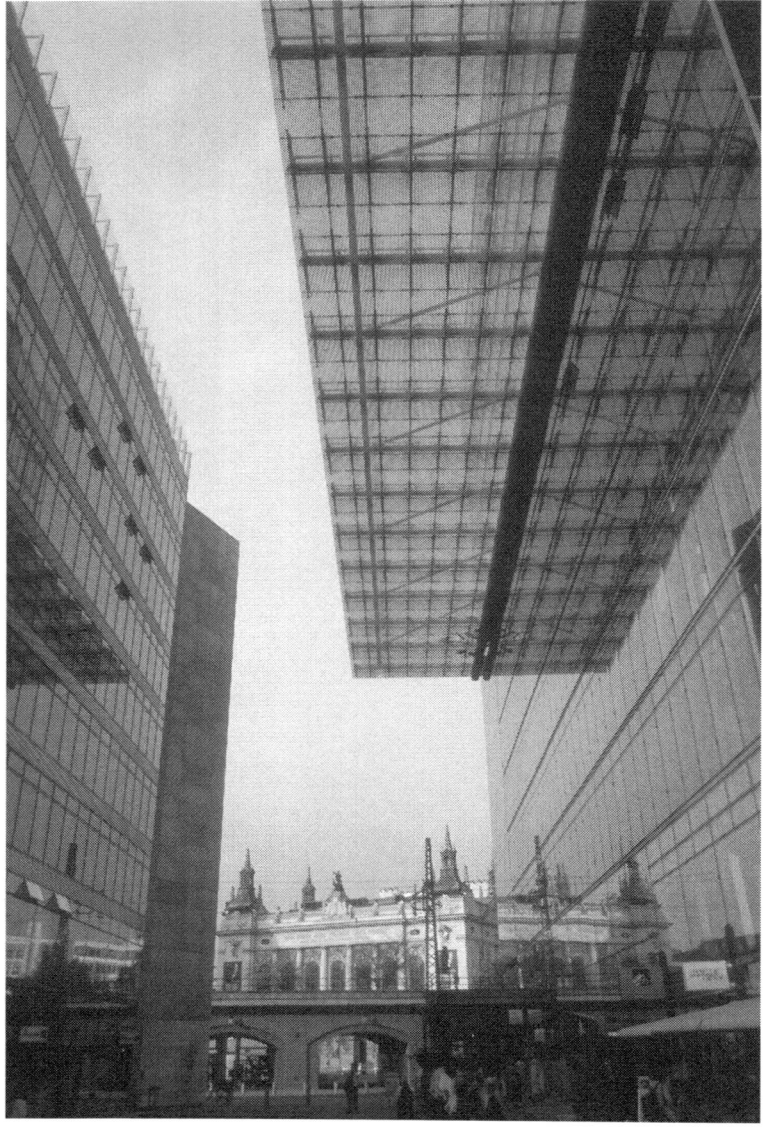

Figure 5. Neues Kranzler Eck

Peek and Cloppenburg Department Store, Kurfürstendamm (framing, kinesis, transparency, triangulation)

The transparent mass of this department store on the Kudamm (figure 6.) appears to be flowing out from under its massive, upwardly thrusting frame. This dramatic dissociation of frame and content thematizes the possibility of overcoming an originary relation, which here takes on the semantic attributes of solid vs. liquid (in functional terms, the transparent shield keeps water off passers-by and prospective customers while at the same time mimicking the attributes of what it is protecting them from). In terms of gender, the transparent, flowing skirt might be thought of as a graceful female counterpoint to the masculine, muscular frame: Peek & Cloppenburg, after all, clothes both men and women.

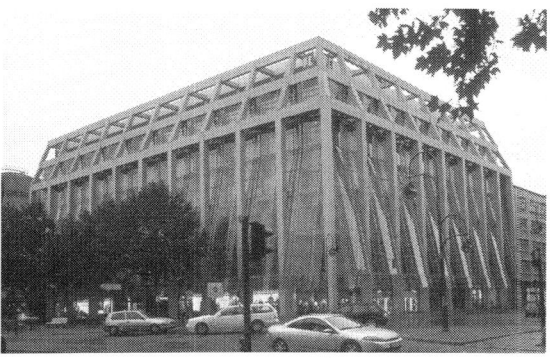

Figure 6. Peek and Cloppenburg

The Baden-Württemberg Office, Tiergartenstraße (theist creation, triangulation)

A wilful, theist architect (Dietrich Bangert) has gutted the building, but in a goal-directed, elegant way made clear by triangulation (figure 7). The horizon lines leading into the building serve to draw us involuntarily into its space, even as we are taken aback by the drastic, non-functional removal of so much matter from a rectilinear volume. Further rectangular incisions in the triangular incision heighten this effect even more.

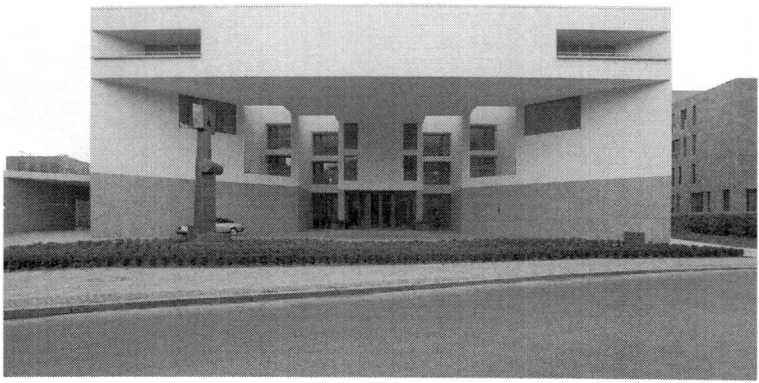

Figure 7. Baden-Württemberg Office

The British Embassy, Wilhelmstraße (theist creation, triangulation, framing)

Because of its bright, arbitrarily selected colors and playful shapes the British Embassy (figure 8.) near the Pariser Platz might superficially seem postmodern. Once more, however, a theist gesture of "I taketh away and I giveth" informs the buildings character more than anything else. In general, it looks as if the architect, Michael Wilford, first eviscerated the building and then placed an enormous triangular form in it pointing back directly out to YOU. The odd feeling of being drawn into the building and at the same time repulsed by it is

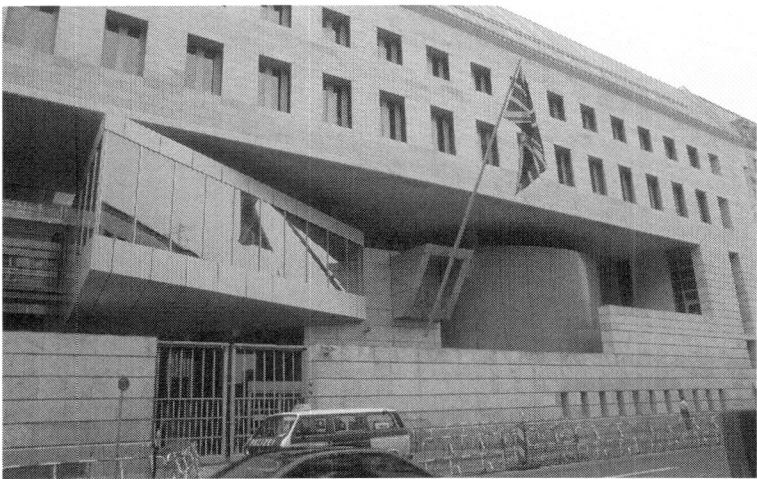

Figure 8. British Embassy

strengthened by the absence of window frames allowing you to find your bearings – the horizon lines recede in such an acute way that you have the impression of no connection between facade and what is behind it (once more a case of a frame dissociated from its content). The total effect is more than a bit unsettling. The building is massive and yet vulnerable, attractive and yet repelling. This paradox is originary and performative rather than cited or semantic. There is no set of previous codes I am aware of that could help us figure out what the building is doing to us.

Indian Embassy, Tiergartenstraße (theist creation, centering)

One of a spate of new foreign embassies in Berlin trying to outdo one another in architectural brilliance (figure 9). It was designed, it would seem, by theistically inspired architects (Léon and Wernik) using a large round cookie cutter.

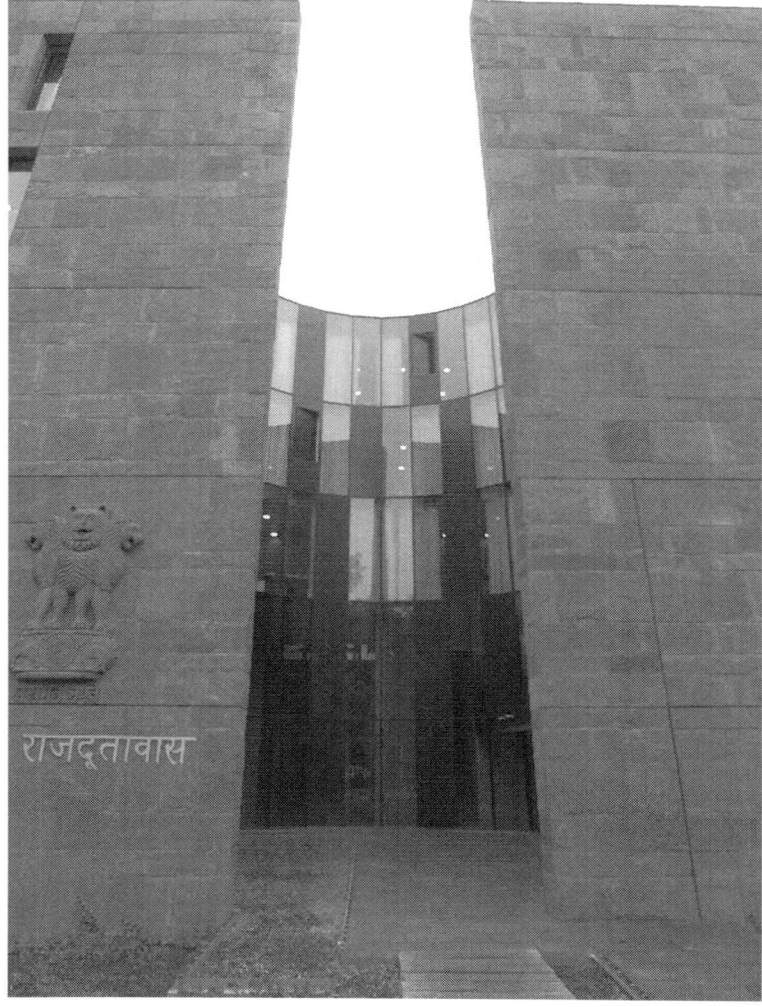

Figure 9. Indian Embassy

The DG Bank, Pariser Platz (framing, transparency, triangulation, theist creation)

The usual line on the DG Bank (figure 10.) is that an overly re-strictive building code for the area around the Brandenburg Gate caused Frank Gehry to design a run-of-the-mill facade, while the real focal point of the building is the bizarre "Horse's Head" conference room tucked away inside. In performatist terms, however, I find that the facade, in its own way, is no less remarkable or complex than the Bilbao museum or any of Gehry's other crumply, amorphous metallic structures. The massive, cut-off columns, which simultaneously frame oversize, movable windows, suggest a powerful upward surge which is paradoxically intensified by being chopped off at the top (that's the theist architect at work again) and by the triangular incline of the transparent window-become-balcony (which suggests overcoming the need for a horizontal frame). The building as a whole is dramatic juxtaposition of upwardly bound, self-transcending transparency and crude, earthbound materiality. On the one hand, Gehry creates a mas-sive, uncompromising frame; on the other, he tries to get rid of it in a series of incompletely realized, irregular, staggered steps (note how the balconies on the second floor create a slightly protruding step or plane setting up the massive, dramatic removal of volume further above).

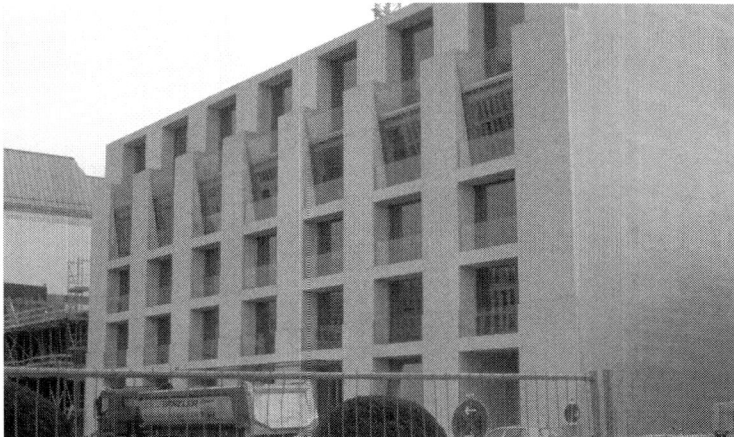

Figure 10. DG Bank

The Paul Löbe Government Office Building, Regierungsviertel (transparency, impendency, theist creation, framing)

Lying between the Federal Chancellery and the Reichstag, the Paul Löbe Building (figure 11.) has the thankless task of linking the massive, brooding Reichstag and the swirling, effervescent Federal Chancellery. Be that as it may, it is still a textbook example of performatist technique. The large chunks cut out of the roof make a transcendent, ineffable frame – the sky – an intrinsic part of the entire architectural statement. This is a common, but very effective performatist device. The spindly pillars of the roof (figure 12.) look as if they could be knocked over with one swift kick (in the aftermath of September 11th, one wonders if the architect, Stephan Braunfels, has had any second thoughts about this impendent feature). The large cuts made in the side of the building are huge theist incisions supposed to make it possible for passers by to observe, at least superficially, just what their elected representatives are up to. After decades of postmodern distrust of visual evidence, performatism – as exemplified in Gans's notion of the ostensive – suggests that truth can be made present and visible in terms of a specifically framed, artificial scene, even as this scene is always open to resentment over what it cannot depict (in this case the abstract or cognitive aspects of

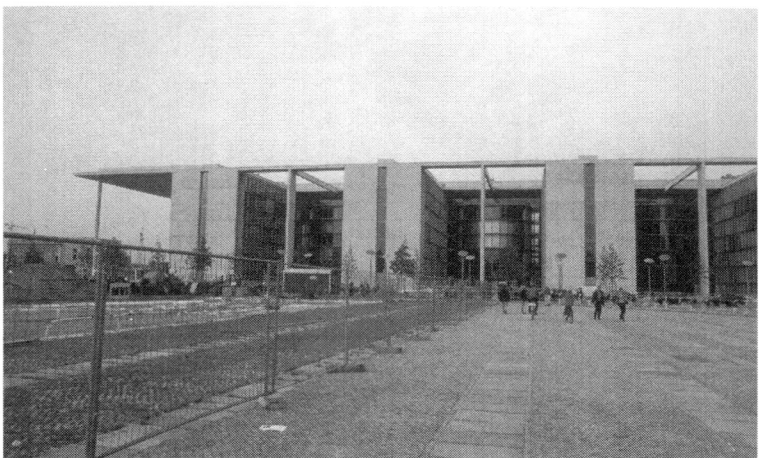

Figure 11. Paul Löbe Building

lawmaking). You don't have to be a hard-boiled cynic to "see through" this particular device, but I think it should be understood together with the total theist message, which implies that the Federal Representatives are also beholden to a higher context of undisclosed origin (German cabinet members have the option of taking the oath of office either with reference to God or without).

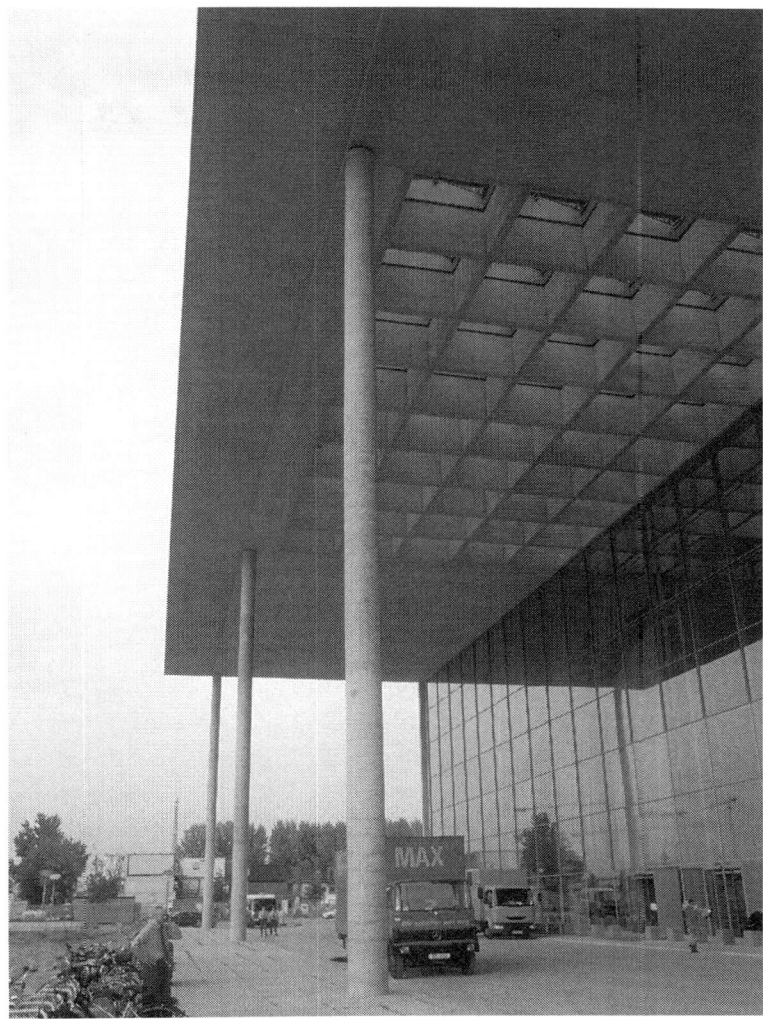

Figure 12. Paul Löbe Building

The Sony Center, Potsdamer Platz (kinesis, transparency, centering, theistic creation, triangulation)

Designed by Helmut Jahn, the megalomaniac German-American architect that critics love to hate, and owned by a multinational entertainment moloch, the Sony Center (figure 13.) is neither *gemütlich* (exuding emotional warmth) nor *volkstümlich* (of the people). It seems to attract visitors not because of any innate charm but because several large cinemas were cleverly located in or near it. Nonetheless, the Sony Center and the surrounding buildings (also designed by Jahn) are all impressive examples of performatist spatialization. The roof, for example, suggests a giant whirligig about to take off on its own in defiance of all notions of functionality or common sense; the odd structure in the middle, by contrast, points dramatically downwards to a center point. Indeed, it looks as if a giant dart had just plunged in the Center's roof, dramatically exemplifying the old Sony Playstation motto "It's not a game." The typical incompleteness of the roof makes the firmament – and even the megalomaniac architect's ultimate inadequacy before it – a part of the total aesthetic statement. Another oddity is the enigmatic, trestle-like frame planted on the building's roof (figure 14). As in many other performatist structures, it seems to transcend both ornamentation and functionality by combining both in a paradoxical way resisting any earthly explanation. Normally, the trestle is found in that epitome of functional ugliness, the train bridge. Planted on the top of a building like this, the trestle becomes an ornament connoting an out-of-place, as yet unachieved functionality that would presumably require us to transcend everything we have known up to now about buildings and train bridges. Unlike postmodernist ornamentation and citation, which is clever and smoothly ironic, this suggests the work of a powerful, yet not perfectly omnipotent hand (that of a theist God or of the architect mimicking Him).

The notion of theist creation also applies to the neighboring Deutsche Bahn Building, which looks as if Jahn took a very large hatchet and chopped it in half (figure 15). Depending on your perspective, it could be either a sign of tremendous power or a bow to something higher, a sublime subtraction of mass demonstrating that less can also be infinitely more.

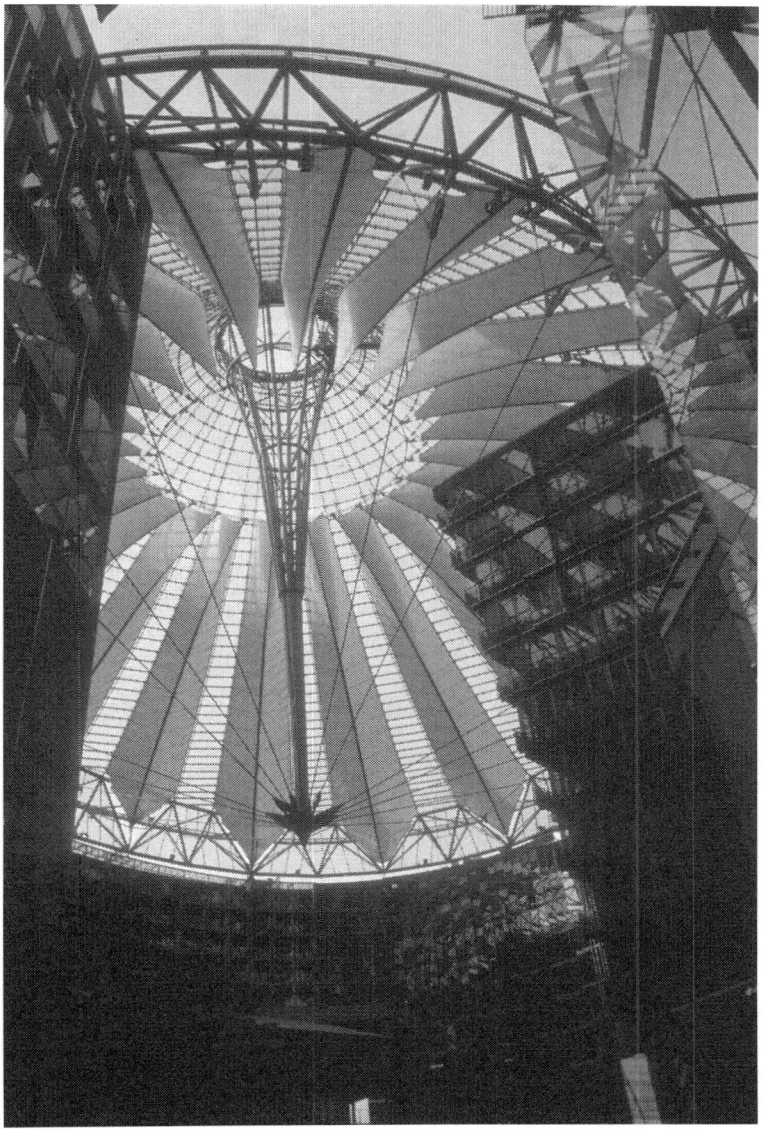

Figure 13. Sony Center

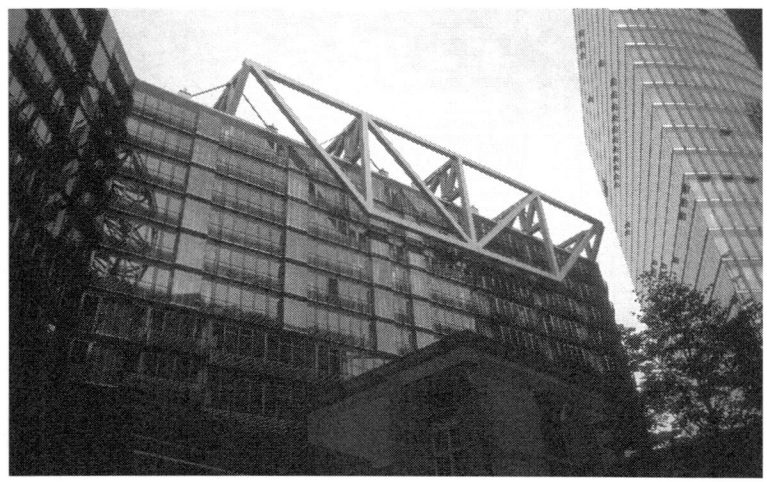

Figure 14. Sony Center

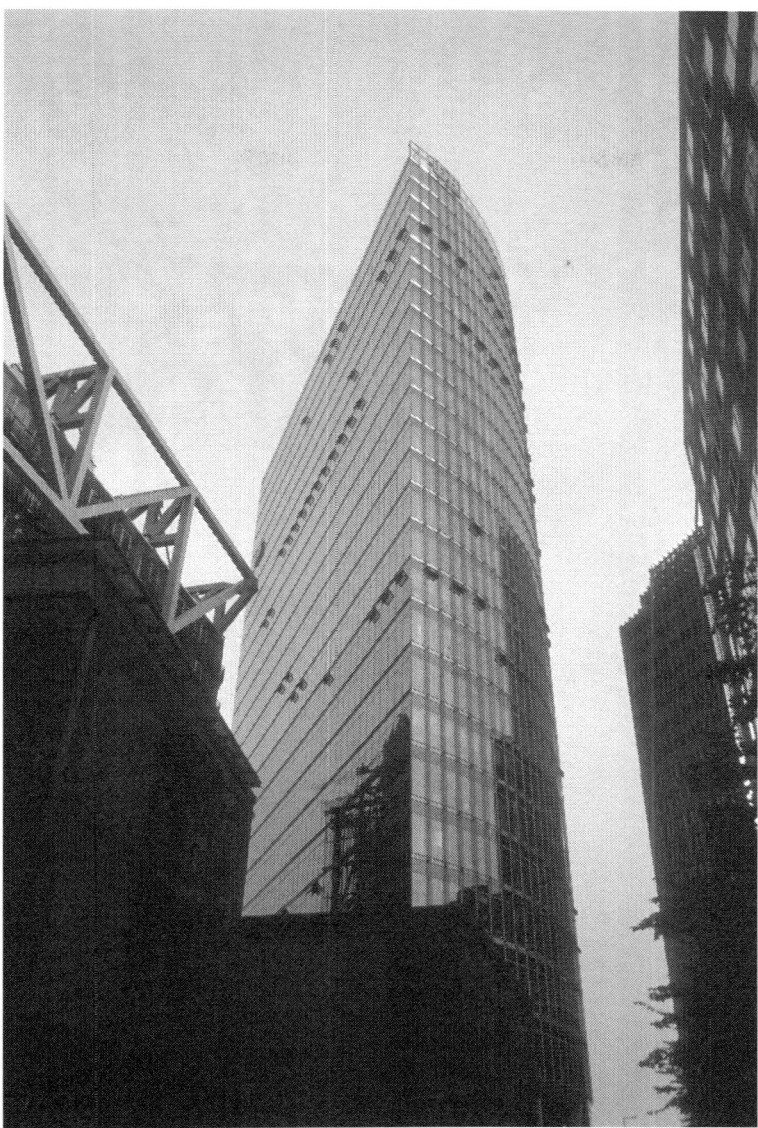

Figure 15. Deutsche Bahn Building

Price Waterhouse Coopers Building, Potsdamer Platz (triangulation, transparency)

This striking Renzo Piano building realizes triangulation and transparency in the extreme (figure 16). Note that the transparent facade of this skyscraper doesn't really reveal any skeletal frame à la Mies. Instead, it accentuates the non-functional, but logically realized acuteness of the triangular frame. This is a typical performatist paradox with a transcendency-seeking resolution. The acute, geometrically rigorous frame thrusting itself out of the building's functional body embodies both ornamentation and functionalism while transcending them both: it is a geometrically defined, rationally conceived, useless ornament whose function is to point upwards and outwards towards an unidentifiable, higher source. If you reverse this function – if you think of yourself being sucked into the space cut out by the building – you are drawn into a newly built, popular shopping district.

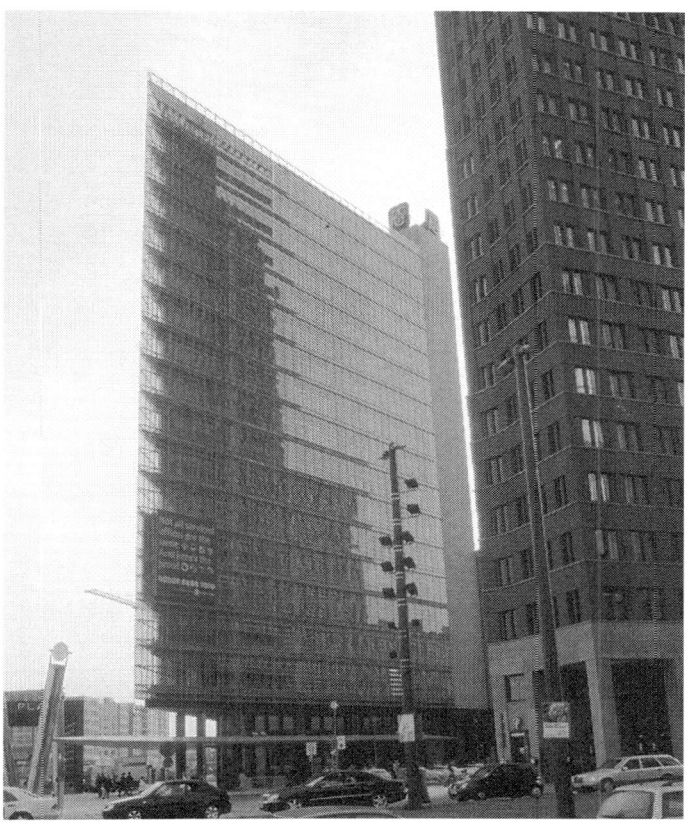

Figure 16. Price Waterhouse Coopers Building

The Treptow Crematorium, Baumgartenstraße (all nine performatist devices)

If you ever have the misfortune to die and be cremated in Berlin, your friends and family will have the good fortune to mourn your passing in this building. Many people think that this is one of the most important and beautiful structures erected in Berlin in the last ten years; indeed, the interest in the Crematorium as an aesthetic object is so great that its administrators have had to hire a private company to conduct tours during cemetery off-hours.

Of all the buildings treated here, the Crematorium is the only one that actually fulfils a sacral function, albeit it one on the fringe of Church dogma (cremation is a pagan, rather than a Christian rite and has become popular in recent years because it is cheaper than a regular full burial). This sacral context, which makes the set to transcendency visible to even the most hidebound cynic, is however not a necessary condition of performatism. Indeed, the architects, Axel Schultes and Charlotte Frank, used almost identical devices in two completely secular buildings (the Federal Chancellery in Berlin, see below, and the Art Museum in Bonn). This more or less self-contained sacral aesthetic (or aesthetic sacrality) is more important than the context-sensitivity typical of postmodernism. Ideally, the performatist leap to the transcendent can take place anywhere, under any conditions.

The Crematorium is a veritable encyclopedia of performatist devices. By all appearances the theist creator seems to have carved it out of a single block (in reality the building is made of plain old poured concrete; figure 17). Slices in the roof (figure 18.) suggest a rationally planned passage to heaven as well as the ease with which even the most solid-seeming material can be made to evanesce. Dematerialization is also suggested by the transparent walls; you can literally see through the entire building. Very effective is also the kinetic manipulation of the façade (figure 18.); its louvers make matter appear and disappear upon command. The ornamental, absolutely superfluous triangulation defining the three ominous smokestacks (figure 19.) suggests upward, transcendent expansiveness while pointing downward, as it were, at three. Not visible in the picture is the incision made in the earth, into which the theist creator has, as it were, laid the Crematorium itself (the actual cremating, which is done by a computer-guided mechanism, takes place underground). Inside, the twenty-nine light-tipped columns arouse universal wonder (figure 20). The columns, which seem to stand around helplessly, like real-life mourners, actually support the roof; the functional brackets at their tips are however made invisible by the light streaming in from on high. It is hardly necessary to comment on how they simultaneously transcend functionality, materiality, and "mere" ornamentation.

An at first curious, but on second thought absolutely characteristic feature is the egg suspended from a barely visible wire hung from the ceiling above a round pool (figure 21). Here, Schultes and Frank are evidently citing pagan symbols of originary unity.[16] The mourner will have no trouble deciding what is more important: the performative, magical representation of that unity or the derivative, ironic fact of its citation. Also striking are the curiously tiered walls of the Crematorium with their regular rows of holes and casket-like incisions with sand piles at their base. The holes contain lights which, when lit, performatively suggest the dispersion of matter from within; the sand piles suggest the dissolution of matter into dust. These and other devices used

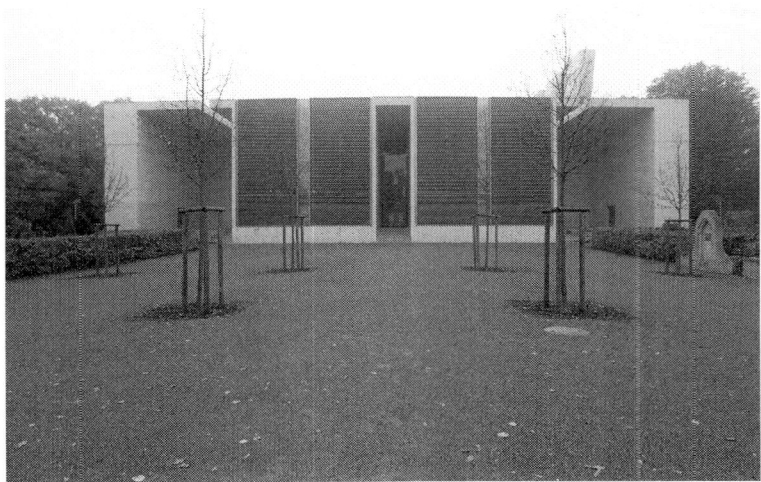

Figure 17.

in the Crematorium are suggestive of non-Christian sacral structures (the Temple of Karnak, the Great Mosque in Cordoba, Stonehenge etc.) without, as far as I can tell, really citing them directly. The point is not to quote but to create what Schultes calls "suggestive spatiality"[17] or, as he also once put it, "a new, primeval convention, an architectonic imperative."[18]

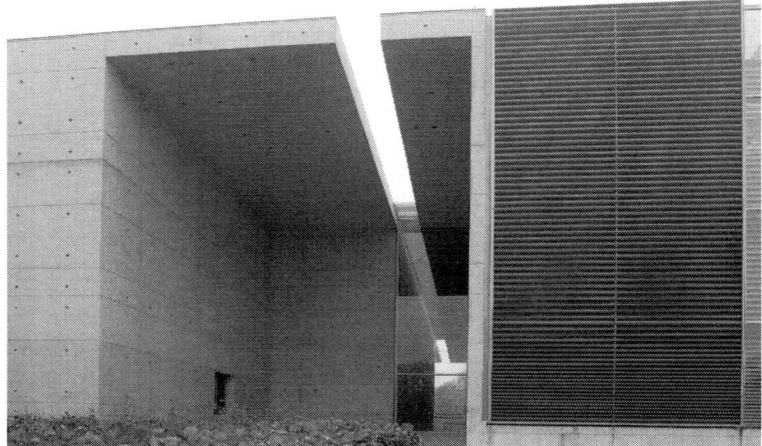

Figure 18.

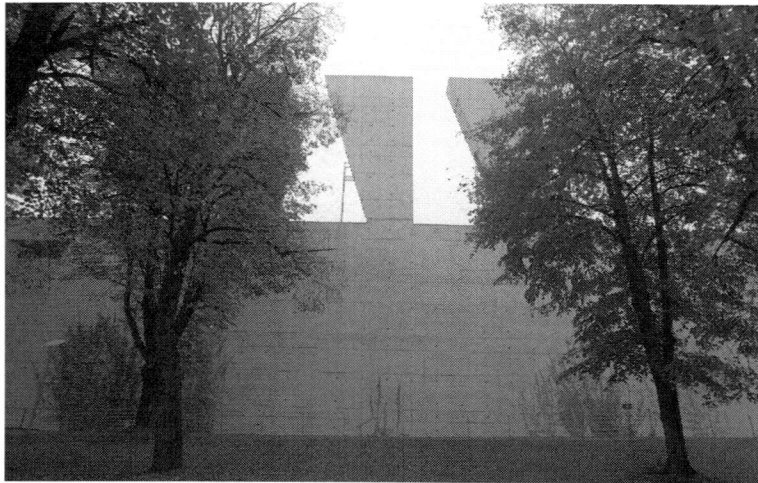

Figure 19.

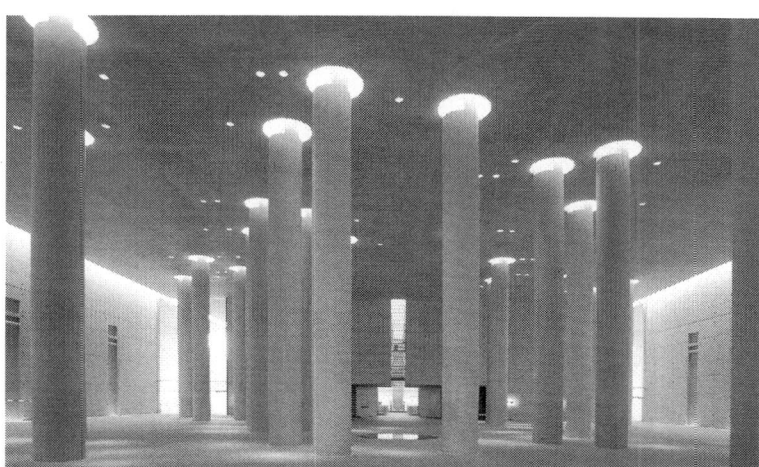

Figure 20.

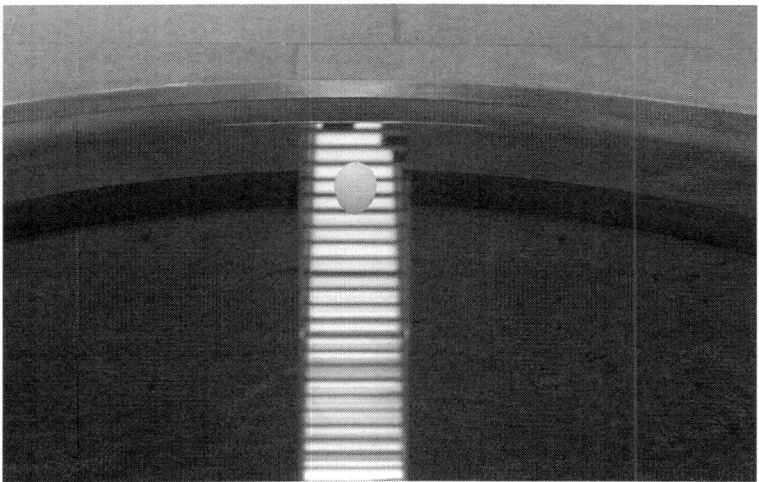

Figure 21.

The Federal Chancellery, Regierungsviertel (transparency, kinesis)

Dubbed the "Chancellor's Washing Machine" by the general public, this swirling, grandiose structure (figure 22), which is the seat of executive power in Germany as well as the Chancellor's home, has been accused of being gigantomanic and excessively garish.[19] Like the Reichstag, the Presidential Chancellery, and the Paul Löbe Building it makes an important positive statement about political culture in today's Germany. In each case, the decision-making bodies involved could have opted for staid, emotionless structures suggesting stability, bureaucratic efficiency, and consensual continuity – the reassuring hallmarks of postwar German politics. Instead, the vacuum that resulted after German reunification was taken as a chance to fit out Germany with an architectonic face beholden to no particular previous historical style and conveying open, uplifting qualities. This is most certainly one case where the fall of communism has had a direct aesthetic expression: the building definitely makes a post-millennial statement in Gans's sense.[20]

The Chancellery itself is a good deal larger than my picture suggests. It is flanked by two massive office blocks, and from the distance its boxy exterior does indeed resemble a giant, outlandish household appliance (the popular idea of the building as a gargantuan washing machine fits in well with my notion of transcendent functionalism). The facade, which is the most striking and widely photographed feature, works by radically disassociating frame and content in both vertical and horizontal space. As in the Treptower Crematorium, it is possible to see through the vast building entirely; the structure seeks in this way to disavow its own materiality. Wings have been sliced into the roof suggesting both flight and the overcoming of matter; the flight theme is echoed further below by the pterodactyl-like roof stretched out over the entrance. The profusion of chopped-off pillars suggests theist wilfulness mitigated by natural growth (the trees on top). On the horizontal level, the first floor appears to be dissociated entirely from the ground floor; similarly, the louvers behind the pillars dissect and "move" space performatively. On the ground, the oddly configured grass strips repeat the wing patterns above and point us toward the entrance. In general, the building "opens" out towards us and tries to draw us into its space, which is then made to dematerialize as much as possible. This effect of openness, transparency, and upwardly bound movement is entirely conscious and political. Schultes wanted to make this German equivalent of the American White House as open to the public view as possible, and was bitterly disappointed that a Citizen's Information Center he designed was not built in front of the Chancellery.[21]

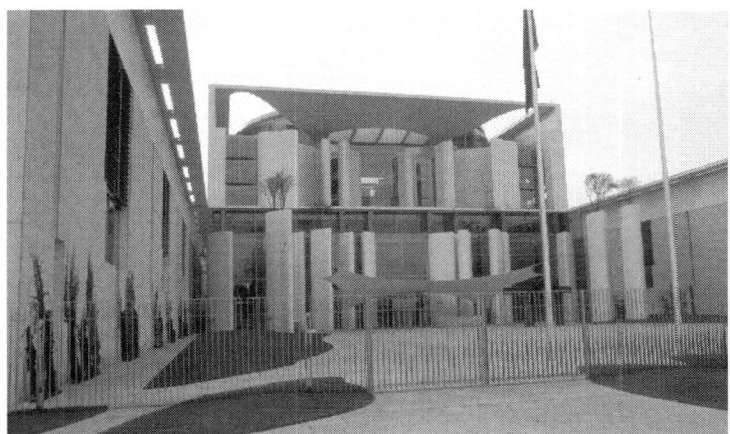

Figure 22. Federal Chancellery

The Presidential Chancellery, Tiergarten (wholeness)

Designed by upstart architects Martin Gruber and Helmut Kleine-Kraneburg, the Chancellery is a shiny anthracite hatbox (figure 23.) that connotes wholeness while at the same time managing to integrate its natural surroundings into itself visually. The building reflects, but in a humane, inclusive way, and not in the cool, metallic-sunglass-style typical of postmodernism: black and white, nature and culture merge amicably on its receding, self-effacing surface.

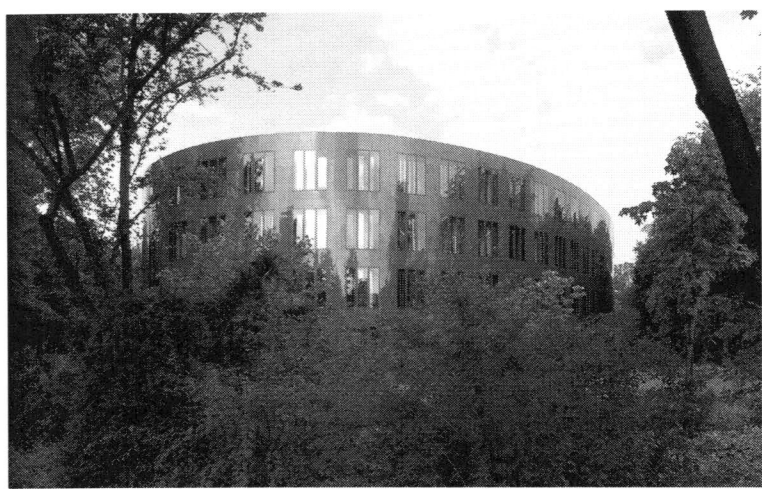

Figure 23. Presidential Chancellery

The Lemon Office Building (closure + triangulation, impendency, transparency, theist creation)

Figuratively speaking, this is performatism's way of squaring the circle (figure 24). Triangulation, which normally involves stylizing convergence and divergence, is combined here in a paradoxical way with circularity and wholeness. Seen from the road, the Lemon Building seems to float over its base, which is marked by crisp incisions that seemingly undermine its wholeness and stability – all the work of architects (Léon and Wohlhage) not quite of this world. In this structure, the occupants of the building unwittingly participate in the performatist plan: undrawn, the window shades realize transparency; drawn, materialization. This spontaneous individual activity of the building's users – something modernist architects disdained as a gross disruption of their rigorous symmetries – is now integrated into the total aesthetic scheme.

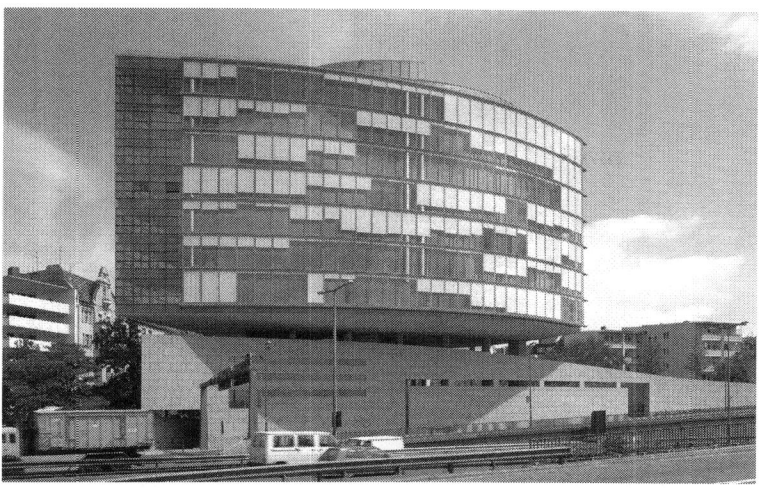

Figure 24. Lemon Office Building

GSW Tower, Kochstraße (transparency, kinesis, framing)

The sail-like structure on top of this building (figure 25.) as well as the peculiar transparent facade work together to create a chimney-like draft that cools the building (designed by Matthias Sauerbruch and Louise Hutton). This demonstrates that performatist devices need not be non-functional in reality – they just have to look that way. In this case there is also still a certain overlap between post-modern and performatist visual language. The sail on top can be said to cite 1950s-style buildings[22] and the red-pink-orange color of the awnings is no doubt still a frivolous, postmodern touch. No longer postmodern, however, is the way in which they interact with the transparent frame to suggest dematerialization. The awnings, whose number and arrangement is constantly changing as their users pull them up and down, put on a striking, spontaneous performance while suggesting that material things are being suspended in thin air. The frame itself appears entirely dissociated from its content, which is yet another frame.

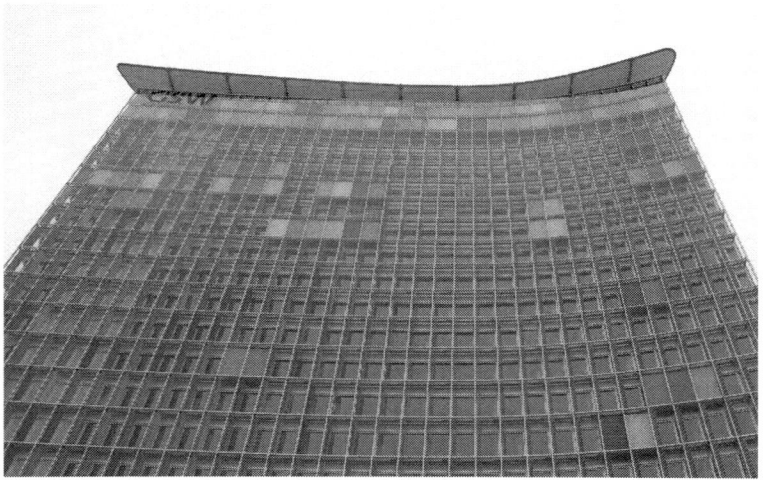

Figure 25. GSW Tower

The Family Court, Kreuzberg (framing, generativity)

This building by the quadrant-loving German architect Mathias Oswald Ungers still has ties to the postmodern aesthetic. It cites a presumably functional unit, the square or grid, and treats it as a superficial ornament rather than as the external expression of an inner functional principle (figure 26). Here, though, it seems to me that Ungers transcends postmodernism by using the square as a generative unit that unfolds in a dynamic second dimension (on the building's facade) and in a third dimension (the empty frame beside it, figure 27). In both instances the square is more than a mere ornament or a simple bearer of functionality. On the two-dimensional plane the kinetically ever expanding squares demonstrate generativity (if observed from the top right to the bottom left) or, in a way more natural to the eye, reduction to originary unity (if observed from the bottom left to the top right). The disassociation of frame and content that we have observed elsewhere is realized in an especially radical way off to the left. The frame's contents seem to have taken off for parts unknown, leaving the functional structure behind as a useless ornament

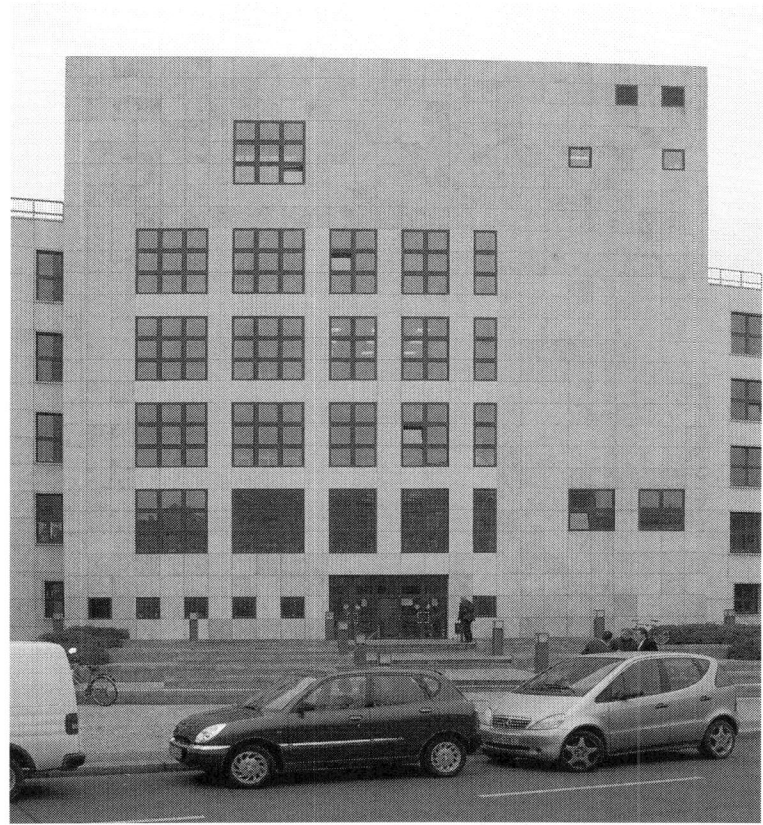

Figure 26. Courthouse

reminding us of a just transpired transcendent event. Ungers, whose manifesto "Towards a New Architecture" (1960) was a harbinger of postmodernism, has more recently expressed himself in ways suggestive of performatism and originary aesthetics. In remarks about his Landesbibliothek in Karlsruhe he notes that the building be designed it supposed to "look as if it had always been there from the very beginning."[23] In emphasizing the "uniqueness" [*Einmaligkeit*] of the building, Ungers rejects the notion of following an "eclectic principle." Rather, he "decomposes" aspects of other structures to form timeless architectonic invariants striving for perfection. His technique consists of "a play of formal elements which remain the same independently of historical development and which are employed in varied form and in the most varied epochs in different works of architecture."[24] This "iconographic principle," as Ungers calls it, resembles the sacral practice of icon painting: "Just as the icon is the original image [*Urbild*] and in the course of time is perfected ever more, so too does the process of assimilation consist not just in banal imitation, but also in ever new interpretations of what are essentially the same architectonic elements."[25] His plan for the Library is thus "not just the extension of an already existing architectonic concept, but also its continuation in the sense of a search for perfection."[26]

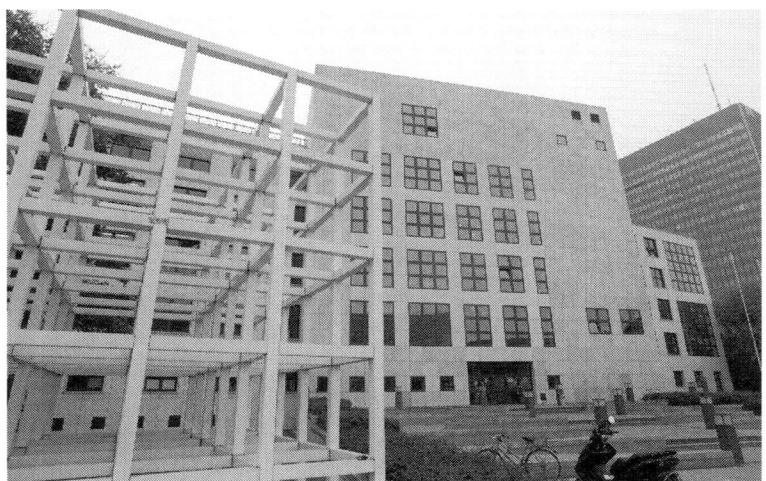

Figure 27. Courthouse

The Jewish Museum, Berlin Mitte (kinesis, theist neglect, incomplete triangulation)

Daniel Libeskind's Jewish Museum (figure 28.) is a deconstructivist, late-postmodern structure that however shares numerous devices with performatism (just as deconstruction itself shares certain theoretical positions with Gans's generative anthropology and performatism). One of the most striking differences between deconstructive and performatist architecture is the former's metaphysical pessimism. Although manifestly theist – it stylizes an act of originary creation/destruction rather than citing previous styles – the Jewish Museum suggests the wilful neglect of a theist God: the cuts in the building look like an evil Other has slashed the building with a giant razor (fig. 29). Generally speaking, triangulation is either lacking (forms are simply oblique) or is incomplete, as in the cuts on the facade. The slanting, squat steles topped by greenery are more suggestive of gravestones than of structural devices; together with the rest of the building they suggest a world gone awry but slowly trying to set itself right again.

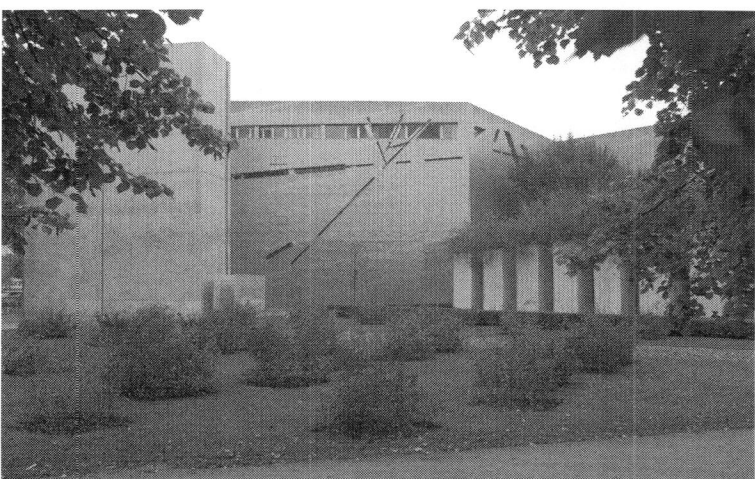

Figure 28. Jewish Museum

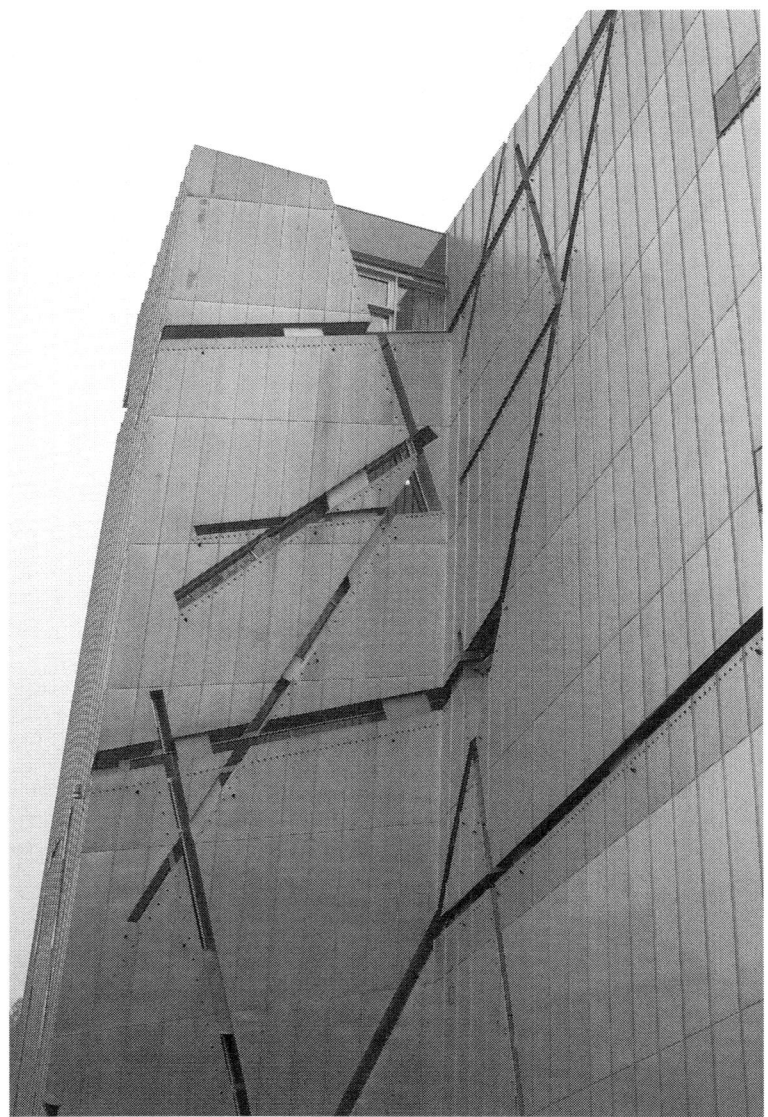

Figure 29. Jewish Museum

Chapter 5

Performatism in Theory: The New Monism

When I first began charting the course of post-postmodernism in the late 1990s, I assumed I would be setting out on already well-trodden paths. Academic criticism, after all, is an extremely competitive, specialized field, and it seemed unlikely that legions of highly trained scholars would have failed to notice the widening gap between the classic descriptions of postmodernism and actual cultural practice. Judging by name, at least, a basic shift in thinking was already taking hold in academia. At the University of Konstanz, where I was teaching at the time, a large research project in the humanities had been titled "Literature and Anthropology" – signaling a rather unpostmodern shift of interest to the human. Colleagues everywhere were grumbling openly about the treadmill-like state of poststructuralist theorizing. And, books with promising titles like *Life After Postmodernism*[1] suggested that someone out there was seriously considering that there might be an "after" after all. Given all these signs of disaffection, I was sure that I would be stepping into a vibrant, already well-established discussion.

I was wrong.

As it turned out, the mechanisms that made postmodernism into one of the most theory-saturated literary epochs ever also prevented its norms from being exposed to any sort of historical self-critique. One of the main culprits, I quickly discovered, was the split, belated concept of sign running through all of postmodern thought. Although colleagues in all disciplines were perfectly ready and willing to discuss terms like "the human," "monism," or even "performatism," the result was invariably the same. The provocative otherness of the concept in question was quickly assimilated back to whatever poststructuralist paradigm my interlocutor happened to favor. While expressing vague acquiescence with the notion that postmodernism wasn't quite what it used to be, no one was willing to abandon the seemingly inexhaustible possibilities of signifying-after-the-fact in favor of a concept of sign that proposed to plunk maudlin-sounding topics like belief, love, presence, and beauty in the center of critical discourse.

In literary criticism and cultural studies the situation turned out to be rather the same. A quick look at *Life After Postmodernism* confirmed that it looked pretty much like life *during* postmodernism – full of theoretically refined, but resolutely posthistorical positions. And, a survey of the major critical journals – even the ones nominally devoted to literary history – revealed a complete lack of interest in formally describing or naming the post-postmodern epoch.

As I've already recounted in my introductory remarks to this book, my search for a historically oriented monist theory quickly narrowed down to Eric Gans's concept of generative anthropology and its notion of the ostensive (and, later, post-millennialism). Gans's monism, however, does not stand alone. Although generative anthropology remains the most user-friendly and productive theory of its kind, there are a number of other monist concepts that have succeeded – with varying degrees of success – in freeing themselves from the endless regress and epistemological fence-straddling common to post-structuralist discourse. The following survey is intended to give a brief overview of some current monist theories and consider their usefulness for describing the shift to a performatist culture.

My short foray into the new monism starts in a kind of semiosphere reserved for two theories that are monist in design but lack certain crucial features that would enable them to leave the gravitational field of posthistorical discourse. As a result, they continue to orbit endlessly around the very kind of postmodern paradoxes that their authors intrepidly set out to overcome.

Pragmatic Performatism: "Against Theory"

In America, the most widely discussed monist concept up to now has been Steven Knapp's and Walter Benn Michaels' campaign "against theory," which was launched in the early 1980s.[2] Viewed in performatist terms, Knapp and Michaels place author, sign, and recipient within the bounds of a single frame. Signs only mean things because human subjects intend them so for other people; interpretations by those other people, for their part, can only seek to reconstruct those intentions through the signs provided by the work. All three elements meet in a unified performance that cannot be reduced to any one of its parts. Attempts to isolate and favor any one part of this unity – be it the mark or trace after the fact (poststructuralism) or the author before the fact (hermeneutics) lead to logical absurdities in the way interpretation is defined and practiced. For example, by radically separating human intention from the sign, poststructuralists like Paul de Man wind up positing the existence of signifiers that "mean nothing" – a definition suggesting, in effect, that they are mere sounds and no longer even signifiers at all.[3]

With their concept Knapp and Michaels establish an airtight primary frame that would choke off all "theory" – all attempts to intervene one-sidedly in the basic semiotic relation linking author, sign, and recipient. As such, interpretation acquires a distinctly performative, rather than an epistemological, cast. Different people interpret what they believe is someone else's intent, and the best or most convincing interpretations of the signs conveying that intent compete for acceptance. Individual subjects constitute themselves by expressing intentions in which they necessarily believe; their beliefs make their own selfness accessible to others, who in turn make their own selfness available through the act of interpretation. Belief, rather than knowledge, becomes the motor of interpretation, and the subject, rather than the signifier, its agent; the benchmark of historical criticism becomes pragmatic and performative.

Unfortunately, Knapp and Michaels never moved beyond this first argumentative step. The fatal flaw of their monist scheme – at least from the performatist perspective – is that it lacks an outer frame relating the act of interpretation to human culture on some higher level. If Knapp and Michaels' neo-Peircian, pragmatic concept really were operative, culture would consist of endless clusters of unified interpretative performances jostling one another until one or the other comes up on top. The poststructuralist notion of culture as endlessly proliferating textuality would be replaced by a pragmatic, anti-theoretical notion

of endlessly proliferating primary frames or interpretative performances. The history of culture would become a chain of interpretative
acts elbowing one another for primacy, with "theory" – or what's left
of it – tagging harmlessly along behind. Knapp and Michaels' scheme
turns out to be atomistic and, in end effect, very nearly tautological.
Before interpretation, as it turns out, there is just interpretation, and
after interpretation – still more interpretation. For this reason, apparently, Michaels was himself never able to develop a positive concept of
post-postmodernism.[4] His work lacks an outer frame – a *theory* – that
would link the atomistic, belief-centered monism of anti-theory with
some overarching construct around it. Inasmuch as it stays true to its
name, anti-theory rules out any synthetic concept of literary history or
culture; its own claim to novelty remains restricted to the analytical,
nuts-and-bolts realm of argumentative logic.

This is most evident in the scene devised by Knapp and Michaels
to dismantle "theory." In their by now well-known scenario, waves
mysteriously inscribe a pantheistic poem by Wordsworth on a sandy
beach – suggesting an originary confrontation with the possibility of
a higher, transcendent intent.[5] The authors, however, in keeping with
their strict anti-theoretical agenda, don't extend their analysis to the
structural significance of belief for the development of culture as a
whole. This rules out any Durkheimian insight into religion or cult
as the basis of secular culture, and it rules out any semiotic insight
into history as the alternation of two basic, competing sets towards
the sign – of which Knapp and Michaels' stringent anti-theory is just
one variant. Although in itself a groundbreaking step forward into the
new monism, anti-theory was unable to formulate its own innovative
contribution in epochal terms.

Paranoid Performatism: Boris Groys's Under Suspicion

As far as I am aware, the only critic to realize the crucial importance
of giving the new a formal theoretical justification has been the provocative Russo-German art historian and essayist Boris Groys.[6] Like
Knapp and Michaels, Groys began his critique of poststructuralism
using a single-framed monism and taking performativity as the main

benchmark of innovation. Groys's basic strategy, first set forth in his book *Über das Neue*[7] [On the new], was to jump-start history again by redefining epochal innovation – "the new" – as performance (Groys calls it an "event"[8]). Groys posits the existence of two realms: the every-day or profane world and the privileged realm of the archive. Innovation – and with it the historical development of art – is determined by what gets into the archive and what is expelled from it over the course of time. Groys argues that there is no "secret" guaranteeing the inclusion of a profane object in the realm of artistic value. Neither market manipula-tion, nor the Freudian unconscious, nor authenticity, nor otherness, nor any other rule formulated by discourse itself is capable of regulating entry into the archive. The reason for this is that all discursive rules themselves are subject to a performative mechanism arising out of the tension between the archive and the profane, undifferentiated world of otherness around it. According to Groys, valuable things in the archive gain their value by presenting the profane other in a new, exciting way. Unfortunately, the luster of this presentation begins to dim at the very moment that it gains general acceptance in the realm of the archive. In other words, as soon as a theory of the profane is canonized within the archive it loses precisely that mysterious bond with the profane, other world that made it attractive to the archive in the first place.[9] The search for a new interpretation of the profane other can then begin anew.

Using this performative theory of cultural innovation, Groys has no trouble disposing of the main conceit of posthistorical discourse. Deconstruction's zigzagging, trace-guided strategy of coupling new with old and old with new does not end history, since a quick glance at its intellectual predecessors confirms that deconstruction's specific way of showing that there is nothing new is itself something new.[10] Although Groys's performative, monist redefinition of history has an undeniable logical charm to it, it is, like "anti-theory," dangerously close to turning into an airtight, arid argument. If we take Groys at his word, the only irreducible, constant element in history is a perfor-mative mechanism that devalues its canons as soon as it grows bored with them and replaces them with new ones. For someone familiar with the tradition of Russian literary theory, the whole thing sounds suspiciously like a warmed-over version of the Russian Formalist

notion of automatization and deautomatization, which reduced literary history to a simple dichotomy of musty old canons and dazzling
new shock effects. As Groys himself realized, this two-dimensional,
mechanistic definition of historical innovation wasn't enough to grasp
the historical process in all its profundity.

With this in mind, Groys returned to the problem of the new in a
second book entitled *Unter Verdacht* [Under suspicion].[11] In trying to
describe the "cultural economy"[12] determining historical innovation,
Groys introduces two new structural features to his model. The first
addition is a unified sign encompassing a "submedial space" in addition to signifier and signified; the second is what he calls a "submedial" subject manipulating that space. In more conventional terms, you
could say that Groys introduces an ontological, an anthropological,
and a transcendent dimension to the sign. For Groys, signs are no
longer composed of signifiers and signifieds that freely combine and
disperse in the endless ebb and flow of signification. Rather, signs have
the purpose of conveying to us something fundamental and mysterious about being without our ever really being able to pinpoint what
that relation is. Groys calls this profound, hidden realm below the
signifier-signified relation the "submedial space." This space, like the
profane realm outside the archive, appears to the archive as an ineffable other. Unlike the profane realm, though, the submedial space is
already *inside* the archive; it forms the substrate of the valued objects
of art within that privileged space. The archive, in other words, now
has a horizontal dimension (pertaining to the transactions between
valued and profane things) and a vertical one (pertaining to a "deep,"
ontological or submedial realm and a "superficial" or merely semiotic
one). The point of including things in the archive is to plunge into
an abyss of speculation on being; the archive itself, however, must
always do this by transcending its own closure – by reaching outside
of itself – to renew the search for what is at the root of existence. The
archive, as the highest repository of cultural value, is now, in any case,
implicated in "deep," inner questions along with regulating economic
transactions between the valuable and the profane.

In contrast to his first model, which left the question of agency open, Groys now introduces a half-human, half-transcendent

subject into his scheme. According to Groys, in dealing with the archive we always suspect that an unknown someone – a "submedial subject" – is manipulating the submedial space to his or her own ineffable ends. The workings of the media in the archive are hence always "under suspicion" of being misused or abused for someone else's purposes. Although this suspicion can never be entirely eliminated, it is possible to diminish it somewhat with what Groys calls the "forthrightness effect" [*Effekt der Aufrichtigkeit*].[13] This means that even though it is impossible to be truly candid or forthright about the (unknowable) workings of the archive, the effect of this can be temporarily achieved when someone seems to reveal to us the "real" workings of ontological or submedial space. According to Groys, this revelation occurs mainly by way of paradox, alterity, and surprise. Signs that seem most forthright tend to be "first of all, new, unusual, and unexpected and, second of all, poor, base, and vulgar."[14] To sum all this up, the basic workings of culture are rooted in a never-ending process of revelation that seems to be manipulated by a malevolent subject with distinctly theist capabilities – a devious God of small things, as it were, who is really a projection of our own jealous insecurities and desires.

Whatever one happens to think of Groys's individual conclusions, his monist model of media culture is in structural terms directly comparable to both generative anthropology and performatism. Like Gans's originary or ostensive sign, Groys's concept of submedial space breeds resentment that must be constantly assuaged through new acts of signification, valuation, and regress to an unreachable origin. And, like performatist constructs, Groys's model of media culture consists of a double frame (archive and sign) presided over by a distinctly theist subject. In spite of these similarities, however, Groys's attempt to formulate a "media ontology" never quite crosses the threshold of postmodernism. The reason for this is Groys's tenacious, typically poststructuralist insistence on favoring knowledge over belief. Since Groys "knows" that ontology is a bottomless pit, and since he "knows" that there is no submedial subject or God of culture, he has no particular interest in getting involved in the day-to-day workings of the archive itself. Having demonstrated with epistemological means that poststructuralist discourse is really an ontology, he is content to walk off with the grand prize for epistemological criticism but not to take an ontological stand himself – thus, in effect, repeating the basic argumentative gesture of poststructuralism. Accordingly, the last section of *Unter Verdacht* rounds up and interrogates the usual suspects – Derrida, Bataille, Mauss, Lyotard etc. – but says nothing about the across-the-board switch to monism now going on in contemporary culture. One leaves Groys with the suspicion that although he himself has intuitively grasped the new, monist turn to a spatially framed apprehension of being, he still feels more comfortable playing the old, postmodern game of trying to get in the last epistemological word at all costs. This is why Groys prefers to talk about the new in the abstract, as a transcendental, empty category, but not as an immanent state or way of being – unless, of course, you happen to think that "being" means getting constantly hoodwinked by a unseen, malicious Other. Groys, like Michaels, leads us to the promised land of post-postmodernism but is unable to enter it himself.

As these two examples show, the minimal conditions for overcoming postmodernism would seem to be, apart from holding to a monist concept of sign, a synthetic, rather than merely analytical, methodology and the unequivocal grounding of discourse in ontology instead of epistemology. The two following theories that I would like to discuss in greater detail – Peter Sloterdijk's spherology and Jean-Luc Marion's philosophy of givenness – not only meet these criteria in full but also add, respectively, a cultural-historical dimension and a phenomenological one to the existing body of monist, no longer postmodern theory.

Effervescent Performatism: Peter Sloterdijk's Spherology

One German philosopher who has had no qualms about switching over to a monist, spatially defined ontology of culture is Peter Sloterdijk. With his massive 2,400-page trilogy *Sphären* [Spheres][15] Sloterdijk has tried nothing less than to show that all human culture is based on discrete psycho-social spaces that he divides into "bubbles," "globes," and "foams." Although not wholly original in its basic premise about the importance of closed-off, spiritualized space – Mircea Eliade has said something similar before[16] – Sloterdijk far exceeds Eliade in the boldness of his philosophical vision and the scope of his cultural commentaries, which range from the beginnings of civilization to the present day and include discussions of such wildly diverse topics as prenatal mother-child bonding, mesmerism, Heidegger's concept of Being-in-the-world, and the history of air-conditioning. Sloterdijk's own discourse in fact exemplifies the ebullient "foaming" [*Verschäumlichung* {sic}] that is the focus of his third volume. Rather than building up a carefully articulated philosophical edifice step by step, he surges from one encapsulated sphere or topic to another, demonstrating as he does their basic phenomenological unity in diversity.

As with the other theories discussed here, the outlook of spherology is explicitly postmetaphysical. Sloterdijk is interested neither in returning to the old global unities of classical metaphysics (at one point, he calls his own method a "critique of round reason"[17]) nor in restoring the whole, well-rounded subjects that were once thought to reside within them. Instead, he suggests that all human culture arises in what he calls spheres, which he defines as spatial encapsulations, spheres, or "bubbles" [*Blasen*] enabling a dyadic, intimate bond to develop between at least two people:

> The sphere is the interiorized, developed, divisible round space that people live in insofar as they succeed in becoming human. Because living already always means creating spheres both small and large, humans are the beings who erect round worlds and gaze off into horizons. Living in spheres means creating the dimension in which people can be contained. Spheres are spatial creations that act like immune systems for ecstatic beings upon which the outside exerts its influence.[18]

Translated into the by now familiar terms of performatism, this means that the basic unit of human existence is an artificially created frame privileging inside over out but not excluding the external world entirely; the inner world must constantly "maintain, reconstitute, and improve itself in the face of the provocation that is the outside."[19] Unlike generative anthropology, Sloterdijk's argumentation lacks any causal explanation of the originary spherological scene; he simply posits it as a universally empirical given, using as he does the biologically suggestive metaphor of the immune system and stressing its creative, artificial nature with evocative terms like "innenhaft" [having the character of interiority], "Schöpfung" [creation], "erschlossen" [opened up for use, made accessible], or "bilden" [to form]. God, rather than being an outside entity, is the emotive froth atop this creative, bubble-blowing performance: "God is an ecstasy arising out of the idea of competency, which encloses the world and the subjectivities embedded within it."[20] For Sloterdijk, our own secular, technological striving is the one, rationalized side of a much older unity of outwardly directed ecstasy and creative competence. Sloterdijk does not, of course, wish to concoct a crypto-theological justification for modern science. However, he does note that the most spectacular areas of research in the "living sciences" – the brain, the genome, and the immune system – can hardly be reconciled with intensified self-reflection on what is human. With the "becoming explicit" of these and similar implicit relations, might we not, as Sloterdijk asks, be confronted with "something completely idiosyncratic, alien, different, something that was never implied or expected, and that can never be assimilated to our thinking?"[21] In such a case we would be dealing with a technological, object-based newness that could not be routinely assimilated into either what traditional phenomenology calls self-reflection or what poststructuralism calls discourse. For Sloterdijk, the transcendent returns again as a promise and problem through the medium of scientific discovery.

As this line of thinking makes clear, Sloterdijk is less interested in *aesthetic* framing – in bracketing knowledge to bring forth beautiful belief – than in what might be called *technical* framing – a way of making things explicit by means of a creative, spatially delineated performance that continually redefines the boundaries of the phenomenal world while invigorating our perception of it. Here, Sloterdijk is evidently following in the antique philosophical tradition that stresses *technē* and subordinates the experiencing of beauty to a way of knowing (a predecessor of sorts is Heidegger in his essay "The Origin of the Work of Art"[22]). And, Sloterdijk's notion that we acquire knowledge by making the implicit explicit is, as he himself emphasizes, lifted directly from Leibniz's monadology – the crucial difference being that the spatially limited bubble replaces the Leibnizian fold, which meanders endlessly through the arabesque, ineffable Whole of a constantly shifting reality.[23]

The third salient feature of Sloterdijk's spherology is its recourse to a specifically theist, dyadic argument that frames, unifies, and renders immanent the old metaphysical call for a unified, self-sufficient subject and a preexistent origin. According to Sloterdijk, the mythological origin of the sphere is neither individual nor divine, but lies in the paradoxical, coextensive reciprocity between a theist source and the subject he creates in his own image: "man [der Mensch] is an artificial product [Kunstgebilde] that could only be created all at twice [auf zweimal] {sic}."[24] In his following excursions into cultural history Sloterdijk justifies this "pneumatic reciprocity,"[25] or "bipolar intimacy"[26] between the inspiring source [*der Hauchende*] and its inspired recipient [*der Angehauchte*] on a wide variety of levels resisting reduction to any one particular discipline, category, or time. *Sphären I*, for example, contains discussions of the myth of Adam's creation; a history of "interfacial relations"; an attempt to position prenatal mother-child relationships before Lacan's mirror stage; a synoptic treatment of angels, twins, and tutelary gods; an intellectual history of the "fascination with proximity," and a good deal more. *Sphären II*, for its part, deals with the grand but ultimately fruitless metaphysical attempts to encase the world in all-encompassing "globes." *Sphären III*, which treats the ills afflicting and potentials residing in (post-)modernity, discusses the breakdown, aesthetization, and technologization of spheres as well as their re-formation and proliferation in the guise of plural ontologies that Sloterdijk calls "foams" and "anthropogenic islands" (he suggests nine different island categories bearing names like the "thanatope," the "ergotope," the "erototope" etc.).

For obvious reasons, it is not possible here to go into any of these topics in any detail without oneself falling victim to what Sloterdijk calls his "cornucopia complex."[27] It is, however, striking how Sloterdijk, using mainly mythological examples, arrives at a concept of dyadic reciprocity structurally similar to Gans's and in a sense confirming

it on the level of originary mythology. Although lacking both a semiotic dimension and a causal explanation of its origin, Sloterdijk's
spherology insists no less than generative anthropology on a framed
scene in which a dyadic, coextensive relationship between two founding figures results in a necessary intuition of personified divinity and
initiates the beginning of culture.

Although his own spherology is manifestly monist and most certainly no longer postmodern, Sloterdijk says little or nothing about
the possibility of an epochal turn – something odd in a book that
otherwise reflects intensively and exhaustively on all aspects of (post-)
modern existence. The main reason for this seems to lie in Sloterdijk's
one-sided fixation on spatiality and, in particular, in his effervescent
postmetaphysical concept of foams. The foams – the multitude of spatially organized, ontologically founded mini-realms that have spread
out to replace the all-encompassing "globes" of classical metaphysics –
bear a deliberate structural resemblance to Deleuze and Guattari's uncontrollably proliferating rhizome.[28] Sloterdijk, in fact, calls the foams
"rhizomes with an inside space" [*Binnenraum-Rhizome*].[29] The rhizome, as the reader may recall, consists of an unbounded network of
intersecting, relationally determined, node-like positions that lack any
ontological center, origin, ground, or end. These nodal positions (like
Leibniz's monads and Deleuze and Guattari's schizophrenic subject in
their *Anti-Oedipus*) have nothing specifically anthropological about
them; they are beholden only to the shifting patterns of energetic relationality coursing through them and not to any "outside" source like
the human. Sloterdijk, for his part, imposes precisely this unified human ground or frame on the rhizome's anti-human dualism, breaking
it up as he does so into countless cells or bubbles existing together "in
lateral annex formations, in flat condominiums, or co-isolated associations."[30] Unlike Deleuze and Guattari, who are content to gyre and
gimble in the rhizome's endless, internally given relationality, Sloterdijk is not satisfied with taking an extended postmetaphysical bubble
bath in his own foams. Instead, he suggests the possibility of a higher
perspective, akin to that of a satellite photo, that would capture the
"unstable, momentary synthesis of a teeming agglomeration"[31] made
up by the foams. If this "momentary synthesis" would be given a

temporal dimension, too, it would be possible to place Sloterdijk a step ahead in time of the rhizomatic theory that he has surpassed with his own innovative monism.

Taken in the most general philosophical and mytho-theological terms, it would seem that Sloterdijk begins with a theist bubble-built-for-two and allows it to proliferate in "neomonadological,"[32] neo-Leibnizian fashion (with the possibility of taking a quick theist look at the whole thing from above, in the manner of a tutelary god or *observator*, a subject touched on by Sloterdijk himself in *Sphären I*[33]). The question nonetheless arises as to how the theist bubbles interact with one another, communicate, and multiply as psycho-social entities. Sloterdijk is for very good reasons unwilling to resort to an energetic, non-human explanation of how the bubbles expand and proliferate as foam – for this would lead him straight back into the deist, dualist fold of Deleuzian poststructuralism. At the same time, Sloterdijk also avoids the Kantian tradition in which a collective more or less unanimously perceives phenomena as social or aesthetic facts. Instead, he seeks an answer to the problem of communication by resorting to a presemiotic, quasi-biological notion of mimesis or imitation advanced by the 19th century French sociologist Gabriel de Tarde.

Tarde is particularly intriguing from the viewpoint of generative anthropology and performatism because of his contrary position to Durkheim in the development of French sociology.[34] Originally considered a serious alternative to Durkheim's more structured neo-Kantian approach, Tarde's radical monist, neo-Leibnizian attempt to ascribe all interpersonal relations, social structures, and cultural developments to the effects of imitation had faded into obscurity by the mid 20th century. Following Deleuze and Guattari, who revived Tarde's line of thinking in *A Thousand Plateaus*,[35] Sloterdijk uses Tarde's concept of mimesis to explain how his windowless spheres manage to communicate with one another in spite of themselves: "agreement among them [the spheres, R.E.] doesn't occur through direct exchange between the cells, but rather through the mimetic infiltration of similar patterns, excitations, infectious goods, and symbols into each one of them."[36] For similar reasons, Sloterdijk sees his "erototope" operating according to René Girard's pre-semiotic notion of erotic, triangular mimesis.[37] Eros is accordingly not "a dual-libidinous tension between an Ego and an Other, but a triangular provocation."[38] Projected onto a global stage, this sort of erotic and social jealousy comes to resemble the problem of resentment as outlined by Gans. Sloterdijk sums this up in the following way: "If the cultural theory were to pose a question to the twenty-first century, it would be this: whether modernity can bring its experiment with the globalization of jealousy under control."[39]

The distinction between spherology and Gans's generative anthropology resides not only in the lack of a semiotic perspective, but also in Sloterdijk's assumption of a postcapitalist, mimetic exchange mechanism that would, as it were, submerge both traditional contractual and naturalistic explanations of human coexistence in a gigantic bed of foams.[40] This is, obviously, not the proper place to stage a High-Noon-style showdown between Gans's neo-Kantian semiotics and Sloterdijk's neo-Leibnizian energetics. It is, however, interesting to observe how two major lines of poststructuralist thought are extended and corrected in the new monist thinking. Gans clamps a unifying frame around the Derridean concept of sign to make it monist; Sloterdijk does the same to Deleuze and Guattari's rhizome.

Sloterdijk's spherology, although unable or unwilling to address its own temporality, offers a rich grab bag of themes, topics, projects, and perspectives for the coming performatist epoch. The first, most notable project is a massive revision of cultural history from a monist perspective. This revision applies in particular to postmodernism, which Sloterdijk assimilates to his notion of spheres without so much as batting an eyelash – or engaging in the withering sort of analytical criticism practiced in anti-theory. Another innovative move vis-à-vis postmodernism is the revival of science as a revelatory *technē* rather than as mere fodder for translation into discourse. And, Sloterijk's off-the-wall, "round" sociology of foams or anthropogenic islands offers an alternative to the "square," Durkheimian tradition that is more attuned to the analysis of social convention. From the literary or cinematic point of view, the theme of spatially conditioned human proximity developed by Sloterdijk has a direct relevance for performatist plots, where it is played out continually in spheres, frames, cubes, rooms, and cages.

Summing up his own results in *Sphären III* in an oblique way, Sloterdijk allows one of the participants in an imaginary round-table discussion to speak of his work as "postpessimistic"[41] – thus explicitly confirming the metaphysical optimism that is characteristic of performatism and anathema to postmodernism. Also congenial to performatism is Sloterdijk's interest in paradoxality. In his imaginary discussion, he has another critic note how an oxymoronic, spherological discourse would allow "the conversion from a monotonously pessimistic science to a sad-happy one" that would correspond to a "contemporary form of the *docta ignorantia* ["doctrine of learned ignorance," R.E.]."[42] Precisely this paradoxical, artificially induced conflation of outer knowledge and inner ignorance plays a central role in performatist aesthetics – and in the phenomenology of the next monist author to be treated below.

Phenomenological Performatism: Jean-Luc Marion's Being Given

As I have pointed out in passing,[43] performatism is a kind of phenomenology turned inside out. Instead of bracketing belief in order to achieve knowledge, performatist works bracket knowledge using artificial, manipulative means in order to achieve belief – a strategy that explicitly exploits Derrida's critique of the Kantian frame. Instead of being neutral or secondary, the brackets are now a crucial part of the aesthetic experience itself: they exert a tangible, coercive effect on the observer. Inside the bracket or frame "old," distinctly metaphysical relations regarding love, beauty, unity etc. are once again made operative without however attaining universal validity (the fact that there is a palpable "outside" underlines their particularity and undercuts their universal truth-value). The main conceit of performatist works is that this immanent inner unity might be, or should be, transferred *en bloc* to the outside realm – a conceit that is, of course, not provable or necessarily doable in any real way. Seen this way, performatism appears as a kind of reversal or parody of the Derridean frame, which deconstructs the old phenomenological *epokhē* by demonstrating that

the brackets themselves – and not the enclosed content – are the crucial part of the whole phenomenological enterprise. Performatism, in
other words, bends the Derridean scheme inward by assigning the
brackets an aesthetic-compulsive, rather than an epistemological, va-
lence and by restricting what would otherwise be metaphysical premises to a purely immanent domain. Aesthetically mediated belief
– experienced in a phenomenological frame or scene – and not the
fluid, constantly receding positions of semiotically mediated, a posteriori knowing gains the upper hand.

   This bending inward of the Derridean deconstruction of phenomenology is admittedly an ad hoc strategy – I am more concerned
with defining performatism in term of specific aesthetic devices rather
than working out a philosophical program of my own. However, it
is all the more interesting to observe how a professional philosopher
and theologian goes about reversing the Derridean deconstruction of
phenomenology in a similar, albeit more exacting way.

   The philosopher in question is Jean-Luc Marion, who has been developing a phenomenological counter-strategy to deconstruction since
the late 1980s. In the following remarks, I'd like to focus on Marion's
major work *Being Given*,[44] which has striking structural similarities to
the projects of generative anthropology and performatism. Accordingly,
the angle of approach will be typological rather than philosophical
in the strict sense of the word. Rather than attempting a critique of
Marion's individual arguments, I would like to demonstrate his more
general affinity with Gans's and my own semiotically based concepts.
With its distinctly Kantian, aesthetic tilt, Marion's phenomenology
also presents a distinct counterpoint to Sloterdijk's emphasis on technologically mediated knowing and neomonadological foams.

   Marion's phenomenological point of departure is what he calls
givenness, which he opposes to the traditional phenomenological
preoccupation with objectness (Husserl) and Being (Heidegger).
Marion, in other words, seeks to shift the focus of phenomenology
from a positivistic apprehension of things or an existential interpretation of man's condition to the analysis of a purely immanent domain
(givenness) involving the relations between a giver, a givee, and a gift.
Translated into performatist terms, Marion establishes givenness as an

outer frame in whose immanent boundaries certain irreducible value transactions take place. This immanent domain in turn contains a starting point for a new synthetic, upsurge – an inner frame – that when taken to its outer limits would transcend the immanent field of givenness itself. In short, Marion formulates a performative phenomenology of givenness that has important repercussions for the study of art, culture, and religion.

Marion begins by defining givenness in terms borrowed directly from Kantian aesthetics. Using an "ordinary, indeed mediocre"[45] painting as the starting point of his discussion, Marion suggests that its givenness is dependent neither on the material status of its objectness (what Heidegger calls subsistence or *Vorhandenheit*) nor on the ability of the given to be used or manipulated in practical terms (the ready-to-hand, or *Zuhandenheit*). Drawing on the terminology employed by Groys, you could say that the painting's givenness can neither be traced back to the material substrate of its signs (paint, canvas, etc.) nor to the way it is manipulated in economic or pragmatic terms (e.g., placed in or removed from a museum). Unlike Groys, Heidegger, and Derrida, however, Marion refuses to subsume the beauty of the painting to a search for truth: "Beauty is accomplished and abolished in the truth."[46] Instead, Marion draws on the Kantian definition of beauty as something corresponding neither to a concrete end nor to a concept: "the painting [...] obeys a finality for which no concept provides the objective representation."[47] The catch here is the *deliberate mediocrity* of the painting – something alien to Kant's argumentation. Since the banal painting has no special attraction to us above and beyond its own visibility, its analysis is, according to Marion, applicable to everything else, for "then all ordinary phenomenality, whose paradigm it would be, could also be reduced to a given."[48] In Groysian terms, you could say that Marion privileges a cultural object inside the archive, but deliberately weakens its pretensions to lasting or "eternal" value – the painting in question is in fact close to being ejected from the archive entirely. Conversely, Marion's definition also raises the chances of mediocre objects *outside* the archive being included in it at some future time. The result is a distinctly Kantian definition of givenness in terms of what might be called weak beauty. By definition, this weak, phenomenal beauty transcends the bounds of any archive and can be found in all of cultural reality.

If the phenomenality of the painting is not subordinate to pragmatic ends, to concepts, to truth, or to the archive, then just how does it work? Unlike Groys, who at this point reverts to a non-committal, purely epistemological account of how cultural value is churned out in a process of endless regress, Marion takes a specific ontological stand. To the ontic visibility of the painting is now added an "upsurge" or "coming forward"[49] that can be said to "impose"[50] itself on the viewer. As Marion suggests, "it is no longer a matter of seeing what is, but of seeing its coming up into visibility [...]."[51] It is not really the viewer that does this, but the painting itself: "the initiative always falls to the painting itself, which decides, as a long-closed barrier yields, to let us reach what is all too visible for us to be able to represent it as a mere being."[52] The painting thus moves from invisibility to visibility by appearing in its imposing, binding givenness to a viewer who must "fall in alignment" with its "immanent axis."[53]

The term Marion uses to describe this movement – anamorphosis – is both auspicious and uncannily familiar.[54] For anamorphosis is an almost literal translation of the phrase *per formam* – "ana" means "movement across" and "morphosis" pertains to form. At its core, then, the new phenomenology of givenness is a kind of *performance* in the sense that I have been establishing it throughout this book. Seen in this way, anamorphosis corresponds in pictorial or visual terms to a primary frame binding author, art work, and viewer in a single, dynamic, binding unity. As we have however seen beforehand, simply establishing this performative unity is not enough (as the case of "against theory" demonstrates). We must also address the problem of how this inner frame relates to things outside and above it (as marked by an outer frame) and how this relation affects the subject that is caught in its phenomenological "lock." Before turning to these questions, however, it is first necessary to deal with the deconstructive critique that presents itself as an unavoidable given in any discussion of gifts, giving, and givenness.

The main obstacle on the way to defining an immanent domain of givenness is without a doubt Derrida's well-known deconstruction of Marcel Mauss's essay *The Gift* in *Given Time*.[55] Derrida's demolition

of Mauss's "insane"[56] essay is a crucial challenge not only to any phenomenology of giving, but also to the entire project of reviving the Durkheimian tradition, which suggests that originary, socially given sacrality
continues to influence and organize even advanced secular culture.

Derrida's by now classic exposition demonstrates with devastating
efficacy that Mauss's essay on the sacral economy of the gift is a kind
of metaphysical shell game in which the very conditions used to define
the gift at the same time work to exclude its appearance. Taking Mauss
exactly at his word, Derrida shows that the gift can only function as
a gift when a) it isn't part of the exchange system that it's supposed
to organize; b) the givee isn't aware of it; c) the giver isn't aware of it
either; and d) the gift doesn't itself ever achieve presence. Put in phenomenological terms, the gift can only appear when it has been bracketed
out of existence from the very start. The only real gift you get from
participating in this economy, it would seem, is that of insanity – since
anyone who believes in the monist unity underlying it would have to be
completely off his rocker.

Marion does not dispute Derrida's analysis, and, indeed, he runs
through it again in some detail in order to confirm its basic veracity.
Marion's aim is not to refute Derrida's deconstruction but to take it a
step further – to undertake an even more radical bracketing that allows
us to focus on the purely immanent side of the gift as opposed to the
metaphysical side reinscribed – and rendered ridiculous – by Derrida.
As Marion notes, Derrida is first and foremost interested in a general
critique of metaphysics rather than in working out a positive phenomenology of the gift: "in identifying the possibility of the gift with its
impossibility, this contradiction [i.e., the one uncovered by Derrida,
R.E.] states the essence of nothing at all, therefore not of any gift whatsoever."[57] If we are to talk about the gift it is, according to Marion,
necessary to speak about it in terms of its *possibility*, rather than impossibility. This, in turn, can only take place beneath the threshold of the
metaphysical-economic model used by both Mauss and Derrida:

The standard model of the gift in fact eliminates the gift – at
least the gift as complete loss, such that it would imply a break
of the circle and a suspension of the gift's return, of the gift in

return. If the truth of the gift resides in the payback, the truth lowers it to the status of a loan.[58]

Marion's response to this metaphysical-pragmatic model is to undertake what he calls a "triple *epokhē*" revealing precisely that immanent phenomenality supposedly written off forever in Derrida's general critique of metaphysics. This triple *epokhē* or bracketing of givee, giver, and gift involves a move that, as I have mentioned above, owes a great deal to Kantian aesthetics. For in order to recover the gift in its phenomenological immanence, Marion must sever it from all purposive and metaphysical ties. In this realm of redoubled bracketing, Marion is able to reveal numerous phenomenal manifestations of noncircular, uneconomical giving that were swept under the rug in the course of Derrida's deconstruction. Marion can show convincingly, for example, that it is possible to bracket the givee when the gift is anonymous, or when the givee is an enemy or an ingrate (someone incapable of, or unwilling to, indulge in reciprocity). As a case in point one can take the ingrate. Even as he asserts the metaphysical principle of self-identity ("I don't owe anything to anyone") his conduct "lays bare the pure immanence of the gift"[59] since the ingrate shows that the gift "is perfectly accomplished without the givee's consent."[60] With his ingratitude, in other words, the givee shows that the immanent, anti-metaphysical performance of the gift – its "losing itself without return," its break with "self-identity"[61] – is so real a threat in phenomenal terms that it becomes something well worth denying.

This surprising revelation of phenomenological immanence applies no less to Marion's way of bracketing of the giver and the gift, which I can only touch on here in passing. It will suffice to say that Marion's phenomenological readings appear strikingly refreshing and rich when read against the background of Derrida's merciless, predictably aporetic dismantling of Mauss. Thus Marion has no trouble showing that it is indeed possible to bracket the gift *as an object*, for this is precisely what takes place when power is bestowed on someone or when someone gives his or her word (power and confidence are not objects that can be exchanged). Marriage vows have this character, too. If you were merely to give yourself as a sexual object when getting married, it would lower the entire institution of marriage to something akin to prostitution; the phenomenological function of marriage vows is to deny this purely material or economic relation.[62] Similarly, the simple case of inheritance suffices to show how giving need not depend on any form of reciprocal economic (and metaphysical) exchange. If the giver doesn't physically exist any more, any exchange mechanism is rendered void to begin with – and the phenomenality of giving is once more confirmed as something that doesn't require the giver's metaphysical or pragmatic presence.

The most elegant move on Marion's part, possibly, is to show that *différance* itself can be made the object of giving. This evidently holds true in the case of indebtedness to an inaccessible giver. For in "recognizing its debt the givee's consciousness becomes self-consciousness, because the debt itself precedes all consciousness of it and defines its self."[63] The givee, in experiencing the non-repayable debt as anterior to his own consciousness, is constituted by this lack, just as the gift itself is constituted by its own lack of a giver, who is in turn determined by his own lack of a gift. Givenness, then, consists in a kind of double or even triple origin, with each member of the triad always already being preceded and anticipated by the others: "Differance therefore passes from the giver to the gift given, then from the gift given to the givee."[64] Instead of acting as an epistemological universal solvent that can eat through anything ontological that it touches, *différance* is now encased in a frame that turns it into the content of an irreducible, real performance that breaks its metaphysical circularity and passes it *onward*, into a new, open-ended teleology. (This may be see in analogy to the simpler case outlined by Groys, in which deconstruction's specific way of sabotaging the new can itself be partitioned off and identified as a distinctly new performance impervious to its own internal, merely epistemological critique of innovation in its irreducible filiation with the old.)

In his analysis, Marion explicitly denies any dependence on a sociological or anthropological model.[65] However, his phenomenological argumentation would seem to be confirmed by Erving Goffman's sociology of everyday behavior, which suggests that people are surrounded by previously given, invisible, but nonetheless socially evident frames staking out domains of trust, power, decorum, stigmatization etc.[66] The degree to which these domains "modulate" (Marion's term regarding givenness[67]) or become subject to "keying" (Goffman's term regarding frames[68]) would then be open to a mixed phenomenological and sociological analysis. And, to the extent that Goffman continues the line of approach begun by Durkheim, in which socially given sacral frames continue to determine secular behavior,[69] it would seem entirely possible to reconcile Marion's thought with a post-metaphysical anthropology of sacred social origins or givens. While it is not possible here to delve further into either the sociological or anthropological implications of Marion's phenomenology, it would be possible in principle to recapture many of its insights in the pragmatic realm that Marion excludes in the pursuit of a philosophically rigorous argumentation.[70]

Having confirmed that Marion's phenomenology is not simply a return to metaphysics as understood by Derrida, I would now like to address some of the issues involved in Marion's definition of givenness. Assuming that the visual performance or anamorphosis works as it does, it is legitimate to ask of it the same questions directed at antitheory and Groys's monist theory of suspicion. How does "givenness" differentiate and develop? Where are its boundaries? Who or what mediates it? And, finally, does it have any self-consciousness of its own epochal innovation?

As I have already suggested, one of Marion's major affinities with performatism consists in his modifying Kantianism in such a way as to cast givenness in terms of a weak, non-conceptual beauty that imposes itself on the viewer in a unified visual performance (the "becoming visible" of a given object for a subject, or anamorphosis). This mild but sweeping aestheticization of phenomenal reality is in turn accompanied by another crucial move owing a great deal to, but also correcting, Kant. This move, whose importance for founding the new monism cannot be overestimated, is the turn to Kantian intuition (*Anschauung*), which Marion places firmly before the concept:

> To be sure, intuition without concept is as blind as the concept without intuition is empty; but blindness counts more here

than vacuity: even blind, intuition still gives, while the concept, even if it alone can make the given seen, remains as such
perfectly empty, therefore quite incapable of seeing anything
whatsoever. Intuition without concept, though still blind, never-
theless gives material to an object, while the concept without
intuition, though not blind, sees nothing, since nothing has yet
been given to it to see.[71]

This radical privileging of intuition is, of course, at odds with Kant
and most of Western philosophical tradition (including deconstruction, which "feeds" on already existing binary concepts). From Marion's point of view, philosophy traditionally favors phenomena poor
in intuition (i.e., logical and mathematical phenomena that are often
unreal[72]); keying in on these phenomena, in turn, blocks out access to
a whole wealth of phenomena both "extreme" and "common-law" in
nature (regarding the latter, he names "the beings of nature, the living
in general, the historical event, the face of the Other in particular"[73]).
As Marion emphasizes, "none of the real phenomena with which we
traffic daily and obligatorily can be analyzed adequately, and what
is more, they are barely even granted the right to appear."[74] Apart
from these everyday givens, the focus of a phenomenology of givenness would be on phenomena that Marion calls rich in intuition or
"saturated"; they would be phenomena that "would give *more, indeed
immeasurably more*, than the intention would ever have aimed at or
foreseen."[75]

Once again, Marion's notion of saturation is heavily indebted to
Kant's aesthetics. For in Kant's notion of the aesthetic idea (as interpreted by Marion), "intuition is no longer exposed in the concept; it
saturates it and renders it overexposed – invisible, unreachable not by
lack, but indeed by an excess of light."[76] In the aesthetic idea, in other
words, the concept is occluded by the intuition of an object that now
unfolds, to use Kant's words directly, in its own "free play."[77] And
this "free play," as Marion suggests, is not just qualitatively beautiful in the narrow Kantian sense, but must also be opened to include
the quantitative dimension of the sublime. Given these conditions,
it is now possible to reconstruct the field of givenness in its entire

phenomenal range. It stretches, degree by degree, from the intuitively apprehended, weakly beautiful becoming visible or anamorphosis of a phenomenon to the outer bounds of a sublime, heavily saturated intuition arising when a phenomenon exceeds its own conceptualization in paradox. The inner frame (marked by anamorphosis) and the outer frame (marked by the sublime, dazzling occlusion of the concept in paradox) reveal themselves as part of one and the same immanent field. At the same time, they serve to delineate that field from mere unmediated materiality and from any metaphysical concept purporting to regulate that field from without.

While it isn't possible here to treat Marion's discussion of saturation and paradox in anything other than a cursory way, it is worth dwelling briefly on four "topics of the phenomenon" suggested by Marion near the end of his exposition – topics derived from the saturation of the Kantian concepts of quantity, quality, relation, and modality.

Marion calls the first such topic "the event." The function of the event is, stated most simply, to make history once more possible. The event "is not limited to an instant, a place, or an empirical individual," but "covers a physical space such that no gaze encompasses it with one sweep" and "encompasses a population such that none of those who belong to it can take upon themselves an absolute or even privileged point of view [...]."[78] The paradigm of this kind of event is the battle, "which makes itself of itself, starting from a point of view that it alone can unify, without any unique horizon."[79] The resulting "plurality" or "proliferation of horizons," "forbids constituting the historical event into *one* object and demands substituting an endless hermeneutic in time"; out of this endless hermeneutic eventually results a "historical community."[80] Although Marion suggests that the event has an "epoch-making" function (it "delimits a homogenous duration and imposes it as 'a block'"[81]), he does not go into detail as to how such a "homogenous duration" could impose itself upon the supposedly endless range of hermeneutical positions. For my purposes it will suffice to say that Marion succeeds in refocusing our attention on the phenomenological origins of history – his starting point is the saturated battle and not the polyunsaturated discourse about the battle. However, he remains vague on the crucial question of how epochal or framed time imposes itself on historical discourse after the event. Clearly, this is a line of argumentation demanding some sort of explication of the temporal "block" or epoch.

Marion links the second topic, that of the "idol," with the previously discussed model of painting and of anamorphosis. The difference is now that instead of a weak, mediocre "upsurge," he allows for the possibility of a highly saturated, aesthetically dazzling performance on the part of the work of art. This is the domain of aesthetics proper, or, to use Groys's institutional term, the archive. Because in the case of the idol intuition always "surpasses the concept [...] proposed to welcome it" the result is a continual renewal of aesthetic experience: "The intuitive given of the idol imposes on us the demand to change our gaze again and again, continually, be this only so as to confront its unbearable bedazzlement."[82] Unlike Kant – upon whose notion of beauty and sublimity this is based – Marion denies the common necessity of this bedazzlement, suggesting instead that the idol provokes an "ineluctable solipsism"[83] comparable to Heidegger's *Jemeinigkeit* or Mineness. For the time being, it will be sufficient simply to note Marion's insistence on aesthetic solipsism, which stands in direct opposition to Kant's aesthetic collectivism arising out of the necessarily same reaction of different observers to the beauty of the object.[84] (The reason for Marion's un-Kantian insistence on the solipsism of aesthetic experience is theological and reveals itself shortly thereafter.)

With the third topic, "the flesh," Marion introduces a specifically erotic and emotional component to his saturated phenomena. The flesh marks the invisible point where contact of what feels with the felt exceeds any relational category around it, as in ecstasy, agony, grief, feeling, orgasm etc. To this general list of "auto-affections" Marion also adds culturally or philosophically more specified borderline states such as "the evidence of love," Proust's "living remembrance," or Kierkegaard's "fear and trembling."[85] Needless to say, the flesh remains personal due to its overwhelming immediacy. The experience of the flesh also ends in solipsism, although of a more radical variety than was the case with the idol (the flesh "gives me to myself"[86]). Marion's discussion of the flesh, in any case, would initiate a monist phenomenology of intuitive affect – and not simply tack already always conceptualized signs onto the bare behind of presemiotic physical experience, as is now the practice in deconstruction and postfeminism.[87]

Finally, Marion speaks of "the icon," which represents the "ultimate point"[88] of anamorphosis and resides on the very outer rim of the immanent. From the performatist point of view, the icon is a stand-in for that theist, ineffable subject which may or may not exist outside the realm of immanent givenness (depending, of course, on what you believe or suspect). The icon, according to Marion, is an Other that imposes its own face and gaze onto the spectator in such a way that he or she gives itself over entirely to its silent force. The gaze and the face of the Other can only be "endured," and not reduced "to the rank of a constituted spectacle";[89] the icon in this way exceeds what turns out to be the mere aestheticity of the idol. Similarly, the icon breaks through the solipsism of both the idol and the flesh. Transfixed by the icon, the spectator renounces his "own transcendental function of constitution" and becomes what Marion calls a "witness," i.e., someone constituted first and foremost by an other, personified gaze allowing no reflexivity. Accordingly, Marion assigns to the icon the power of synthesizing the other three aspects of saturation previously discussed. Like the event it "demands a summation of horizons and narrations";[90] like the idol it "begs to be seen and reseen,"[91] albeit in a mode of endurance rather than enjoyable bedazzlement; and like the flesh it affects the I so intensely that it loses its transcendental bearings in a kind of selfless ecstasy. With the supremely potent, barely resistible figure of the icon, Marion reaches the limits of the immanent field first established in the inner frame of "weak" anamorphosis.

Even for someone unfamiliar with Marion's professional credentials, it is hardly surprising at this point that his discussion now takes an explicit theological turn. Having synthesized the saturated phenomena of the event, the idol, and the flesh in the mediating, Christlike figure of the icon, Marion leaves the sector of the immanent and begins to expound upon the possibility of a "saturation of saturation" in Christian revelation – something he doesn't even pretend to justify in purely immanent terms. How are we to deal with this (not entirely unexpected) leap into transcendence? Are we being "framed" so that we have no choice but to accept a purely theological interpretation of givenness? Or – what is no better – are we supposed to discount Marion's immanent phenomenology of givenness because it originates outside the frame, in open metaphysical space?

The answer, at least from my perspective, is a double "no." Seen from an epochal bird's-eye view, Marion's own argumentation mere-ly recreates the typical narrative structure of performatist works in general. Marion begins by establishing an immanent field composed of a double frame. The inner frame – anamorphosis – encloses im-mediately given objects of perception and draws them into the phe-nomenal field; the outer frame – the icon – marks the outer bound-ary separating that field from an unknown Outside. Within this field, surprising, innovative things happen – not least because it op-erates the exact same way that any other aesthetic field operates (by occluding conceptuality and practical finality). Having encouraged us to accept this immanent field of argumentation (itself saturated with many surprises), Marion then goes a step further and *tran-scends it himself*. In an authorial performance of his own, he dares us to accept a transcendent, or outside, explanation that we can only believe in or reject. What is relevant here is not the actual content of Marion's outside solution, which can't be proven one way or another. Rather, it is the fact that it reinforces and gives direction to our previous position, which has been to assume the *stance of a believer per se*. As critical individuals, we have every right to remain skeptical about Marion's doubly saturated Revelation. However, we have been compelled by the immanent force of his argument to assume, at least temporarily and intuitively, the *possibility* of its truth within what is in effect an aesthetic frame. Whether we like it or not, we have been made to take on the phenomenological stance of *believers*. Whe-ther of course we continue to maintain this stance on a conceptual, "outside" level is quite another issue – for most secular individuals this will not be an option at all. However, many secular individuals – including myself – have no difficulty at all maintaining this at-titude on the *intuitive, aesthetic level*, where there is no need (and where there are no means) to express belief in a dogmatically bind-ing, conceptualized way.

In essence, all performatist works do the same thing. They begin by creating a compelling immanent scene – an aesthetic "given" whose intrinsic or immanent logic imposes itself forcefully on the viewer or reader (anamorphosis). This "givenness" is by nature saturated with scenes, relations, images etc. that acquire an entirely new, paradoxical logic within the context of the frame – a logic that is experienced intuitively and objectively by the observer as something that must be believed (the observer usually has little or no choice in the matter, short of ignoring the work entirely). This half-intuitive, half-coercive experience of aesthetically mediated belief in conceptually implausible givens sometimes comes with strings attached from outside. For example, at the end of a movie we may be asked to accept what is ultimately a transcendent explanation, as in *American Beauty*. More often than not, though, this explanation is simply deferred; the plot resolution is offered as a new given that can be taken up again in the future (this is the case in "realistic" works like *Idiots* or *Simple Stories*[92]). The fact that we are made aware that there is an "outside" to the aesthetic frame or field of givenness doesn't render its immanent logic invalid. It does, however, encourage us to take on a synthetic attitude causing us to reach out past the given frame and solve the problem at hand in a new, perhaps more successful way. This synthetic "set" of performatism towards transcending any given frame leads to a basic metaphysical optimism, even if the concrete, immediate results happen to be very meager.

Another productive perspective opened by Marion's phenomenology is the juxtaposition of a closed, solipsistic subject and an open subject "set" to transcendence; this subject is so susceptible to saturated givenness that it practically waits for the icon to come along and mesmerize it. While Marion is clearly prejudiced toward this latter type of religious sensibility, he accurately captures the spatial poles between which the subject must move if it is to overcome its own limitations in a performance (a topic discussed previously in Chapter One). The closed or solipsistic feeling of self is needed to focus the self enough to achieve an aim or intent; this aim or intent must however by nature lead outside the frame of the subject formulating it. Obviously, secular aesthetics and religious phenomenology differ greatly in what paths such a transcending of closure can take. Here, Sloterdijk's ebullient account of intimate dyadic relationships is probably closer to the pulse of post-postmodern life than is Marion's mode of abject waiting-to-be-called.[93]

One way of testing Marion's own notion of phenomenal givenness in terms of practical aesthetic judgments is to try it out very briefly on a movie like *American Beauty*, which encourages belief both explicitly and implicitly in the way I've described above. As I'd like to show, Marion's own theory is not an "icon" staring the work down into a state of sheer, passive compliance. Rather, when applied, his theory itself succumbs to the anamorphosis exerted by the work upon it. *American Beauty* confirms, but at the same time ironically twists and turns the central intentions of Marion's phenomenology within the movie's own givenness or aesthetic frame.

One of the visually most highly saturated moments of the movie is the becoming visible of Angela at the high-school basketball game that Lester at first doesn't at all want to attend. Lester, entranced by his first sight of the what is evidently a female idol, brackets players, cheerleaders, and spectators to focus entirely on Angela, who gives herself as an erotic object by returning Lester's gaze in kind (the camera cuts from Lester's bracketed vision to Angela's equally bracketed perspective, which shows Lester sitting alone on the high school gymnasium's bleachers). Seduction, as Marion says, "plays itself out by constituting it first in and through the response, which alone can attest it by rendering it, for the first time, audible and visible."[94] This invisible unity of call and response is given to us, in turn, and shows itself, through the medium of film. Later, this merely erotic unity will be transformed into the synthetic, totalized response to givenness that Marion calls "responsibility." Lester will feel himself not just ethically responsible for Angela as the Other (he does this, too), but achieve an expansion of self ("I'm great"[95]) and a synthetic, passive vision of the world's beauty that is consummated in the gift of death bestowed on him by Colonel Fitts ("I can't feel anything but gratitude for every moment of my stupid little life..."[96]).

This synthesis, however, remains unmediated by an icon in Marion's sense. The only figure even vaguely reminiscent of the icon is, arguably, Ricky Fitts, whose own gaze, as mediated by the video camera, is anything but unreturnable and unendurable. In fact, the medium of video itself makes his gaze readily accessible both to us and to various characters in the movie (the Colonel and Jane). If anything, Ricky is an intermediary for the icon: he has the ability to gaze back at the Other through the medium of the dead Face, which he makes memorable by capturing it on film.[97] (Interestingly enough, when looking at Lester's face after the latter's death, Ricky participates in pictorial anamorphosis literally: he must slant his head in an unnatural way in order to look eye to eye with Lester.)

This moment of reciprocity with the supposedly unbearable gaze of the Other is, obviously, alien to Marion's theologically justified phenomenology. For what Ricky perceives or intuits in the face of the Other is not the window to pure, blinding transcendence, but a mixture of sublimity and beauty: it is the gift of God back to the viewer. *American Beauty*, in other words, "recycles" the spiritualized aesthetic givenness that in Marion's theology is simply the first, transitory step towards receiving a gift that is so totally saturated as to defy any representation whatsoever. *American Beauty* seeks to intensify saturation in the here and now (hence the paradoxical title); Marion would defer its completion to the hereafter.

A final note is in order on the similarities between the phenomenology of givenness and Eric Gans's concept of ostensivity that I've been using throughout this book. In Marion's phenomenology, as we have seen, the saturated phenomena work to subvert, occlude, and exceed all conceptuality, finality, and intentionality. As such, the saturated phenomena may be thought to send out what Marion characterizes as a "call" to a particularly receptive post-metaphysical subject that he names "the gifted." Rather than realizing metaphysical goals such as the preservation of discrete self-identity,[98] the gifted subject "is completely achieved as soon as he surrenders unconditionally to what gives itself – and first of all to the saturated phenomenon that calls him."[99] In its originary mode, the call and the "responsal"[100] of the gifted bear a striking resemblance to the ostensive ur-scene outlined by Eric Gans. Here Marion's version of the originary moment:

For every mortal, the first word was always already heard before he could utter it. To speak always and first amounts to passively hearing a word coming from the Other, a word first and always incomprehensible, which announces no meaning or signification, other than the very alterity of the initiative, by which the pure fact gives (itself) (to be thought) for the first time.[101]

Unlike Gans, Marion has no concept of mimetic conflict that generates the "pure fact" of the first word and the "very alterity" of its initiative. However, his phenomenological synopsis can be assimilated to Gans's semiotic notion of the originary, ostensive scene with surprising ease. In both cases, the originary subjects constitute themselves as humans through the givenness of the sign, which, although nominally passed from one speaker to an Other as a spontaneous "gift," can be constituted as such only after the Other accepts it intuitively, rather than semantically or conceptually. At the same time, this acceptance engenders a "saturated," tension-filled paradox by relinquishing the object that the sign designates as a gift to a givee who, technically speaking, cannot accept it in full without destroying the equilibrium of the originary scene.[102] And, as in Marion's scenario, *différance* is passed on down the line without vitiating the original unifying and violence-deferring power of the originary ostensive sign.[103]

Within the frame of this originary scenario, intuition (*Anschauung*, literally "the looking at" what is given) may be considered the flip side of the ostensive (the "showing of" the sign and its spontaneous acceptance by another protohuman in place of the coveted object). For both giver and givee of the word (protohuman one and protohuman two in Gans's scenario), the word shared by them is correctly experienced as a gift from without, for it creates them as much as they create it. Much the same can be said to apply to Marion's originary call: "the call [...] individualizes me, because it separates me from all property or possession of the proper by giving it to me and letting this proper anticipate its reception by me and as me."[104] For both Gans and Marion, the givenness of the first sign necessitates structural speculation on what is "beyond" the given. Neither, however, are dependent on this kind of speculation to establish their basic arguments. Marion, for example, divides his own exposition into a rigorously immanent, post-metaphysical argumentation and an openly theological one; Gans, for his part, has no systematic theology apart from a certain historically justified sympathy for monotheism.

Gans and Marion would also have no trouble agreeing that there is nothing authentic about their originary situations; both, in effect, accept and continue Derrida's critique of classical metaphysics in a monist mode. The gift of language, as Marion says, is "originally non-originary"[105] because it always comes from the Other. For Gans, the originary scene lacks any pure or ideal relationship of adequacy between sign and thing or sign and self; the triangular relationship between rival protohumans and the sign can't be reduced to any one part or any one combination of parts. If anything, the opacity of unseen, personal selfness – its striving for metaphysical closure – engenders resentment and endangers the intuitive, collective reconciliation made possible by the gift of the sign.

Obviously, there are also numerous differences between the two theories. Although both are grounded in paradox (which Gans considers a semiotic necessity[106] no less than Marion considers it a phenomenal one), their respective arguments quickly veer off in secular and theological directions. In Gans's minimal scene the paradoxical substitution of the sign for the thing creates both reconciliation and resentment; from the very start, the ostensive scene is rife with a mimetic, centrifugal tension whose continual resolution-through-deferral sets a history in motion that is "the story of our liberation from the sacred."[107] Although the name-of-God – Gans's term for the originary sign – cannot be forgotten, it can very well indeed be displaced from the center of society. Gans's thinking is more "realistic" than Marion's in the sense that his theory accepts and justifies the prevailing order brought forth by liberal democracy and market capitalism (both divert mimetic desire away from a sacred center that would authoritatively regulate all societal tensions – a secularizing, centrifugal tendency of which Gans approves). Marion, by contrast, would reinstall the sacred center by assigning the "icon" a synthesizing, superior role in what would otherwise be a free-wheeling phenomenal interplay of history, idolatry, and carnal experience.

Marion's phenomenology is a productive complement to Gans's generative anthropology and to performatism in general. In particular, it would seem possible to make practical use of a phenomenology of givenness by emphasizing its aesthetic, paradoxical elements over the theological, hierarchical ones – something which is implicit anyway in the unpredictable movement of anamorphosis upon which Marion's theory is based. *Being Given*, in any case, confirms the possibility – and necessity – of continuing the post-metaphysical project begun in postmodernism with new, specifically monist means.

Summary

In my discussion of Gans's generative anthropology, Sloterdijk's spherology, and Marion's phenomenology of givenness I've tried to dispel two widespread, mutually confirming assumptions. The first is that the only viable kind of theory derives from the notion of sign as something belated, uncontrollable, and split apart from its referent; the second, that the new monist, unified concepts of sign are simply repeating old, well-known metaphysical errors. In a purely formal sense, of course, all three monist theories do indeed start out with poststructuralist notions of sign (or, in the case of Sloterdijk, with the energetic-organic concept of the rhizome). The new monism however frames and unifies these concepts in a distinctly different way that, no matter how you twist and turn it, is no longer compatible with the basic semiotic credo of poststructuralism. The crux of this difference shows itself most directly in the new monism's *framed reduction to the originary*. The focus is no longer on the wildly proliferating, secondary relations that signs indisputably enter into after they've been around for a while, but on the basic – one could say *a priori* – conditions necessary for the sign to come about in the first place. This "givenness" of the sign (Marion), its "ostensivity" (Gans), or the "binary reciprocity" of its creators (Sloterdijk) suggest that the creation of the very first sign must have involved a spontaneous, object-related, inspired unity of two human intuitions rather than an ironic, after-the-fact suspicion that signs were being arbitrarily or deviously tacked onto some ontological *fata morgana*. While all three monist theories allow for the possibility of deceit, resentment, or abuse after the fact, they all agree that these aspects are secondary to the logic of the original founding scene. And, in normative terms, all three theories agree that it is now imperative to tap into this originary or primary scene again so that we may renew and revitalize our attitude towards art, ethics, religion, and reality in general. The result is a paradoxical, oxymoronic, or saturated *return to metaphysics using postmetaphysical means.* This means that the grand metaphysical postulates – presence, center, love, beauty, truth, God etc. – all return, *but only insofar as they can be apprehended as immanent relations.* To adhere to this proof of immanence in the most rigorous way possible is a common goal of all three theories.

The second move crucial to the new monism is the revitalized notion of *performance*, or the move from immanence to transcendence. The anamorphotic upsurge (Marion), the creation of new bubbles, globes, and foams (Sloterdijk), or the leap from a horizontal to a vertical plane in the originary scene (Gans) mark the transcendent striving of the human forces inside the frame, their attempt to extend their apprehension of givenness, their creative intimacy, or their reconciliatory scene to the entire world around them. The goal of performatism, stated most simply, is to analyze this transcendent striving in the realm of culture after the fact.

Chapter 6

Performatism in Art

Anyone following the international art scene for the last ten years or so will have no trouble identifying developments that are difficult to reconcile with the practice and theory of postmodern art. These include a renewed interest in beauty and the discipline of aesthetics, a new seriousness or lack of manifest irony, a renascence of painting (as opposed to performance art and installations) as well as the imposition of unified authorial intent on the represented world. As in other branches of culture, however, no critic and no artist up to now has been willing to connect the dots, as it were, to form the picture of a whole epoch that is opposed to postmodernism and that is gradually beginning to replace it. In the follow remarks I would like to show that art – no less than literature, philosophy, film, and architecture – has entered into a stage that can best be understood using the monist, no longer poststructuralist or postmodern concepts of performatism.

Here as elsewhere in this book it isn't possible to provide anything resembling an exhaustive, step-by-step description of how performatism took hold in the world of art. To keep the discussion to the point, I have limited myself to five well-known artists working in three different kinds of media: Vanessa Beecroft in performance art, Andreas Gursky and Thomas Demand in photography, and Neo Rauch and Tim Eitel in painting. All the artists are important figures in their fields; all belong to a generation that came to prominence in the mid-to-late 1990s. These artists, in spite of their seeming diversity, are not pursuing idiosyncratic, unrelated styles or concepts, and they are not merely new twists in the endlessly unfolding field of postmodernism. Rather, they are part of a broader pattern of innovation that is entirely in keeping with the move towards monism in the other arts as well as in theory.

Before I start describing performatism in art, a few additional explanations are in order. In the hypothetical originary scene as described by Eric Gans, there are three basic positions that may be taken in regard to the ostensive sign (which arises in intuitive mutual agreement between two or more heretofore speechless protohumans and as yet has no signified or meaning).[1] If the thing is perceived as blocking access to the transcendent, reconciliatory power of the sign, the result is the sacral, or religion. Alternately, if the sign is perceived resentfully, as blocking access to or obscuring the material thing, the result is the political, or a grab for power that nonetheless still has to "go through" the sign to get what it wants[2] (the various neo-Nietzschean schemes common to poststructuralism would reduce the sign to this function alone). Finally, when attention oscillates between the closed unity of sign and thing, this creates a sense of distance that allows us to experience the sign-thing relation as beautiful.

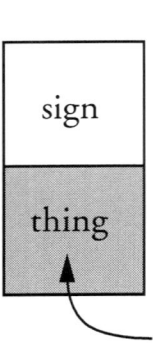

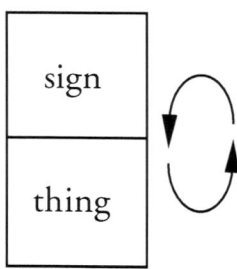

The Sacral

The thing is perceived as a hindrance to appropriating the transcendent sign.

The Political

The sign is perceived as a hindrance to appropriating the immanent thing.

The Aesthetic

Attention oscillates between sign and thing, enabling us to achieve a distance to them and regard them as beautiful.

The result is a concept of art corresponding in many regards to the definition advanced by Kant in his *Critique of Judgment*: the aesthetic is below the threshold of concept (*ohne Begriff*), without interest (*interesselos*), necessary (*notwendig*), and is pleasing (*erzeugt Wohlgefallen*).[3] Unlike the original Kantian model, however, this scenario is impervious to the kind of deconstruction practiced by Derrida on Kant in his *The Truth in Painting*, which exposes the contradictions arising when Kant tries to separate "pure," disinterested beauty from the impure, practical concepts that are needed to mediate it.[4] In the case of the ostensive sign, by contrast, all *three* basic modes – the sacral, the political, and the aesthetic – are rooted in the originary relation between sign and thing and are prior to concept; the disinterested aesthetic sign is not any "purer" than the interested approaches to the sign beside it and is not compromised by exposure to concept.[5] This trinitarian division of labor is crucial to explaining how performatist art maneuvers through the Scylla of high modernist Kantianism and the Charybdis of postmodern, neo-Nietzschean irony to establish a truly new monist mode of representing reality.

There is now a broad consensus among art critics that high modernist, non-representational art fits in well with the basic precepts of Kantianism (as filtered through the writings of formalist critics like Clement Greenberg).[6] Modernist art operates below the threshold of concept, abjures practicality, strives for a self-referential, formal purity and, if it is good, imposes itself necessarily on the viewer's intuition. Through this self-referential search for purity, modernist art may be said to strive for a semiotic unity of artist, work, and viewer. This kind of art, which reached its apogee in the Abstract Expressionism of the early 1950s, was swept away in the 1960s by what most critics now refer to as postmodern art, or, as the case may be, anti-art. This art is beholden to ironic conceptuality, constantly undercuts the boundaries between art and practice, uses disgusting objects to discredit the notion of essential, thing-bound beauty, and, by virtue of its unrelenting irony, forces the viewer out into a vast contextual expanse from which there is no returning to a pure, unmediated appreciation of the art work at hand. The philosophical roots of this kind of concept or performance art are Hegelian (its conceptual *Inhaltsästhetik* is directly opposed to Kantian *Formästhetik*) and Nietzschean, in the sense that the artists are constantly trying to smash through our conceptual illusions by representing them ironically in deliberately flawed or repellant works of anti-art. The semiotics of postmodern art are indisputably dualist: value and meaning accrue to things after the fact, by virtue of their position in a particular context.

This sweeping displacement of a monist sign and value system by a dualist one would seem to confirm the dichotomous notion of art history championed by Heinrich Wölfflin and his followers. Moreover, it suggests that the course of art history might one day be renewed by a direction diametrically opposed to the semiotic dualism, insistent irony, and ludic conceptualism of postmodernism. Unfortunately, although most art critics are becoming aware that the "triumph of anti-art" (McEvilley) has turned out to be a Pyrrhic victory, there has been no attempt to conceive of the new, pro-art trend in positive epochal terms. Thus, even when a shrewd critic like Boris Groys (whose ideas are treated in detail in Chapter Five) is able to conceptualize the new, he is unable or unwilling to link that conceptualization with contemporary artistic practice. Similarly, a mainstream critic like Arthur C. Danto, who moved from rejection of anti-art to grudging acceptance and appreciation, is now once more edging towards a Kantian position: in a recent series of lectures he concluded that beauty is an anthropological constant and "one of the values that defines what a fully human life means."[7] Unfortunately, Danto is still unable to part with a specifically Hegelian approach to art that he links with the analysis of "embodied meaning"[8] – which is to say that art or art appreciation remains in his view a conceptual rather than an intuitive endeavor (in the Kantian sense). My own approach takes exactly the opposite tack. To understand the present epochal shift in art we must, I believe, jettison entirely the notion of concept and return to a specifically intuitive notion of art that is nonetheless distinct from modernist formalism or traditional Kantianism.

The most direct way to explain how this new monism works in art is to recur once more to the notion of the double frame, which consists of two interlocking parts: the primary or inner frame (the ostensive sign) and the outer frame, or work frame. My basic assumption –

confirmed by observations in other media – suggests that contemporary artists have intuitively or unconsciously turned to latter-day variants of the ostensive sign to avoid the endless regress and increasingly strained ironies of classic postmodernism, and that they place an outside frame – an ironclad clamp or lock – around that sign to insure that its aesthetic efficacy remains unbroken.

As such, the new epoch may best be defined as the becoming-conscious of the ostensive, which up to now existed as a latent, but unrecognized force in all culture.[9] The teleological closure resulting therefrom – the notion that the originary semiotic scene has reached its historical fulfillment in the present epoch – is unavoidable, since it is not possible to think outside history and anticipate what the *next* epoch is going to be without having gone through this one first. In this sense history *always* appears to have ended, since it's not possible to view history from an ahistorical, transcendental perspective.

As noted above, the ostensive sign or inner frame can be experienced in three ways: as sacred, as political, and as aesthetic. The aesthetic is not a separate, pristine realm of its own, but arises when someone takes advantage of a modality offered by the sign in its most basic state. As soon as you step back to regard the sign as it oscillates between being a sign and being a thing, you automatically lose interest in instrumentalizing it for material or sacral ends. For this reason beauty in performatism has no intrinsic formal properties except that of closure; it arises in a reflexive, intuitive distance to the ostensive sign, which is nothing more than a closed mental frame that has been placed around a thing and a signifier. Performatist beauty is not an essence, but is constructed in the intuitively experienced distance to a closed inner frame encompassing an undecidable relation between a sign and a thing.

This postmetaphysical, relational notion of beauty-as-closure is diametrically opposed to the modernist notion that beauty can be achieved by eliminating representation, promoting flatness (Greenberg) or otherwise purging the art work of "extraneous" devices. At the same time, this concept of the aesthetic is no longer postmodern in the sense that it accords the aesthetic a discrete status of its own, rather than treating it merely in terms of a conceptually or ideologically guided, anti-artistic grab for power. In performatism, then, beauty exists necessarily, but it is a "weak," constructed beauty whose only formal property is that of closure.[10]

The second crucial element of the performatist concept of art is that of the outer frame.[11] The outer frame creates a discrete inner space within a context and – in direct opposition to postmodern practice – forcibly cuts that space off from the surrounding context and from what may variously be described as conceptuality or discourse. The result is a curious expansion of the intuitive minimal space marked by the ostensive sign to some selected part of reality at the expense of discourse and concept – a move that is deeply inexplicable to a postmodernist and deeply pleasing – in the sense of *Wohlgefallen* – to an performatist. In performatist art, the lock between outer and inner frame creates a field of artistically imposed intuition that causes viewers to align themselves with that intuition in a specific way – in a performance. This forcible manipulation of the viewer within the bounds of an intuitively constructed, closed, and categorically organized artificial field is the central device of performatist art.

Inasmuch as the outer frame is forcibly imposed from without, it may be experienced as the sublime, intimidating product of a higher, powerful will. This distinctly authorial or theist effect stands in direct opposition to the deism of postmodern art, in which the authorial position recedes in an endless *mise-en-abyme* of undecidable, catch-me-if-you-can irony. In performatist art, the result is what might be called a will to beauty rather than to power (what elsewhere in this book I have called "Kant with a club," or "Kant with a hammer").[12] Although there is no preexisting metaphysical guarantee that beauty or sublimity can be achieved, the entire work is nonetheless "set" towards achieving those effects, and coerces the viewer into receiving them.

Just how do these abstractions translate into concrete works of art? In the following analyses I'll try to show how double framing works in visual terms, and how certain characteristic themes and devices of performatism are realized in contemporary performance art, painting, and photography. My observations, incidentally, are often in agreement with those made by art critics writing without any theoretical agenda and with the self-assessments of the artists themselves. The crucial problem as I see it is not so much to recognize individual devices as to point out that artists working in completely different media are involved in a larger epochal shift involving not just other artists, but also writers, filmmakers, architects, and philosophers.

Performatist Performance Art: Vanessa Beecroft

Performatism was not conceived originally with art in mind, hence the odd-sounding collocation in the heading above.[13] However, since performance art has become almost entirely synonymous with the anti-art of postmodernism,[14] it seems necessary to point out that there is a performatist performance art, too.

The most striking representative of a no longer postmodern performance artist that I have been able to find is Vanessa Beecroft.[15] Superficially, Beecroft's performances bear all the trappings of "classic" performance art: they are offensive or merely titillating to many people in the general public, they don't involve any particular skill in the way they're set up, and they raise doubts as to whether what she is doing is really "art."[16] Also, Beecroft's mildly scandalous public behavior and well-publicized personal problems help round off the image of the performance artist as eccentric exhibitionist,[17] and her performatively enacted themes, which include femininity, voyeurism, and power relations, seem to place her squarely in the mainstream of postmodern discourse.

Beecroft's performances all follow one basic formula, with occasional exceptions and minor variations. A group comprised of one sex (usually female[18]) is presented to the public in a closed space to which public access can be tightly regulated (usually a gallery, a museum, or, more recently, upscale fashion stores). Depending on the plan of the performance, the women range from entirely nude to entirely clothed; Beecroft also employs body paint, wigs, makeup, and the like to alter and unify their appearance. In addition, the performers are given instructions that effectively keep them from performing. Often they are told to stand phalanx-style for about an hour, after which they are free to assume any position they want, as long as they do not move too quickly or interact with the audience. The performers are normally not allowed to speak, so that the performance remains entirely visual. The performances are in addition rather long – about 2-3 hours – and, by all accounts, physically and mentally strenuous for the performers. The artist herself does not participate in any of the performances and is often not even present when they are put on.

Given the well-known details of Beecroft's personal life – she suffers, or suffered, in any case, from an obsession with eating – it is tempting to explain her art as an attempt to work off gender-related pressure exerted by a male-dominated society. In fact, this victimary posture marked Beecroft's very first impromptu performance in Milan in 1993, where spontaneously engaged performers were meant to interact with a diary recording her obsessive eating habits.[19] Accordingly, there has been no shortage of attempts to interpret her art as a statement on gender and/or link her with postmodern artists like Cindy Sherman, who deliberately scramble conventional markers of masculinity and femininity in order to demonstrate the belatedness and constructedness of gender.

If Beecroft's art demonstrates anything, though, it is not the constructedness of *gender*, but the constructedness of *sex*. In fact, proceeding from the givens of her performances, it is impossible to draw any direct conclusions about gender whatsoever.[20] The only thing you can say about her nude women is that they're women, and not men or perhaps hermaphrodites, and the only thing you can say about her fully clothed men in U.S. military uniforms is that their gender orientation – whatever it may happen to be – is entirely opaque. What Beecroft's performances do is to drastically cut off the performers (and herself) from whatever social and sexual roles they might happen to have in real life. The space of the performance is a specifically aesthetic frame constructed around the originary sign of the human body and excluding, as much as possible, the social context that normally affects or "genders" our perception of that body. Of course, this does not mean that the outer frame excludes *everything*, and it does not suggest that the inner frame around the body is constructed in an entirely natural way.

Two examples should suffice to demonstrate this. Although the outer frame or work frame of Beecroft's performance eliminates most markers of social origin, there are, as a rule, always traces of outside socialization and style – the most notable example being the sailors' uniforms or various fashion accessories that the performers (who are often professional models) are made to wear. Where they do appear, the outside traces are, however, made uni-form,[21] so that it becomes essentially impossible to "perform" gender heterogeneously in the way that someone like Judith Butler conceives it. Secondly, the body, as the inner frame of Beecroft's performances, has nothing essentially natural about it. It is an originary construct particular to the performance and *exists as an origin only within the confines of the work frame itself.* Thus, even the presumably natural color of pubic hair is rendered opaque in that performance where Beecroft has the models appear with shaven pudenda and blonde wigs (VB 46). Wigs, paint, hats, and cloth strips (in the *Pontisister* project[22]) all demonstrate the constructedness of the origin or inner frame, even as the outer frame shuts out context and its endlessly shifting ironies that would cause that origin to dissipate in discourse.

Of course, it's always possible to disregard the discreteness and particularity of the double frame and suggest, as one German art critic did, that a performance of women clad only in pantyhose (VB 55) would have turned out completely differently had it been put on in the gritty Turkish quarter of Berlin rather than in the genteel ambience of the Tiergarten district, where Mies van der Rohe's New National Gallery is located.[23] This sort of criticism remains, however, entirely external to the performance itself, which is reduced to little more than a device for producing different effects in different contexts (something that, incidentally, applies indiscriminately to *all* works of art – and to everything else, for that matter).

It has also been argued that the real driving force behind Beecroft's art is her anorexic-bulemic condition and depressive tendencies, which are supposedly played out indirectly by the performers. This focus on pathology, which has been developed systematically by Christine Ross in her *Aesthetics of Disengagement*, is not especially compelling. While it is undoubtedly true that the obsessiveness of the artist is forcibly projected onto the performers, and while it is also true that the givens of the performance make them tired and uncomfortable, it is not especially clear why the net result is a discourse of

depression. The reason for this curious diagnosis lies in Ross's definition of depression as a "dimensional state"[24] rather than as a category. Although Ross concedes that Beecroft's performers "cannot be
designated depressed"[25] and are not "represented in a state of pathological depression,"[26] she nonetheless maintains that they "enact key
scientific symptoms of depressive disorders"[27] in spite of this. In Ross's
typically poststructuralist thinking, "being depressed" is a shifting
set of external symptoms rather than a categorical state that you are
"in" (baring oneself in public in a group is presumably the last thing
a clinically depressed person would want to do). However, being "in"
something – the closed work of art – is precisely the situation of Beecroft's performers.[28] Postmodern criticism of this type is still possible,
as these examples show, but it is unable to grasp these performatist
performances in positive terms or – what is even more telling – to get
inside of them at all.

When you do get inside the performance – and you have to do
so to appreciate it fully – you are exposed to a specifically authorial
or theist will. This opaque, genderless will confronts viewers with a
uniquely constructed originary situation for which there is no *concept* – no norms or previously established rules of conduct.[29] As Dave
Hickey notes, "in these tableaux [i.e., in the performances, R.E.] we
are denied both the privacy of contemplating a representation and the
intimacy of participating in a real encounter."[30] In effect, the frame
of the performance forces both male and female viewers to oscillate
between a direct, physical appreciation of the women and the spontaneous search for a socially acceptable attitude within the frame that
is not offensive or threatening to others. This intuitive impetus, in
conjunction with the particular givens of the performance, creates a
specifically aesthetic experience, rather than an erotic or merely social
one. In daily life, this sort of thing occurs only when we are confronted with what Erving Goffman calls breaking frame, which is to
say a massive breach of protocol in conventional, normed situations.[31]
In Beecroft's art, by contrast, the "break" is internalized and becomes
an aesthetic paradox: it acts as an autonomous norm forcing us intuitively and spontaneously to work out norms of our own that are
binding only in one particular context.[32] This context, in turn, forces

pleasure upon us but – not least because of its paradoxical construction – is unable to deliver that pleasure in full. What is at stake here is not the "failure" of this project (which in epistemological terms is a foregone conclusion) but the communal success of the intuitive acts of individuation resulting from it. The participants, in other words, spontaneously form an originary, aesthetically organized community underneath the threshold of concept, and the performers achieve a kind of minimal individuation in spite of – or perhaps precisely because of – their isolation from discourse.[33]

The results of Beecroft's performances are, as noted above, aesthetically ambivalent. Although there is a distinct, almost classical will to beauty in force (the focus on the nude body), the interplay and oscillation between personal pleasure and spontaneously constructed role-playing vis-à-vis others keeps a "pure," classically Kantian apprehension of beauty from arising (the kind of intuitive appreciation that Greenberg was looking for when assessing abstract painting). The aesthetic, in other words, is confirmed in Gans's sense as an originary anthropological construct and not as an ineffable anthropological essence. This constructedness is, incidentally, also apparent in the categorical set-up of many of Beecroft's performances: hair color (sometimes augmented by brightly colored wigs) and various ornaments are used to create simple, usually color-coded categories within the performances. The result is a kind of primitive Kantianism – one might call it Kant with a fright wig – that imposes half-natural, half-artificial aesthetic categories on viewers' intuition.[34] This intuitive, categorically organized experience is not a belated effect of discourse or a set of pathological symptoms being created under laboratory conditions. Rather it is the direct Other of discursive experience and its immediate, implacable rival.[35]

Interestingly enough, Beecroft incorporates both the ostensive and imperative mode in Gans's sense into her art.[36] This, I think, is the best way of explaining her interest not just in scantily clad women, but also in uniformed, rigidly posed sailors. As she herself notes of her performances with sailors, "I wanted to see how [...] military rules of conduct rub off on aesthetics."[37] The sailors, no less than the women, appear here beneath the threshold of concept: in the closed space of the museum they impose an imperative order on spectators, albeit in an autonomous, non-practical way that visitors would otherwise not be able to experience. The perhaps legitimate objection that Beecroft is avoiding an ideological critique of the military by limiting herself to a specifically aesthetic venue is however based in its most extreme form on a notion of art that regards any autonomous and intuitive personal experience (be it of order or of anything else) as a sham to begin with. It is however precisely within this imposed free space of autonomous selfhood that the aesthetic moment resides, and it seems that after many years of being effaced and dissipated in postmodernism it is making a comeback of epochal dimensions.

Performatist Photography: Andreas Gursky's Aesthetic Theism

It is no understatement to describe the changes that have occurred in art photography over the last fifteen years as dramatic. Like the anti-art of postmodernism, photography of the 1970s and '80s delighted in freakish, unattractive themes and a seemingly amateurish *mise en scène* of its material. The striking, disturbing images of Lee Friedlander, Annie Leibowitz, Nan Goldin, and Diane Arbus, to name just a few, may be taken as tokens of this general tendency. In Germany, postmodern photography found an original incarnation in the influential work of Hilla and Bernd Becher.[38] The Bechers specialized in pictures of peripheral, unattractive industrial objects like water towers, winding towers of coal mines, or grain silos, all of which were photographed in the same, deadpan way from the same position against flat gray skies. Taken alone, the pictures do not beautify the formal elements of their quotidian subject matter (the way Edward Weston squeezed formal beauty out of curvaceous bell peppers). Taken together, though, they form a discourse documenting the fascinating endless differences in the visual language of functional architecture. Given the heritage of German photography, it was also evident that the Bechers were doing for industrial capitalism what August Sander once did for people with his *Stammmappen*;[39] they were creating a kind of systematic register documenting individual types. The pictures also acquired an added poignancy because many of these industrial objects were falling into disuse or being torn down; the pictures came to document the slow decline of an entire industrial region. The photographer was in any case no longer a creative individual taking artsy pictures of odd or perhaps even beautiful objects, but a kind of performance-artist-with-a-lens organizing and presenting us a deliberately drab visual discourse with socially critical implications.[40]

This discursive, anti-aesthetic approach was given a more explicit ideological spin by Thomas Struth, a pupil of the Bechers, who in his *Unconscious Places* (1987) photographed cities in the early morning to look as if they were entirely unlived in, if not to say unlivable. It is no accident that the vanishing lines in some of his bleak urban scenes lead towards distant, diminutive church spires, which seem unable to compensate in iconic terms for the desolation that the receding perspective is coldly thrusting toward them. The dour irony of this and similar projects by Becher pupils[41] made one of the richest countries in the world appear economically stagnant and spiritually barren. The point is not, of course, whether this pictorial analysis was true in strict empirical terms. It did, however, reflect a widespread disaffection among intellectuals with what was perceived as a repressive state and a self-satisfied, morally indifferent postwar society.

All this began to change sometime in the mid-to-late 1990s. In hindsight it seems obvious that two separate developments worked together. First, postmodernist anti-art was beginning to exhaust what seemed like an unlimited plurality of possibilities for sawing off the branch upon which it was sitting. Although there was no dearth of concepts to subvert, the ironic gesture involved in doing so was becoming increasingly predictable and easy to duplicate. While conceptual art did not simply disappear overnight, there has been a noticeable tendency – particularly in Germany – towards the "classic" medium of painting and away from jumbled installations and crudely provocative performance art. Secondly, the rapid, revolutionary switch to a market economy in Eastern European countries and the globalization process in general made capitalism – whatever one happened to think of it in political terms – into a universal, inescapable economic and cultural reality.[42]

The results of both these developments converge in the photography of the West German Andreas Gursky (b. 1955). Gursky,

who was originally a student of the Bechers, began by making photos aimed at humdrum subjects and steeped in the dualist irony of
postmodernism. His *Bochum, University (Bochum, Uni* 1988),[43] for
example, shows a university terrace with a massive, honeycombed,
poured-concrete roof that blocks off our view of the upper sky. A few
students stand scattered beneath the roof, with a natural panorama
of fields and forest faintly visible in the background haze. Another
work from this period, *Ratingen* (1984),[44] shows a park forest road
marked with two parallel red-and-white circular traffic signs signaling "no entry" to vehicles; a few visitors stand scattered around
the entry path to the forest, perhaps preparing to leave or preparing
to enter. The "message" in both cases is hard to miss. In *Ratingen*,
the arbitrary, doubled cultural sign (a simulacrum of itself) acts as
a barrier to a nature that acquires its "natural," privileged position
precisely by virtue of the sign; the photograph confronts us visually
with the undecidable duality that lies at the core of all postmodernist
thought. In *Bochum, University*, the roof protects us – perhaps overly
so – from nature while at the same time interdicting our access to the
transcendent openness of the sky.[45] Humans are indeed present, but
they seem randomly positioned and pursue no particular goals. Nature, for its part, appears as a hazy promise in the background – so to
speak under erasure, both there and not there. When taken together,
Gursky's two photographs cut us off vertically from transcendent experience and horizontally from a natural one: the photographs thrust
us back into the condition of endless, undecidable immanence that
is postmodernism.

Other early Gursky photos, however, project an openness and a
hint of transcendent experience lacking in those of his postmodern
contemporaries. The most notable example is his 1989 color photograph of a Ruhr Valley bridge (*Ruhrtal*), which may be said to mark
symbolically the gateway out of postmodernism and into performatism. The photo shows a tiny human figure beneath a tall highway
bridge that forms a dark diagonal band running across the top of
the picture from left to right. The miniscule figure is framed by
the two tall, slender pillars of the bridge and the grass embank-
ment on which he is standing; in the background there is a flat gray

Becher-like sky. The dynamic, diagonally inclined bridge, though, is more than just another inert industrial object waiting to be visually archived; the open expanse of flat gray sky (which takes up most of the picture) is more than just a neutral backdrop, and the human figure – evidently a fisherman – seems to be caught in a state of open potentiality rather than one of ironic undecidability.[46] *Ruhrtal* doesn't contain any of Gursky's later trademark techniques or motifs – the eagle's-eye perspective, the digital manipulation, or the brightly colored matrices of things, buildings, and people. However, the picture's evident lack of irony and its optimistic opening up of space foreshadow the direction his no-longer postmodern aesthetic would take in the future.

In the more recent analyses and appreciations of Gursky's work there is a broadly held feeling that Gursky is something other than postmodern (and certainly no longer compatible with the aesthetic championed by the Bechers). However, this feeling is seldom expressed in a resolute way, and is invariably couched in terms applying well to Gursky's art but not to anyone else's. In the following remarks I would like to set forth a thumbnail sketch of Gursky's art that will allow us to place him not in some sort of differentially defined individual niche after postmodernism, but in the broad context of the epochal shift that is performatism.

My starting point is the double frame, which is to say the lock between a theist, authorial perspective and a personal, human one. Gursky's pictures are normally taken from "on high" and because of this create the effect of sublime distance to their objects (Gursky himself speaks of an "extra-planetary" perspective[47] and notes that he is interested in humans as a "species" in their environment and not as individuals[48]). This theist perspective, which overwhelms the senses more than it pleases them, keeps his pictures from descending into the uncritical celebration practiced by commercial photography. The first immediate effect of his photography is thus to totalize the things or activities we see within a large, but highly selective frame. This sublime totalization, however, can only function as a whole because it is confirmed by categorical order existing at a lower, human level. Gursky himself puts it like this:

You never notice arbitrary details in my work. On a formal level, countless interrelated micro and macrostructures are woven together, determined by an overall organisational principle. A closed microcosm which, thanks to my distanced attitude towards my subject, allows the viewer to recognise the hinges that hold the system together.[49]

Due to the high resolution of the pictures (and also to digital manipulation) this sublime, theist perspective is anchored in sharply defined, digitally manipulated images that practically force us as viewers to focus on small individual things and their formal, ordered relationships – in short, to experience beauty.[50] The eagle's-eye view, in conjunction with high resolution, an often unnaturally deep field of focus, and brightly colored, enigmatically ordered forms encourages us to work out intuitive categories of order which, when synthesized in our mind's eye, confirm the original totality confronting us in the first place. Here, too, the effect is Kantian in the special performatist sense I have been using all along. As Gursky says, "[...] the history of art seems to possess a generally valid formal vocabulary which we use again and again."[51] One must add, however, that this formal vocabulary is not entirely "natural" or a priori but is imposed on the viewer through a totalizing, highly selective gaze and through digital manipulation. In this performatist Kantianism, nature and art are framed by a theist artist in such a way as to be indistinguishable – and we wind up believing in this unity whether we want to or not.

This unity can also be seen in Gursky's photo of a landfill (*Ohne Titel XIII*, 2002) and of one of Jackson Pollock's drip paintings (*Ohne Titel VI*, 1997), which are simply different versions of the same thing caught in different stages of constructedness. The drips are a kind of garbage that Pollock deliberately placed on canvas to form random, but beautiful patterns; the garbage in the landfill forms beautiful patterns partly by chance, partly through digital manipulation by Gursky. As in all performatist art, these larger frames or totalized unities are nothing more than giant-size versions of the original ostensive sign, which is that place where nature (the thing) and culture (the sign) are intuitively framed for the first time through spontaneous, mutual agreement and form a communal, divinely charged field deferring conflict. Gursky's specific feat is to position himself on the outside of the frame, as it were, as a quasi-divine being with a totalizing perspective that at the same time allows individual access to categorically mediated, beautiful thingness. The price of this aesthetic theism is however that we are never absolutely sure what is real and what has been digitally manipulated – and usually have no way of knowing if the artist doesn't tell us. The net result, as in all performatism, is to create an artificially framed aesthetic field that we *believe in* even though we are aware of the artificial, manipulative conditions behind it.

This aesthetic theism also causes Gursky's photographs to radiate a metaphysical optimism that is entirely alien to postmodernism. This is most evident in the way Gursky presents space. In the postmodern photographs of Ruff and Struth, space – even outside, presumably open space – is presented as claustrophobic (typical examples are Ruff's *Haus Nr. 8 III*[52] or Struth's *Shinju-ku [Skyscrapers]*[53]). In Gursky's art, the opposite is true. Even when Gursky in *Copan* (2002) photographs essentially the same thing as Struth does in *Shinju-ku* (the massive facades of ugly high-rise buildings) the variegated colors and ordered patterns in Gursky's facades work to dematerialize their oppressive volume.[54] In Gursky's work, in fact, even the most closed and oppressive inner space imaginable – that of a jail in *Stateville, Illinois* (2002) – appears radiant and open; light shines through the outside windows of each cell into the inner courtyard, from whose center the picture was taken. In Foucauldian terms, this panoptic perspective would at first seem to make the photographer (and ourselves) complicit in the prison's confining, punitive function. This centering, however, can be interpreted in quite another way: it allows us to apprehend the possibility of universal redemption for the inhabitants of the cells, who appear framed by miniscule cubes of light.[55] The principle of spatial transcendence realized in the earlier *Ruhrtal* (the tiny figure surrounded by a large open frame) is now repeated a hundredfold in more constricted circumstances – but with an optimistic refraction of light suggesting the possibility of individual transcendence.

The inevitable question arises as to whether Gursky would not do better subjecting globalization to an ironic pictorial critique of the sort developed by Ruff, Struth, and others and also employed by Gursky in some of his early work. These ironic techniques, as noted above, include strategies of exposing the conceptual dualities conditioning our "natural" vision and of "returning to the real" – photographing depopulated, constricted space so as to suggest oppression and spiritual emptiness. Although it is no doubt possible to employ these and similar techniques in a critique of global capitalism, it would prevent us from ever capturing globalization pictorially in its own terms, as a total phenomenon. If global capitalism really is as spiritually empty, ugly, arbitrary, and claustrophobic as the postmodern critique maintains, then it is fair to ask how it managed to unfold such a world-encompassing, universal dynamic in the first place. This question, I believe, finds a more convincing answer in Gursky's method than in Ruff's or Struth's. For in Gursky's photography we experience the totalizing, dynamic, overwhelming effect peculiar to globalization itself. While not "critical" in the postmodern sense that requires us to take the position of a peripheral victim, Gursky's work forces us to experience a distinct sort of ambivalence regarding the activities or things portrayed. Because totalization *imposes* beauty and order on us, and because we remain aware of this circumstance in spite of our enjoying its details, we are also forced to develop an intuitive resistance towards it. This resistance operates not through concept, but through the apprehension of categorical equivalencies arising between different totalities. Taken together, the pictures of the Kuwaiti stock exchange, the North Korean mass assemblies, and Vietnamese basket-weaving factory (and, of course, all of Gursky's other photos relating to global society) form a categorical assemblage of totalities whose imagery could be reapplied in a potentially critical, discursive way to the reality around us. The fact that Gursky doesn't express this criticism himself in words is less his problem than our own. The point is, however, that an effective critique of globalization must first apprehend the dynamics of globalization itself in order to counter that dynamic in an effective way. In this regard the type of art pioneered by Gursky may indeed play an instrumental role in future critiques of globalization that move beyond the neo-Nietzs-chean, localized positions typical of postmodernism and prescribed by poststructuralism.

Thomas Demand: Bracketing the Real

Perhaps the most unusual and inimitable performatist photographer of today is the German Thomas Demand, who was originally trained as a sculptor. Demand first painstakingly recreates scenes (usually interiors) out of folded paper and cardboard on a 1-to-1 scale, then photographs them with a large-format camera or films them (the model is destroyed after the picture is taken). The large-scale pictures are in turn displayed without frames in laminated Plexiglass on patterned backgrounds, giving the impression of being direct incisions in the wall.

From the performatist point of view, Demand's technique may be said to radically reduce photography to an experience of theist willpower and originary, categorical intuition. This claim may at first seem curious because Demand's draws heavily on familiar media images relating to juicy, discourse-laden subjects like brutal crimes, corrupt politics, and dramatic historical events – typical examples being his *Tunnel* (a film moving through a life-size facsimile of the tunnel in which Lady Diana died); *Corridor* (depicting the hallway where the mass murderer Jeffrey Dahmer lived); or *Office* (showing a looted office of the Stasi, the East German state security service). Indeed, the standard postmodern way of describing Demand's pictures is in terms of the absent things that they purport to represent: they are said, for example, to "capture moments that refer to a greater event, a before and after."[56] Seen from this epistemological perspective, the visually stunning, large-format pictures are mainly there to make us conscious of a lack: "Demand's *Bathroom* [a picture relating to a notorious German political scandal, R.E.] points to the evasions and ultimately to the failure of photography's attempts to understand the violence behind the apparent ambiguity of political life."[57]

However, upon examining these photographs more closely – it would perhaps be better to say intuitively – it becomes apparent that we can derive them from media images only through descriptions of their titles, which function in much the same way that the *inscriptio* and *subscriptio* did in Baroque emblems: they ascribe meaning to what is otherwise an inexplicably constructed, rather arbitrary looking scene. If you did not have the *subscriptio* provided by Demand in his interviews, Lady Di's tunnel could be anyone's tunnel; Jeffrey Dahmer's corridor anyone's corridor; and the looted Stasi office anyone's act of vandalism anywhere. Demand's constructive technique evidently disturbs the causal connection leading from reality to the photograph so much that it must be artificially supplemented with outside discourse[58] (even the generic titles, which in conventional terms are indisputably part of the photograph's presentation, don't help much in figuring out what his pictures are about).[59] Demand's photographs, in other words, create discrete aesthetic spaces accessible primarily, if not exclusively, to intuition; like Beecroft's performances, they are far enough below the threshold of concept that they must be reconnected to the practical world around them artificially. If anything, in fact, the photographs act as indices not of reality, but of categorical experience: the tunnel is a scene prefiguring *all* threats emanating from tunnels, the corridor is *any* lonely person's corridor, the looted office *any* retributive act of destruction. Demand isn't providing us with failed representations forcing their failure upon us after the fact; instead, he's supplying us with a set of ostensive aesthetic *categories* that can be used by us a priori to construct or approach quotidian reality anew. This *category art* is, in effect, the opposite of, and successor to, the concept art that has dominated our aesthetic experience for the last thirty years or so.

My assessment of Demand's art as a positive act of creation is not alone. As Michael Fried has pointed out in an important recent article in *Artforum*, Demand's photographs aren't about lack or failure; they're about imposing the intention of the artist on the spectator. As Fried writes, Demand tries

> to replace the original scene of evidentiary traces and marks of human use – the historical world in all its layeredness and compositeness – with images of sheer authorial intention, as through the very bizarreness of the fact that the scenes and objects in the photographs, despite their initial appearance of quotidian

"reality," have all been constructed by the artist throws into conceptual relief the determining force (also the inscrutability, one might say the opacity) of the intention behind it.[60]

Translated into the epochal terminology of performatism, you could say that the theist artist Demand occludes discourse on the level of the sign-object or inner frame by depriving it of all but the most minimal features necessary to make it identifiable as a real-world object. For the viewer, the only adequate way of approaching these constructed minimal objects is, *nolens volens*, through intuition.

This intuition, however, is not indeterminate or up to the individual position taken by the viewer, as is the case in what Fried calls minimalism or literalism. Instead, Demand's inner frames are imposed on viewers through the opaque will of the theist artist; the viewer experiences the whole of the work as an uneasy mixture of beauty, uncanniness, sublimity, and discursivity (which is tacked on, as it were, as an afterthought by the imperfectly theist artist confirming the existence of a world outside his own creative scene[61]). This "ontological project"[62] as Fried calls it, radically reverses the entire program of postmodernism. We are no longer dealing with an anti-image demonstrating the failure of the visual sign to represent reality, but with a unique, originary construct that relocates the apprehension of reality in a "divine" aesthetic act uniting creator, object, and viewer. And, if we inject the notion of category into Fried's analysis, the will of the artist can be integrated intuitively into the consciousness of the viewer and projected back out again onto the real world. My only real complaint about Fried's analysis is, of course, that he doesn't go far enough: he explicitly leaves the question of an epochal shift open.[63] This gap can easily be filled, though, by reference to a theory of performatism.

Performatist Painting

Arthur C. Danto's *After the End of Art* (written in 1995) ends with a discussion of the end of original style in postmodern painting. In his remarks on the American Russel Connor and on the Russian emigré duo Komar and Melamid, Danto notes that the task of the artist is no longer to paint in any new style (since everything has presumably already been tried out) but to ironically juxtapose already known, mutually exclusive codes. The result is a comic art practiced by what might best be described as highly gifted pranksters; in the case of Komar and Melamid, for example, the performance surrounding the work of art ("America's Most Wanted"[64]) is more important than the work itself. Faced with the imminent dissolution of art into what looks like a running series of practical jokes, Danto retreats to an essentialist, above-the-fray Hegelian position affirming the continued existence of art in different historical settings. Art, which is always "about something" and always "embodies meaning"[65] no matter how mundane or trivial its subject matter may be, can do so in completely different ways under completely different historical conditions, in accordance with the prevailing zeitgeist. Although Danto several times invokes the name of Heinrich Wölfflin – the scholar virtually synonymous with an epochal concept of art history – he understandably makes no attempt to speculate on how and when the end of art could actually end. Art in 2005 will no doubt be completely different from what we imagine it today, he continues, but the main thing is that it will still be identifiable as art.[66]

Some twelve years later the situation in art has indeed changed in a way that would hardly have been imaginable in 1995. There has been a massive resurgence of paintings that are no longer comic, ironic, or composed entirely of self-conscious citations of other styles. The most talked-about younger artists are painters or photographers rather than performance artists, and the art they have been producing has a feel to it that is not readily captured using the terminology of postmodernism. This development has, of course, not been lost on art critics, who have begun to use heretofore suspect words like "ontology," "immediacy," "beauty" or "totality" to describe the new works in a positive way. Obviously, I have no quarrel with these assessments. However, I would insist that the changes they describe must be treated as epochal in nature, and not simply as incremental innovations or yet another new proof of postmodernism's sheer endless mutability.

This epochal perspective is Hegelian in the sense that it assumes that art can be said to progress in diametrically opposed leaps and bounds, and that certain types of art can appear only in certain times or epochs. It is, however, non-Hegelian in the sense that the motor of this progress is located in a basic, insoluble conflict between semiotic monism and semiotic dualism and not in the zeitgeist, in shifts in concept or style, or in a particular mode of argumentation "accidentally" always favoring one side of the equation. In this regard there can be no end of history in the Hegelian and/or postmodern sense. The seeming "triumph" of one semiotic mode over the other invariably causes its methods to congeal into conventional norms that in time would choke off the free space that makes art what it is. The only way out of this trap is to break with normative convention as it stands and adopt the position of its semiotic Other. The problem we are facing today is that art has intuitively taken this step some time ago but art criticism has not. It is still caught up in a discourse that can only conceive of art in terms of differential shifts within the Same, but not in terms of a leap towards an intuitively experienced unity of artist, work, and observer that transpires on the level of the sign and not on the level of concept. The case of Danto shows that even a moderate Hegelian with a soft spot for Kant isn't going to get us out of this posthistorical bind. For to do so, we are all going to have to in some way become neo-neo-Kantians and semiotic monists – at least until that posture, too, exhausts its creative and analytical possibilities.

Closed and Open Horizons: Bulatov, Gursky, and Eitel

The most direct way to describe the shift to monism in painting (and painterly photography) is to show how a certain conceptualist motif is cut off from concept and forced to float in the intuitively perceived and categorically defined free space of the performatist frame.

My starting point is the work of Erik Bulatov, one of the most important Russian conceptualist painters of the 1970s and 1980s. Like the other conceptualists, Bulatov used techniques comparable to those of Western pop-art, but with a uniquely Soviet point of reference. His perhaps most well-known painting, *Horizon* (*Gorizont*, 1971–72),

seems at first to be done entirely in the pseudo-naturalist style of Socialist Realism: it depicts a group of fully clothed people on a beach
walking away from the viewer towards the ocean horizon on a bright
sunny day. A closer look reveals that the canvas is divided into four
horizontal stripes of kitschy, highly saturated color: the yellow sand
of the beach, the dark blue of the water, an abstract, broad red band
where the horizon should normally be, and the cerulean blue of the
sky. For those familiar with Soviet symbols, the red band blocking the
horizon is not just an abstraction, but is also the ribbon attached to
the Order of Lenin, one of the highest honors bestowed in the Soviet
Union. As Groys has pointed out in his *Total Art of Stalinism*, Bulatov
is echoing a theme of Nietzsche's (who likens the death of God to
wiping out the horizon) as well as staging an undecidable struggle
between Socialist Realism, modernism, and official Soviet power: in
competing for power with Socialist Realism, modernist abstraction
itself becomes indistinguishable from an official insignia of power.[67]
The painting, in effect, exposes previous art movements as a will to
power and power as a will to art. Using a by now familiar ploy of postmodern conceptualism, the artist occupies a liminal, shifting position
that is parasitic on the discourses he is using without being reducible
to any one of them.

Groys would however come to realize in his later essay *Unter Verdacht* [Under suspicion, 2000] that the uncanny elusiveness and unac-
countability of the postmodern artist eventually works to revive the
notion of subjectivity itself. Since the artist has the unique power to
renew value in the cultural archive, he or she inevitably comes to be
regarded as the bearer of some sort of transcendent secret, even if – or
precisely because – the artist's main message is that there *is* no secret.[68]
The result is what Groys calls a "submedial subject," who operates
with consistent success below the level of concept and who because of
that attracts our envy and suspicion.

Because Groys remains rooted in postmodern skepticism, he is unwilling to assign the submedial subject anything more the role of a
Loki – a deceitful, vaguely malevolent prankster-god. This is, once
more, entirely in keeping with a specifically Nietzschean interpretation of the sign, which sees in it only the political and sacral:

Subjectivity is always only the subjectivity of the other, who is assumed to be behind its surface. Subjectivity is what appears to me suspicious about someone else, what scares me – it is what causes me to make lamentations and accusations, to assign responsibility, to struggle and protest – in short, to engage in politics. Only when a hidden God is assumed to be behind the image of the world does one feel moved to take a political stance.[69]

What Groys is unable to grasp is that the autonomous or submedial space inhabited by art may also create an affirmative, constructive projection of its own that can be imposed visually on others on its own terms.[70] In recent art, in fact, it's possible to observe how painters working in the new monism have done just that. These artists use strategies that dampen or defuse suspicion and create positive visual projections within the artificially imposed, but internally free space of intuition.

These strategies are, first of all, evident in the "painterly" photos of Andreas Gursky already treated above. It is particularly interesting in this regard to see what Gursky does with the horizon motif used by Bulatov. This motif is, of course, not original to Bulatov himself. It directly cites Socialist Realist models like Aleksandr Dejneka's *Future Pilots* (*Budushchie lyotchiki*, 1937) and indirectly the work of the German Romantic Caspar David Friedrich, who likes to place observers with their backs turned to us in front of radiant, horizontally organized seascapes or landscapes. In Friedrich's typically Romantic projection, we are not only confronted by a sublime, numinous Nature, but we are also made to reflect on how others reflect on that Nature.

Gursky cites Friedrich's landscapes in several photographs,[71] but the one most relevant for this discussion would seem to be *Rhein II* (Rhine II, 1999). *Rhein II* confronts us with a landscape that is no less spiritualized than Friedrich's and no less artificial than Bulatov's. The large-format photograph, which measures approximately 6 x 12 ft (208 x 387 cm), consists of seven horizontal stripes: a verdant shore at the bottom, a gray ribbon of road, more green shore, a gleaming, mercury-like band of wave-rippled water, a gray strip of shore, the green stripe of the far riverbank, and a flat, grayish-white sky above it. As in Bulatov's painting, we have difficulty deciding whether the photo is entirely natural, though for different reasons. The neatly horizontal bands of land, water, and sky appear so perfectly composed as to be unreal, and critics have in fact associated the photograph with works by abstract artists like Barnett Newman and Agnes Martin.[72] In Gursky's case, though, the effect is not one of ironic undecidability but of a paradoxical unity prior to all concept; the viewer has little choice but to oscillate between these two potentialities imposed on them by the frame of the photo. The two undecidably fused poles of the natural and the artificial are in turn augmented and intensified by the other factors noted earlier: the sublime size of the picture; the set towards form and order; the imposition of categorical intuition on the viewer; and the possibility of transcending the frame of the individual picture and reapplying its givens to other works of art or to nature itself.

Unlike the work of Friedrich and Bulatov, there is no reflection on reflection in Gursky's picture: nature, art, and the observer are all bound together in a framed unity that seems to transcend, rather than undercut, the individual premises upon which that unity is based. And, even if we are aware that Gursky manipulated this scene (he in fact digitally excised a factory that would probably have warmed the hearts of the Bechers[73]), the effect of this epistemological insight on our appreciation of the photograph is nil. Like gender in Beecroft's nude performances and media events in Demand's architectonic photos, the building has simply been bracketed out of existence; it leaves no traces for us to interpret. We know it is out there somewhere, but have no way of connecting it to the photograph without the explicit intervention of the theist artist, who "positions" us along a particular phenomenological axis that in turn forces us to perceive the world anew. The "suspicious" Groysian viewer must either reject the painterly photo's sublimity and beauty out of hand or try vainly to imagine something that isn't there – the factory that would effectively reinscribe the picture in "the real," and ultimately in a particular, identifiable context. Suspicion without concept is, however, nothing more than *belief,* and it is precisely that effect that the picture achieves: it converts skeptics into believers whether they like it or not.

Another variant of the horizon/observer motif can be found in the work of Tim Eitel (b. 1971), a German artist associated with the New Leipzig School. I am not sure whether Eitel is familiar with Bulatov, but many of his paintings appear to cite Friedrich's romantic scenes: naturalistically depicted people with their backs turned towards us walk casually towards or stand in front of the horizon of a beach or field.[74] The effect achieved by Eitel lies somewhere between painting and snapshot photography, without however suggesting photorealism. Because Eitel uses very flat, rich expanses of monochrome paint in his depictions of nature, his pictures take on an abstract quality in spite of their patent realism. The major difference to Bulatov is that the coexistence of the natural and the abstract lacks any ironic tension whatsoever. Nature appears as an abstraction of the theist artist (who "improves" nature by making it more monochrome, saturated in color, and homogenous than it really is). At the same time, the monochrome abstraction is never allowed to dominate entirely: there is always just enough detail to keep it within the bounds of the mimetic.

This applies with no less intensity to the humans caught up in this aesthetically simplified and beautified space. Their own emotional state of mind remains enigmatic and opaque, either because they are turned away from us completely or because when they face us they seem entirely oblivious to the artist-observer.[75] Although not represented in photorealistic detail, the subjects always still evince slight traces of individual taste or character: a particular slouch, a certain kind of handbag, a sport jacket slung over the arm in a characteristic way. In this sense these figures are not stereotypes (as in Bulatov) or mere conduits of Romantic reflection on the sublime (as in Friedrich). Against the mimetic flatness of the surroundings they stand out as uniquely, albeit minimally, human. Eitel's paintings of this sort in fact radiate an enticing, irresistible combination of the theist and the human. The observer is lured into their space by the theistically perfected depiction of nature and by the enigmatic opacity or closedness of the people within that nature – whereupon the aesthetic trap snaps shut: you yourself enter into the intuitive space of the painting whether you like it or not.

This theistically constructed unity of abstraction and realism is even more pointed in Eitel's museum paintings, in which the naturalistic level of the observers seems to overlap with the abstract level of the paintings they are looking at. In *Blue and Yellow* (*Blau und Gelb*, 2002), as in Bulatov's *Horizon*, an abstract stripe (of a black museum railing in the picture's foreground) runs across the breadth of the canvas and appears at first glance to be on the same plane as the Mondrian painting behind it. However, the disruptive illusion disappears quickly when one notices that a human observer is standing between the artificial monochrome lines of the painting and the real, monochrome line of the railing. In Gans's generative anthropology the human is defined precisely as the ability to distinguish between the real as mediated by the sign and the sign itself; in *Blue and Yellow* it is a human subject that allows us to make precisely this distinction in regard to a pictorial representation. Eitel's museum paintings may thus best be described as performative, second-degree representations of the originary, paradoxical aesthetic situation. They create a visual outer frame that forces the observer to participate in the peculiarly human oscillation between signs and thingness that is represented in the inner frame of the painting; what is represented in the inner frame by the artist is performed by the viewer in the outer one. Painter, viewer, and painting all converge within the bounds of one closed frame.

A die-hard postmodernist would no doubt object that Eitel's human figures are trapped helplessly between the representation of the real and the representation of the abstract. However, this sort of "suspicious" interpretation must pointedly ignore the placidly opaque demeanor of the subjects involved. Although in a certain sense they really *are* trapped in the aesthetic space between the real and the sign, they seem neither to enjoy nor to suffer from their predicament: they are suspended, as it were, in an ostensive, originary mode of complete potentiality and don't appear to suffer unduly because of it.[76] The only way to "get behind" their opacity and "get back" to discourse would be to excise the human from the paintings entirely – a move that is however external to the works themselves and that would, in essence, destroy them.

The Aesthetic Workshop of Neo Rauch

One of the main conceits of Russian conceptualism was that capitalism and socialism were essentially the same – both were equally unfree, but capitalism was simply materially better off, and hence less cognizant of its own illusions. As Bulatov himself recently put it, "In the West there is no freedom either, just its semblance. There is no difference between Soviet and Western unfreedom. Genuine freedom is a rupture [*proryv*] running through social reality."[77] In this way of thinking (which is of course not all that much different from Western conceptualism) only the neo-Nietzschean artist has the power to subvert the illusions of both systems by enacting the kind of ironic conundrums described above, which force us to assume a position of otherness vis-à-vis prevailing codes and experience a liminal, tenuous kind of freedom within the cracks opening up in the dominant culture. The fall of communism, however, wasn't just another reshuffling of already familiar concepts. The socio-economic system called capitalism became a universal reality, whereas its chief rival, communism, entered into the realm of the unreal – it simply ceased to exist as a physical entity.

The disappearance of their brand of conceptual "unfreedom" into an ontological black hole provoked different reactions among artists from the former Soviet bloc. While it's not possible here to go into all individual variants, one can speak of three general tendencies. The first might be called art – or business – as usual. Bulatov, for example, continued to work in a similar fashion as before, for example, by placing diagonally receding three-dimensional slogans in front of natural backgrounds (a citation of a Russian avant-garde technique that is lost on most Westerners; see his *Freedom is Freedom I* [2000]). As the critic Victor Tupitsyn has pointed out, these new paintings lack the ironic bite of Bulatov's Soviet work; they appear more like flashy advertising images than the neo-Nietzschean commentary on capitalism they are no doubt intended to be.[78] Others, like Komar and Melamid, who emigrated earlier, had less problems adapting and, as noted above, became adept at turning Western marketing techniques into both tools and targets of their conceptual irony.

A second tendency is what Hal Foster has called "the return of the real,"[79] and which is often thought to be typical of postmodern art in the 1990s. In the Russian context, this applies to anti-artists like Alexander Brener, Oleg Kulik, and the photographer Boris Mikhailov. These artists may be said to take the materiality of the art work *literally*; they destroy other people's art works (Kulik), physically attack observers during performances (Brener), or present the real as abject and debased (Mikhailov). This kind of art rubs our noses in the material existence of the real while conceptually confirming the impossibility (or undesirability) of actually ever appropriating it. In Groysian terms, these artists, driven by an intense, conceptually guided suspicion of the motives of art in general, deliberately try to destroy the materiality of art to "get at" its submedial or ontological source, which (as they are well aware) is reducible neither to materiality nor to conceptuality. Unfortunately, an art that can only approach the real by destroying it or highlighting its repellant character remains trapped forever in the dualism of late postmodernism, which derives a kind of perverse, endless pleasure from experiencing the proximity of the real on the one hand and the impossibility of ever appropriating it on the other. And indeed: the pro forma recognition of the real achieves nothing if the real cannot be experienced as a unity with the sign that represents it. Only this performatist, monist framing, which necessarily takes place below all concept, can in the long run renew today's art.

There are, however, also specifically performatist, non-conceptual reactions to the disappearance of socialism. The best example of this can be seen in the work of Neo Rauch (b. 1960), who is a product of the academic East German art system and came to prominence only after the fall of Communism. Unlike the many East European artists who juxtapose two or more readily identifiable, but incompatible cultural codes in a state of undecidable conceptual irony, Rauch has developed a representational mode of painting that operates entirely below the threshold of concept and cannot be reduced to an ironically conceived stand-off between Eastern and Western discourses.

Rauch's work however also differs from the other performatist artists discussed above because he strives neither for thematic unity nor does he work with simple, intuitively recognizable categories that are

"naturally" accepted by viewers. In fact, his paintings seem to do precisely the opposite: they contain a plethora of irritatingly incongruous
figures, styles, actions, colors, and objects. A typical (comparatively
simple) example is *Pfad* (*The Path*, 2003[80]), which contains three gar-
ishly colored, out-of-scale figures (two male, one female) that look like
they have been pasted onto a monochrome, half-finished blue background. On this background we see a path leading up to a modernist
house on a hill; oddly standing trees, a basket of mushrooms and what
looks like an agave plant border the path, which is marked by a multi-
colored logo reading "Path." The figures carry odd objects, including
a shiny green serpent-like staff, a purse, a pair of branch clippers, and
a liquid-looking green knapsack. Two yellow tubular bars, placed in a
triangular formation and having no apparent function, seem to merge
with the woman's blouse. The figures are expressionless and seem intent on doing something – it is just not clear just what. The one male
figure wears a long, split-tailed cloak that might be from the nine-
teenth century; the other is dressed like a worker, and the woman in
a 1950s style dress and blouse. There is no unity of time or place, and
there is no sense that all this has been achieved through the synthetic
vision of the subconscious (as is the case in true surrealism). More
specifically, we have the apprehension of a distinctly theist, "outside"
artist who inserts things into a frame (hence the collage-like figures)
and who hasn't entirely completed the work at hand.

   Although the different styles used by Rauch can be traced back
to such sources as comic books, East German propaganda art, surrealism, and modernism, they don't compete with one another for
dominance the way they do in conceptualism. The reason for this is
that Rauch's paintings are devoid of any narrative and conceptual pur-
posefulness. This quality, which has been noted by numerous com-
mentators, is formulated most forcefully by Bernhart Schwenk, who
stresses the self-referential qualities of Rauch's paintings:

> Neo Rauch is no teller of tales, even if he works with narrative
> elements and motifs. Rather, his pictures are still-lifes, symbols
> of picture-making; he creates, as it were, an emblemology of
> painting. To experience his pictures thus, the observer must

free himself or herself from the compulsion to read a story into them, from the urge to decipher their meaning. [...] If the observer succeeds in avoiding this trap, the pictures reveal a broad and variegated visual code. Although springing from personal and historical experience, they are self-sufficient creations, metaphorical constellations. They create an exterior framework for a more profound content whose significance stretches far beyond the bounds of art.[81]

In performatist terms, Rauch can be said to create a peculiar inner space that generates neither meaning nor narrative but rather only aesthetic "work" on the part of the observer; it is only this magical, purposeless task that can transcend the jumbled and incongruous givens of the painting. The net effect is that of aesthetic hard labor. The observer is encouraged to work, however this work takes place in a purposeless space using signs that have minimal discursive meaning and minimal ties to reality. This type of labor radicalizes the categorical procedures of performatist art discussed earlier by creating what seem to be idiosyncratic categories and by denying unity at the thematic level. The result is a complex, "saturated" kind of categorical intuition that makes the outside world of discourse seem drab by comparison. Moreover, this inner world becomes the place where history, which has imploded and ceased to develop in both discursive and real terms, is intuitively restarted through the exertions forced upon us by Rauch's art. Rather than dwelling in endless, belated irony, the theist artist tries to restart time using the meaningless, but nonetheless somehow significant fragments of the past and the subconscious to create a perpetually active present. Because it is not anchored in any particular discourse, it allows both *Ossis* and *Wessis* – East and West Germans alike – to take part in it on an equal footing. The result is a unified, East-West aesthetic consciousness that would not be possible in discourse.

Concluding Remarks

Performatism in art is not a programmatic movement,[82] a style, or a moral posture (it does not derive its legitimacy from postmodernism being "bad," "immoral," or "arbitrary"). Rather, performatism marks a positive, specifically historical, across-the-board shift to monism in different media and in works of art having otherwise little or nothing in common in the way of subject matter, motifs, or technique. The problem is not so much that contemporary critics have failed to grasp the innovative achievements of individual artists or works of art. There are, as we have seen, numerous perceptive, trenchant analyses of the new, no longer postmodern aesthetic, and there is a widespread feeling that postmodernism is, for better or worse, on its way out. Nonetheless, critics are still loath to take the next logical step and treat these innovations as part of an historical epoch that is irreducible both to postmodernism and to any one of the old monisms like classicism, neo-Kantianism, or the Apollonian. The reasons for this hesitation are in human and institutional terms entirely understandable. For the only way to understand the new epoch *from within* – from its *own* position – is to jettison practically everything that critics have accumulated up to now in the way of analytical and theoretical tools and start again from scratch within the new monist mindset. Unfortunately, there is no way to get around this specifically historical, self-transcending kind of performance. Any reapplication of postmodern concepts to explain postmodernism's historical Other will simply result in a further reification of postmodernism.

Whether the tag "performatism" will ever be adopted as a name for the nascent epoch is, of course, impossible to say; in a certain sense it is not even crucial to my project. However, there can be little doubt that the things described by performatism – the authorial or theist perspective, the artificial, forced construction of unities, the use of categories rather than concepts, and the set to unified, ostensive signs – are right now the main sources of innovation in contemporary culture and will remain so for some time. What is needed now most in the world of art criticism is a peculiar conflation of Wölfflinian and Nietzschean virtues: the ability to think in historical, epochal dichotomies and the courage to smash through accustomed patterns of discourse and reenter history via the new monism.

Notes

Notes to Introduction

1. "Mapping the Postmodern," *New German Critique* 33 (1984), 5–52.
2. See the illustration in Chapter Four of this book, 154.
3. Typical of the prevailing attitude in academia is the collection *Beyond Postmodernism. Reassessments in Literature, Theory, and Culture*, ed. by Klaus Stierstorfer (Berlin: Walter de Gruyter, 2003). Most of the book is devoted to critical reassessments of postmodernism that do little more than project postmodernism back onto itself using poststructuralist methodology. A small number of the authors (most notably Ihab Hassan and Vera Nünning) discuss unpostmodern trends toward subjectivity, faith, aesthetics, and ethical solidarity in an approving way. None of them, however, is willing to conceive of, let alone name, an epoch that would lie beyond postmodernism.
4. The notion that literary history is determined by two opposing, alternating styles is of course not new. The tradition I am following can be traced back to such authors as Heinrich Wölfflin in *Renaissance and Barock* (Ithaca: Cornell University Press 1966 [orig. 1888]) and Ernst Robert Curtius in his *European Literature and the Latin Middle Ages* (New York: Pantheon, 1953). In Slavic studies, the influential notion of a "primary style" versus a "secondary style" was first suggested by Dimitrii Likhachev in *Razvitie russkoi literatury X–XVII vekov. Epokhi i stili* [The development of Russian Literature from the 10th to the 17th century. Epochs and styles] (Leningrad: Nauka, 1973) and developed in semiotic and semantic terms by Renate Döring-Smirnov and Igor Smirnov in their *Ocherki po istoricheskoi tipologii kul'tury: ...realizm — (...) — postsimvolizm (avangard)* [Outline of a historical typology of culture: ...realism (...) postsymbolism — (the avant-garde)] (Salzburg, 1982). Within Slavics itself there has been no particular interest in applying epochal models to the cultural development after postmodernism.
5. See Herman Rapaport, *The Theory Mess. Deconstruction in Eclipse* (New York: Columbia University Press, 2001).

6. Obviously, the term isn't to be confused with performance the way that Judith Butler or other contemporary theorists use it. The postmodern performance is by definition weak, split, and doomed to failure before it even starts; the subject in such conceptions is little more than a belated effect of circumstances far exceeding its control.
7. Though based on Gans's notion of the ostensive, the concept of performatism was developed independently of Gans's own epochal notion of post-millennialism, which first appeared in his internet journal *Chronicles of Love and Resentment*, No. 209, 3 June 2000 under the title "The Post-Millennial Age" (www.anthropoetics.ucla.edu/views/vw209.htm).

Notes to Chapter 1

1. See his *The Truth in Painting* (Chicago: University of Chicago Press, 1987), esp. 37–82.
2. In this sense, performatism is the opposite of the phenomenological *epokhē*. Phenomenology brackets things to *know* them better; performatism brackets things to *believe in* them better. For more on this see the discussion of Jean-Luc Marion's *Being Given*, Chapter Five in this book, 175–193.
3. The most recent book-length formulation of this theory is Gans's *Signs of Paradox. Irony, Resentment, and Other Mimetic Structures* (Stanford: Stanford University Press, 1997); see also his *Originary Thinking. Elements of Generative Anthropology* (Stanford: Stanford University Press 1993) as well as the numerous glosses and additions in his internet journal *Chronicles of Love and Resentment* at
www.anthropoetics.ucla.edu/views/home.html
4. See, for example, René Girard, *Things Hidden since the Foundation of the World* (Stanford: Stanford University Press, 1987), 7–9.
5. Gans suggests in his *Originary Thinking* that while the idea of God may be forgotten as society becomes more secular, "the process of this forgetting can never be concluded. Even if someday not one believer remains, the atheist will remain someone who rejects belief in God, not someone for whom the concept is empty" (42–43).
6. See his discussion, for example, in *Originary Thinking*: "The pleasure of the esthetic results from the deferral or 'drowning' of the prior displeasure — the resentment — generated by unfulfillable desire.

The esthetic experience engages the subject in a to-and-fro movement of imaginary possession and dispossession that blocks the formation of the stable imaginary structure of resentment, where the self on the periphery is definitively alienated from the desired object at the center" (118–119).

7. The deconstructionist argument about language origin only works if you assume the existence of binary categories *prior* to language. Compare Jonathan Culler's explanation of this in his *On Deconstruction. Theory and Criticism after Structuralism* (Ithaca: Cornell University Press, 1982): "If a cave man is successfully to inaugurate language by making a special grunt signifying 'food,' we must suppose that the grunt is *already distinguished from other grunts* and that the world *has already been divided* into the categories 'food' and 'non-food'" (96). [The italics are my own.] Culler's explanation suggests two models of language origin. In the first, which is absurd, language would originate through a process of infinite regress. Originary language would be preceded by a still more originary language and so on and so forth. In the second, which is entirely plausible, the differentiation already exists in human cognition, where it so to speaks sits around waiting for a linguistic correlate to express itself. Unfortunately, this argument is no longer deconstructive, since it assumes the existence of a signified already existing in human consciousness before the signifier. What is really undecidable here is not the origin of the sign itself (which cannot be *known*) but whether there is a pre-existing "set" in human consciousness towards treating signs and things as unities or dualities. The entire history of culture suggests that both, in fact, are possible, and that the competition between both possibilities is the basis of cultural history.

8. For paleoanthropological arguments see Gans, *Chronicle* No. 52, "Generative Paleoanthropology," 27 July, 1996 (www.anthropoetics. ucla.edu/views/view52.htm). Gans's hypothesis is also compatible with Mircea Eliade's more general observation that religions must be founded in a sacred, holy place at the center of the world. See his *The Sacred and the Profane. The Nature of Religion* (San Diego: Harcourt, 1987).

9. Alan Ball, *American Beauty* (New York: Newmarket Press), 60.

10. Ball, *American Beauty*, 60 and 100, respectively.

11. Ball, *American Beauty*, 60.

12. For more on how the victimary mechanism operates in a religious context see Girard, *Things Hidden*, esp. Chapter 1, "The Victimage Mechanism as the Basis of Religion" (3–47).

13. See also Chapter Three in this book, 97.

14. See his *Frame Analysis. An Essay on the Organization of Experience* (Boston: Northeastern University Press, 1986).

15. The classic example of "keying" is the set of signals that transforms fighting into playing for animals (see *Frame Analysis*, 40–82).

16. Randal Collins, "Theoretical Continuities in Goffman's Work," in *Erving Goffman. Exploring the Interaction Order*, ed. by Paul Drew and Anthony Wooton (Boston: Northeastern University Press, 1988), 51.

17. *Frame Analysis*, 21.

18. *Frame Analysis*, 28–30.

19. *Frame Analysis*, 31–37.

20. The surprisingly good fit between Gans's and Goffman's theories is undoubtedly a result of their common Durkheimian heritage. For more on Goffman's indebtedness to Durkheim see Collins, "Theoretical Continuities"; for more on Gans's own positive appraisal of Durkheim see his "The Sacred and the Social: Defining Durkheim's Anthropological Legacy," *Anthropoetics* 1 (2000) (www.anthropoetics.ucla.edu/ ap0601/durkheim.htm).

21. For more on this see Collins, "Theoretical Continuities," 59–60.

22. *Frame Analysis*, 1.

23. Cf. Goffman, *Interaction Ritual. Essays on Face-to-Face Behavior* (New York: Pantheon, 1967), esp. "The Nature of Deference and Demeanor," 47–95.

24. *Interaction Ritual*, 95.

25. Based as it is on mutually held projections, the Durkheimian tradition is anathema to rigorous deconstructionists as well as other strains of poststructuralism drawing on the illusion-bashing philosophy of Nietzsche. Derrida's own send-up of the Durkheimian projection — his critique of Marcel Mauss's *The Gift* — can be found in in Chapter Two of his *Given Time. 1: Counterfeit Money* (Chicago: University of Chicago Press, 1992). See also the discussion of how Jean-Luc Marion reverses this criticism in Chapter Five, 178–182 in this book.

26. According to Girard's scapegoating mechanism, a collective works off its mimetically generated tension by lynching an arbitrarily chosen

victim, who is then deified after the fact as the group's saviour. In the case of *The Celebration* the scapegoating mechanism has a moral, rather than simply an energetic origin because the expulsion of the father is justified. Here as in many other cases in performatism, an archaic or originary scene returns outfitted with a constructed, modern-day rationale.

27. This occurs in the black comedy *Dogma*, in which two angels decide to return a God(dess) played by Alanis Morissette.

28. Ball, *American Beauty*, 57.

29. See the classic discussions in Jacques Lacan, "The Split between the Eye and the Gaze," in *The Four Fundamental Concepts of Psychoanalysis* (New York: Norton, 1981), 67–78 and Michel Foucault, *Discipline and Punish: The Birth of the Prison* (New York, Vintage Books, 1995), esp. "Panopticism," 195–230.

30. For more on this see Eric Gans's neoconservative critique of what he calls "victimary politics," e.g., in *Chronicle* Nr. 257, "Our Neo-Victimary Era," 2 March 2002
(www.anthropoetics.ucla.edu/views/ vw257.htm)

31. New York: Penguin, 2001.

32. His reading material towards the end of the movie includes *Frankenstein*, suggesting that he is aware of his own monstrosity.

33. Here as elsewhere I've adopted the narratological terminology developed by Franz Stanzel in *A Theory of Narrative* (Cambridge: Cambridge University Press, 1984). Stanzel's opposition of authorial/figural is best suited to describing the homologous relationship between a theist (authorial) creator/creatrix and his or her human (figural) creations. Stanzel himself excludes first-person authorial narration from his well-known tripartite classification scheme.

34. Ball, *American Beauty*, 1.

35. I have treated *Atonement* briefly in "Originary Aesthetics and the End of Postmodernism," *The Originary Hypothesis: a Minimal Proposal for Humanistic Inquiry*, ed. by Adam Katz (Aurora, Colo.: Davies Group, 2007), 59–82.

36. "Buben nizhnego mira" in Viktor Pelevin, *Sochineniya v dvukh tomakh. Tom I. Buben Nizhnego Mira* (Moscow: Terra, 1996), 362–366.

37. "Buben," 366.

38. In his collection *A Werewolf Problem in Central Russian and Other Stories* (New York: New Directions, 1998).

39. In his collection *The Blue Lantern and Other Stories* (New York: New Directions, 1997), 21–62.

40. For more on these terms as used by Jean-Luc Marion, see Chapter 5, 175–193.

41. Michel Foucault, *Herculine Barbin. Being the Recently Discovered Memoirs of a Nineteenth-Century French Hermaphrodite* (New York: Random House, 1980), XIII.

42. See the discussion in her *Gender Trouble: Feminism and the Subversion of Identity* (New York : Routledge, 1990), 23–24.

43. In postmodern literature, this principle is exemplified best in Sasha Sokolov's hilarious novel *Palisandriia* (Ann Arbor: Ardis, 1985), in which the hero, after a life of wild sexual and social transgressions, discovers at the end of the book that he was really a hermaphrodite all along.

44. New York: Farrar, Strauss and Giroux, 2002.

45. Evanston: Northwestern University Press, 2003 [Polish orig. 1998].

46. New York: Knopf, 2000.

47. See his *Topologie der Kunst* (Munich: Hanser, 2003), where he ducks the issue completely.

48. Michaels, *The Shape of the Signifier* (Princeton: Princeton University Press, 2004), 182. For a further discussion of Michaels' antitheory see Chapter Five, 162–164.

49. *Margins of Philosophy* (Chicago: University of Chicago Press, 1982), 20.

50. See in particular Derrida's "Some Statements and Truisms about Neologisms, Newisms, Postisms, Parasitisms, and Other Small Seisms," in *The States of 'Theory': History, Art, and Critical Discourse*, ed. by David Carroll (New York: Columbia University Press, 1990), 63–94; here 65.

51. See his "No Apocalypse, Not Now (Full Speed Ahead, Seven Missiles, Seven Missives)," *Diacritics* 2 (1984), 20–31.

52. See his *Is There a Text in this Class?* (Cambridge, Mass: Harvard University Press, 1982).

53. First introduced in *Chronicle* Nr. 209, 3 June 2000, "The Post-Millennial Age" (www.anthropoetics.ucla.edu/ views/vw209.htm). Gans develops a systematic epochal concept of history prior to postmillennialism in Part Two of his *Originary Thinking*, 117–219.

54. The flip side of the coin is that deist time can also end apocalyptically — see Derrida's "No Apocalypse, Not Now" or Leibniz's assertion in *Monadology* § 6, that the monads can only be created or be destroyed in one fell swoop ("tout d'un coup").

55. See Gilles Deleuze, *Cinema 2. The Time Image* (Minneapolis: University of Minnesota Press 1989), 40.

56. *Cinema 2*, 40.

57. *Cinema 2*, 41.

58. For more on this concept, which has been suggested by Jean-Luc Marion, see Chapter Five, 198–200.

59. For more on this architectonic concept see Chapter Four, 139.

Notes to Chapter 2

1. London: Penguin, 2001.

2. *Hotel World*, 181.

3. *Hotel World*, 30 and 237.

4. *Granta* 72 (2000), 35–54; Polish original "Numery" [Numbers] (1989), cited according to Tokarczuk's story collection *Szafa* (Wałbrzych: Ruta 1998), 10–39. Page numbers refer respectively to the English and Polish editions.

5. "Hotel Capital," 35/10.

6. "Hotel Capital," 35/10–11.

7. "Hotel Capital," 36/11.

8. See also Chapter Five in this book, 168–175.

9. See his *Sphären I. Blasen* [Spheres I. Bubbles] (Frankfurt a.M: Suhrkamp, 2000), esp. the introductory chapter "Die gehauchte Kommune," 17–82.

10. *The Sacred and the Profane. The Nature of Religion* (San Diego: Harcourt, 1987), 22.

11. *The Sacred and the Profane*, 21.

12. *The Sacred and the Profane*, 63.

13. See in this regard Gans's interpretation of Kant in terms of generative anthropology in his "Originary and/or Kantian Esthetics," *Poetica* 35 (2003), 335–353: "The ultimate source of our pleasure in the 'formal finality' of aesthetic representation is not our 'cognitive faculties' but our intuition that the community's shared participation in this finality or representational intentionality will protect us from

mimetic violence. The aesthetic performs a function analogous to that attributed by Durkheim to religious ritual: it reinforces our solidarity with the sacred center and, through its mediation, with our fellow members of the human community" (344).

14. "Hotel Capital," 36/11.

15. See the classic phrasing in § 22 of his *Critique of Judgment*. Kant, of course, suggests that this "necessity" is an expression of absolute cognitive freedom and does not consider the force that the text exerts upon the reader.

16. "Hotel Capital," 39/16.

17. "Hotel Capital," 39/16.

18. "Hotel Capital," 40/17.

19. "Hotel Capital," 40/17.

20. "Hotel Capital," 40/28.

21. "Hotel Capital," 44/29.

22. "Hotel Capital," 45/25.

23. "Hotel Capital," 45/31.

24. *Sphären I*, 40.

25. *Sphären I*, 42.

26. *Sphären I*, 46.

27. In the last volume of his philosophical trilogy *Sphären* [Spheres] Sloterdijk uses the ungrammatical metaphor of "foams" ("Schäume") to describe the inner experience of a modern life "developing in a multi-focal, multi-perspectival and heterarchical way" (*Sphären III. Schäume* [Frankfurt a.M.: Suhrkamp, 2004], 23). "Foams" serve as a post-metaphysical emblem of heterogeneous interiority and dyadic bonding as it occurs in modern and postmodern culture. For more on Sloterdijk see also Chapter Five in this book, 168–175.

28. In the case of Tokarczuk, these regulations are almost certainly derived from C.G. Jung's teachings on dreams and archetypes as well as from Mircea Eliade's studies on religion; readers familiar with Polish can check up on this for themselves in Tokarczuk's essay *Lalka i perła* [The doll and the pearl] (Cracow: Wydawnictwo Literackie, 2001) and her interview in Stanisław Bereś's *Historia literatury polskiej w rozmowach XX–XXI wiek* [A history of Polish literature of the 20th and 21st centuries in interviews] (Warsaw: WAB, 2002), 493–526. In the former book, an essay on Prus's realist classic *The Doll*, Tokarczuk borrows the concept of a higher quasi-divine ego or "observer" from

Jung; the observer encompasses the authorial ego and influences it in a symbolic way that cannot be reconstructed rationally (16–18). The chambermaid, so one must assume, is a personified instrument of the author, who is in turn guided by this higher, originary, and apriori source. In this regard it is significant, as Sloterdijk has pointed out in a different context, that Jung's "observer" is derived from a tradition encompassing both the tutelary gods of antiquity and Kant's transcendental formula "I think" (see *Sphären I*, 426 and 454).

29. "Hotel Capital," 51/34.

30. "Hotel Capital," 47/28.

31. "Hotel Capital," 47/28–29.

32. "Hotel Capital," 48/29–30.

33. "Hotel Capital," 48/29–30.

34. "Hotel Capital," 49/30.

35. "Hotel Capital," 50/33.

36. "Hotel Capital," 41/19.

37. "Hotel Capital," 41/19.

38. "Hotel Capital," 41/19. The emendation is my own: "prehistory" was left out of the English translation.

39. "Hotel Capital," 53–54/38. The Polish Bible translation is much more emphatic; the last phrase reads: "And God will restore that which is past." [R.E.]

40. Edinburgh: Cannongate, 2002.

41. *Life of Pi*, 69.

42. Gans coined the term in *The Origin of Language* (Berkeley: University of California Press, 1981); for his most recent definition of the term see *Signs of Paradox. Irony, Resentment, and Other Mimetic Structures* (Stanford: Stanford University Press, 1997).

43. Cf. Gans, *Signs of Paradox*: "The truth of the originary sign is the birth of the human. The sign is what protects the human community against its potential self-annihilation in mimetic conflict. In the face of this danger, its truth as a gesture of representation rather than a gesture of appropriation is not a foregone conclusion. It is only because the members of the originary community accepted this truth as the revelation of central Being that we are here to speculate about it. They drew back from conflict because they were able to interpret their own acts not as spontaneous movements toward the center but as ostensive signs designating the agent that prevented this movement" (53).

44. The book leaves the question of whether there really is a God open by resorting to the Cabbalistic doctrine of Tsimtsum, in which God creates the world and retracts back into Himself (the Japanese ship carrying Pi and his family is named "Tsimtsum" and Pi himself studies the Cabbala). The doctrine suggests that there is a single origin but that we simply have no way of corroborating it anymore.

45. In this sense performatism reverses the basic procedure of the phenomenological *epokhē*: a situation is bracketed so that we experience beauty instead of acquiring knowledge. For more on Jean-Luc Marion's new monist use of bracketing in phenomenology, see Chapter Five, 193–194.

46. While performatism is an epochal, and not a general theory of literature, it is in keeping with the growing relevance of theories concerned with aesthetics, ethics, and positive reader response rather than with linguistic or epistemological misprision. For more on this turn in literary theory see Winfried Fluck, "Fiction and Justice," *New Literary History* 34 (2003), 19–42.

47. In other words, it does the opposite of the Derridean frame, which mediates in an undecidable way between inside and out. For a further discussion of the frame in performatism, see Chapter One, 2–8.

48. As Eric Gans points out in his "Originary and/or Kantian Aesthetics," "the pleasure in the moment of sharing exists only against a constantly renewed background of 'painful' desire that Kant does not mention"; hence the aesthetic experience "can best be conceived in Kantian terms as an oscillation between the pleasure of beauty and the pain of sublimity" (343). Performative texts in effect guarantee this oscillation by placing around a beautiful center coercive, "painful" frames that remind the reader of the limits of beauty while at the same time making the experience of beauty possible in the first place.

49 London: Picador, 1999; German original: *Simple Storys* (Berlin: Berlin Verlag, 1998). Page numbers refer respectively to the English and German editions.

50. In *What We Talk About When We Talk About Love* (New York: Vintage, 1989), 37–45.

51. This applies above all to stories written before the collection *Cathedral*, which is widely thought to mark a turn towards optimism in Carver's work.

52. This apprehension of menace is in fact often mentioned in connection with reader reactions to Carver's fiction, and it would seem to account for a good deal of its success with upscale readers; see in this regard Adam Meyer, *Raymond Carver* (New York: Twayne, 1995), 22–23.

53. Presumably, Schulze was aware that "Sacks" is a heavily trimmed-down version of Carver's story "The Fling," which uses the same plot but supplies much more detail. In "The Fling," for example, we learn that the cuckolded husband committed suicide in a particularly painful way.

54. *What We Talk About*, 37.

55. *Simple Stories*, 86/102.

56. *Simple Stories*, 89/104.

57. *Simple Stories*, 90/105.

58. *Simple Stories*, 90/105.

59. In Carver's story, it is the adulterous wife who gets religion at an expedient moment: "She got down on her knees and she prayed to God, good and loud so the man would hear" (45); in "The Fling," the cuckolded husband goes so far as to commit suicide.

60. *Simple Stories*, 93/109.

61. *Simple Stories*, 95/111.

62. *Simple Stories*, 201/220.

63. *Simple Stories*, 86/101.

64. *Simple Stories*, 91/106.

65. *Simple Stories*, 91/106.

66. London: Flamingo, 1997.

67. See such polemical non-fiction works as *The Cost of Living* (London: Flamingo, 1999), *Power Politics* (Cambridge, Mass.: South End Press, 2001), and *War Talk* (Cambridge, Mass.: South End Press, 2003).

68 Spivak first used the concept in her article "Deconstructing Historiography," (orig. 1985); cited according to *The Spivak Reader* (New York: Routledge, 1996), eds. Donna Landry and Gerald MacLean, 203–235, esp. 214–215.

69. Spivak, who mixes Marxism and deconstruction, eventually stopped using the term herself, which she said "simply became the union ticket for essentialism" (see the interview with her in *Boundary 2*, 20:2 [1993], 24–50; here: 35). As Boris Groys points out in his

witty essay *Unter Verdacht* [Under suspicion] (Munich: Hanser 2000) this poststructuralist obfuscation of subjectivity eventually leads to its restitution. The less we have a handle on what the agent or subject is up to, the greater is our suspicion that he or she is really there — and pulling off something devious behind our backs (29–43). For more on Groys's theory of suspicion in the media see also Chapter Five in this book, 164–168.

70. "The End of Imagination," in *The Cost of Living*, 144.

71. "The End of Imagination," 145.

72. "The End of Imagination," 159.

73. The two characters, in other words, combine appealing physical qualities with the status of social otherness. For an incisive reinterpretation of Kant's concept of beauty as one of otherness see Tobin Siebers, "Kant and the Politics of Beauty," *Philosophy and Literature* 1 (1998), 31–50. According to Siebers, this focus on beauty-as-otherness need not be unpolitical: "Admittedly, beauty provokes otherness on a small scale — a human scale in fact — but perhaps this is where otherness has the greatest political value, since the small scale forces individuals to confront otherness within their world rather than referring it to an external reality" (37). Roy takes this a step further: at some point, her beauty-as-otherness turns into sameness by allowing an identification across all boundaries of culture and ideology. The "God of small things" — the God of sublimity and beauty — is a global One.

74. *God of Small Things*, 327.

75. *God of Small Things*, 328.

76. As Eric Gans has pointed out repeatedly in his internet *Chronicles of Love and Resentment*, postmodernism's focus on decentered otherness (as opposed to utopian master narratives) leads to an ethical mindset privileging peripheral victims. From Gans's neoconservative point of view, this attitude is productive in its rejection of centralized authoritarianism but unproductive in its reliance on resentment. Roy certainly wouldn't agree with Gans's notion that we should all warmly embrace global capitalism and bourgeois democracy, but her position is consistent with Gans's in that it stresses reconciliation, love, and beauty — and a break with the guilt-producing mode of victimary discourse. For more on this see also the discussion of *The Reader* further below.

77. *God of Small Things*, 176.
78. *God of Small Things*, 333–334.
79. *God of Small Things*, 230.
80. This universalist pretension has been noted by numerous authors. For those still obligated to postmodern norms this can only appear as a sellout: Marta Dvorak, for example, in her article "Translating the Foreign into the Familiar: Arundhati Roy's Postmodern Sleights of Hand," in *Reading Arundhati Roy's* The God of Small Things, ed. by Carol and Jean-Pierre Durix (Dijon: Editions universitaires de Dijon, 2002), 41–61, criticizes Roy for addressing not her "own community but an allogenous one" and for engaging in a "dynamics of domestication and familiarisation" (61) rather than playing up the non-reciprocal otherness of her own cultural experience.
81. See his article "Our History," *diacritics* 3 (1990), 97–115, esp. 105.
82. Gans describes this postideological scenario in the following way ("On Esthetic Periodization," *Chronicles of Love and Resentment* 258, March 23, 2002, www.anthropoetics.ucla.edu/views/vw258.htm): "Where modernist politics is cruel, postmodern politics is victimary. Its scenic imagination, haunted by the image of victimization, conceives an ideal scene without a sacred center, where all is periphery. [...] Postmodern politics has an infinity of tasks; it sees every form of human relation as at least potentially victimary. Where the postmodern esthetic shies from constructing a center, postmodern politics finds in every mode of human interaction a center to deconstruct, construed as the locus, not of sacrifice, but of power."
83. As Phillipe Lacoue-Labarthe puts it in his *La Fiction du Politique. Heidegger, L'art et la politique* (Paris: Bourgois, 1987), the Holocaust is, regarding the West, the "terrible revelation of its essence" ("L'Extermination, est à l'égard de l'Occident la terrible révélation de son essence" [63]).
84. See Eric Gans, *Chronicles of Love and Resentment* No. 120, 13 December 1997, "Victimage and Virtual Inclusion" (www.anthropoetics.ucla.edu/views/vw120.htm).
85. Eisenman's plan was widely criticized in Germany for being too abstract. Eventually, the German government made him include an information center in the concept so as to provide at least some form of historical documentation. For a full account of the debates regarding the Memorial see Bill Niven, *Facing the Nazi Past. United*

Germany and the Legacy of the Third Reich (London & New York: Routledge, 2002), esp. Chapter 8, "The Holocaust Memorial," 194–232.

86. The museum, which was open to visitors while it was still empty, proved to be a popular attraction solely on the basis of its architectonic effects.

87. New York: Pantheon, 1997; German original: *Der Vorleser* (Zurich: Diogenes 1995).

88. See in particular Omer Bartov, "Germany as Victim," *New German Critique*, 80 (2000), 29–40; J.J. Long, "Bernhard Schlink's *Der Vorleser* and Binjamin Wilkomirski's *Bruchstücke*: Best-Selling Responses to the Holocaust," in *German Language and Literature Today: International and Popular*, eds. Arthur Williams, Stuart Parkes and Julian Preece (Oxford: Peter Lang, 2000), 49–66; Helmut Schmitz, "Malen nach Zahlen? Bernhard Schlinks *Der Vorleser* und die Unfähigkeit zu trauern," [Painting by numbers? Schlink's *The Reader* and the inability to mourn] *German Life and Letters* 3 (2002), 296–311; and Ernestine Schlant, *The Language of Silence. West German Literature and the Holocaust* (New York & London: Routledge, 1999), 207–216.

89. Schlink, who is a professor of law and a practicing attorney, "frames" his heroine in a very deliberate way. Hanna's guilt is made explicit by confronting her with an extraordinary situation requiring an easily made act of free choice; the crime is however mitigated somewhat because it is unpremeditated and passive. Also, it remains unclear whether Hanna was simply doing her duty or whether she was "cruel and uncontrolled" like another guard called the "Mare" (see *The Reader*, 118–119). The weak circumstantial evidence of Hanna's brutality is evidently meant to make us decide *in dubio pro reo*.

90. This initiation is symbolically sanctioned by his mother, who sends him to "Frau Schmitz" so that he may thank her for helping him after he was sick in public.

91. *The Reader*, 196.

92. See in particular Long, "Best-Selling Responses": "By accepting the proffered identification with Hanna, the reader can abdicate responsibility for engaging with the vexed moral questions that any serious discussion of the Holocaust necessarily raises" (55).

93. See Bartov, "Germany as Victim": "[...] metaphorically, Michael *becomes* the Jewish victim, both by virtue with his association with

Hanna as the reader, and thanks to the grace of his late birth, which prevented him from becoming a perpetrator. Yet, even as he tilts toward the category of victim, Schlink contextualizes his tale within a framework of emotional numbness and sexual obsession, both of which are above or below morality, since the former is a blank and a void, and the latter is involuntary and uncontrollable. Thus numbness and obsession are a means to avoid responsibility and reject all ethical categories" (34).

94. Both Schmitz in "Malen nach Zahlen?" and Bartov in "Germany as Victim" diagnose Michael as suffering from the syndrome defined by the Mitscherlichs.

95. See Alexander and Margarete Mitscherlich, *Die Unfähigkeit zu trauern* [The inability to mourn] (Munich: Piper, 1988 [orig. 1967]): "[...] we must broaden the insight into ourselves so that we recognize ourselves in those horrifying scenes [...] in which 100, 500 or 1,000 corpses lie before us — corpses of those we have killed. That would mean an insightful, empathetic acceptance of victims long after the time of terror has passed" (82).

96. Schmitz, "Malen nach Zahlen?," 311.

97. See Bartov, "Germany as Victim," 40. If I understand Bartov's use of a Primo Levi quote correctly, this direct experience of Holocaust terror — akin to looking at the Gorgon's head and turning to stone — is impossible anyway; all we can do is belatedly cobble together our ravaged post-Holocaust identity in a quasi-fictional, simulatory way. Hence Wilkomirski's fraudulent memoirs, which mourn virtually, are more acceptable to Bartov than Schlink's inability to mourn at all in the postmodern mode.

98. For more on Goffman's concept of framing and performatism see Chapter One in this book, 10–12.

99. See in particular Goffman's essay "The Nature of Deference and Demeanor," in Erving Goffman, *Interaction Ritual. Essays on Face-to-Face Behavior* (New York: Pantheon, 1967), 47–96, in particular 95.

100. Even *The Reader*'s harshest critics, such as Bartov and Long, agree that Michael's representation of Hanna cannot be taken at face value. Both suggest however that Schlink has not distanced himself enough from Michael's perspective.

101. For a full discussion see his *Things Hidden Since the Foundation of the World* (Stanford: Stanford University Press, 1987), esp.

3–30. Bill Niven, in a similar argument, has linked Hanna's behavior with a "culture of shame" (as opposed to a "culture of guilt"). See his subtly argued and perspicacious article "Bernhard Schlink's *Der Vorleser* and the Problem of Shame," *Modern Language Review* 2 (2003), 381–396.

102. See Niven, "The Problem of Shame,": "It is as if she [Hanna] had hoped to slip back into the role of passive recipient. Realizing that this will not be possible, she escapes, in carefully stage-managed style, into suicide" (395).

103. Typical of this is the line taken by Nancy in "Our History." According to this way of thinking, any "humanist" or "democratic" attempt to project a feeling of social community or hope is an unconscious repetition of the fascist project (115). The only tenable alternative to this kind of self-delusion is the critical act of "taking history to its limit" — with that limit being marked, apparently endlessly, by our attitude toward events now lying three generations in the past.

104. I've treated Pelevin in more detail in my article "Thematischer und performativer Minimalismus bei Eric Gans und Viktor Pelevin," [Thematic and performative minimalism in Eric Gans and Viktor Pelevin] in *Minimalismus zwischen Leere und Exzeß* [Minimalism between emptiness and excess], ed. by Mirjam Goller and Georg Witte, *Wiener Slawistischer Almanach Sonderband* 51 (2001), 233–247; the article compares Pelevin's fictional monism and approach to capitalism with Gans's generative anthropology.

105. Original: *Sedmikostelí. Gotický román z Prahy* [Sevenchurch. A gothic novel of Prague] (Prague: Argo, 1999). The novel has been translated into German as *Die Rache der Baumeister. Ein Kriminalroman aus Prag* [The revenge of the architects. A detective story of Prague] (Berlin: Rowohlt, 2001).

106. *Sedmikostelí*, 64.

107. *Sedmikostelí*, 326.

108. By contrast, Urban's other recent book, *Hastrman* [The water demon] (Prague: Argo, 2001) supplies us with a plausible object of ideological identification. The half-piscine, half-human hero, who in the 19th century acts as a cruel avenger of human hubris, returns in the 20th as a merciless green terrorist. In the end, however, he is able to recognize the superiority of a political or symbolic vengeance over a purely physical one. In this case, Urban draws on Kant directly.

The amoral, fish-like hero, who in the 19th century once boasted of "the starry sky within me and the moral law beside me" (29) becomes a true Kantian in the 20th: he recognizes that the green commune whose members he helps "have at least for the time being foregone their egoism and have become parts of a perfectly functioning whole" (393). Realizing that his avenging function is superfluous, the hero allows himself to be violently and ritually sacrificed for the good of the green cause — something entirely in keeping with the tenets of an archaically founded Kantianism.

Notes to Chapter 3

1. A commune member pretending to be mentally retarded is left by his "attendant" in the company of several fierce-looking motorcycle gang members, who interpret his grunting attempt to leave them as a wish to use the toilet. Assuming that he is truly severely retarded, they have no qualms about helping him urinate.
2. The Derridean approach to framing aims to show that there is no way to discuss intrinsic, inner space without including extrinisic, outer space in it. Hence the frame, which is where inside and outside meet, constitutes itself out of an irreducible duality which, for Derrida, is the paradoxical point of departure and end point of all analysis.
3. It is interesting to note that Erving Goffman's notion of face-to-face interaction works in a similar way. The reliability of interaction is made possible by the "fit" between the self (inner frame) and an outer frame (meaning the physical world, the social ecology and the institutional setting). As Collins suggests in his "Theoretical Continuities in Goffman's Work," in *Erving Goffman. Exploring the Interaction Order*, ed. by Paul Drew and Anthony Wooton (Boston: Northeastern University Press, 1988), "only if the larger frame is properly handled can conversation take place" (51).
4. *The World in a Frame. What We See in Films* (Chicago: University of Chicago Press, 2002), 44–51.
5. *World in a Frame*, 48.
6. 1987, 48–49.
7. See his *Cinema 1. The Movement Image* (Minneapolis: University of Minnesota Press, 1986) and *Cinema 2. The Time Image* (Minneapolis: University of Minnesota Press, 1989).

8. Buddhism, which also plays a role in performatism, is a special case. Although dispensing with the notion of a personal God, Buddhist-influenced fictions such as *Ghost Dog* and *American Beauty* suggest no less than Western theist fictions that reality is constructed around a subject, and that the subject, in order to transcend, must merge with that construct.

9. See Gans's treatment of this in his "Originary and/or Kantian Aesthetics," *Poetica* 35 (2003), 335–353.

10. See "Performatism, or the End of Postmodernism," *Anthropoetics* 2 (2000/2001) (www.anthropoetics.ucla. edu/ap0602/perform.htm).

11. For more on the theory of aspirated inner space developed by Peter Sloterdijk, see Chapter Five, 168–175.

12. Goffman's *Interaction Ritual. Essays on Face-to-Face Behavior* (New York: Pantheon, 1967) warns of this: "If the individual could give himself the deference he desired there might be a tendency for society to disintegrate into islands inhabited by solitary cultish men, each in continuous worship at his own shrine" (58). See also Jean-Luc Marion's critique of solipsism, discussed in Chapter Five in this book, 199–200.

13. For more on the dyadic character of theism see also the discussion of Peter Sloterdijk's spherology in Chapter Five in this book, 169–171.

14. *Cinema 2*, 263.

15. *Cinema 1*, 62.

16. *Cinema 1*, 20.

17. Cf. *Cinema 2*: "[...] the essence of the cinematographic movement-image lies in extracting from vehicles or moving bodies the movement which is their common substance, or extracting from movements the mobility which is their essence" (23).

18. Cf. Deleuze *Cinema 2*: "[...] the sensory-motor schema is no longer in operation, but at the same time it is not overtaken or overcome. It is shattered from the inside. That is, perceptions and actions ceased to be linked together, and spaces are now neither co-ordinated nor filled. [...] It is here that the reversal is produced: movement is no longer simply aberrant, aberration is now valid in itself and designates time as its direct cause. Time is 'out of joint': it is off the hinges assigned to it by behavior in the world, but also by movements of the world" (40–41).

19. *Cinema 2*, 41.

20. See also Fredric Jameson's discussion in his *Postmodernism, or the Cultural Logic of Late Capitalism* (Durham: Duke University Press, 1992), 295.

21. Ethan and Joel Coen, *The Man Who Wasn't There* (London: Faber and Faber, 2001), 26.

22. Sven Spieker, of the University of California at Santa Barbara, suggested to me that Ed Crane's longing for a transcendent world is caused by his being homosexual. At first, this doesn't seem convincing at all. Ed rejects a pass made by Creighton Tolliver, and, if anything, seems to be asexual — he doesn't sleep with his wife and crashes his car after Birdie Abundas makes him an unambiguous offer. However, some small clues indicate that a repressed sense of opposite genderedness plays a major role in his spiritual quest. For example, before Ed is electrocuted, a patch of his leg is shaved in the exact way that Ed shaved a patch of Doris's leg earlier on, suggesting that the only way a man could be treated like a woman in the 1940s is in the death chamber. Also, Ed is writing his story for a men's magazine featuring pictures of half-naked, muscular hunks on the cover — the only type of venue where repressed homosexuality could safely be expressed in the 1940s. If Spieker's theory is true, Ed would not be looking to express his homosexuality in 1940s-style terms — as a "pansy" like Creighton Tolliver — but in transcendent ones as yet unknown to himself, and in fact also to us. Doris (with her masculine, blunt personality and anti-Italian self hatred) and Ed would then be reunited in a Great Beyond where all gender and ethnic distinctions have been overcome for good.

23. *The Man Who Wasn't There*, 104–105.

24. *The Man Who Wasn't There*, 66–67.

25. *The Man Who Wasn't There*, 100–101.

26. As Gans notes in his *Chronicle* Nr. 83, 8 March 19977, "Film Open and Closed," (www.anthropoetics.ucla.edu/views/ view83.htm) the universalization of color in movies and TV "makes impossible the abstract shadow-world of the *film noir* and its closed predecessors." By making an aesthetically "impossible" movie, the Coen Brothers suggest the possibility that any frame of reference can be transcended — as a one-time performance.

27. "After 'After': The Arkive Fever of Alexander Sokurov," 5 May 2003 (www.artmargins.com).

28. "An Ark for a Pair of Media: Sokurov's *Russian Ark*," 5 May 2003 (www.artmargins.com).
29. See the discussion of this in Kujundzić, "Arkive Fever."
30. For more on this see www.dogme95.dk.
31. As outlined in his *Sculpting in Time: Reflections on the Cinema* (New York: Alfred A. Knopf, 1987), 113–121.
32. *Cinema 2*, 40–41.
33. *Cinema 2*, 34–35.
34. Within the inescapable, treacly real time of the shot Sokurov and Büttner use numerous tricks to speed up or modulate our apprehension of time, most notably through camera movement and/or the use of music. Also, as Oliver Baumgarten has noted in an article in the internet version of the film magazine *Schnitt* (www.schnitt.de/filme/artikel/russian_ark.shtml), Büttner uses ersatz-cuts to compensate for the lack of the real thing. When things start to slow down, for example, he does a closeup (of gloved hands, for example) and then swings the camera around to a long shot with full depth of field, thus simulating the mechanics of the cut within real time.
35. "Archive Fever."
36. Although even this argument seems forced sometimes. The classic artistic (and clinical) figure of the melancholic doesn't *move*. If the camera stroll through the Hermitage is supposed to exemplify melancholy, then it's a pretty lively variant of it.
37. You could probably also argue with Deleuze that Leonard's type of consciousness is a "spiritual automaton," a highly restricted reaction to outside impulses directed by a single, deeply embedded memory. However, in Deleuzian and Bergsonian terms Leonard's condition embodies "bad" time — a series of presents that are chopped out of the flow of time and then pasted back together again. It is only in the pathological dysfunctionality of this minimal setting that the theist and deist conceptions can meet.
38. Andy Klein, in his "Everything You Wanted to Know about Memento,'" *Salon Magazine* 28 June 2001 (www.salon.com), invested enough energy for five film reviews in trying to untangle *Memento's* plot and came to the conclusion that it doesn't work even on its own terms: "the only way to reconcile everything is to assume huge inconsistencies in the nature of Leonard's disorder. In fact, in real life, such inconsistencies apparently exist, if Oliver Sacks is to be believed. But

to build the plot around them without giving us some hints seems like dirty pool."

39. See his *Chronicle* Nr. 269, 31 August 2002, "Mulholland Drive." (www.anthropoetics.ucla.edu/views/vw269.htm).

40. See, for example, Nr. 42, 11 May 1996 "Tarentino Transcendence" (www.anthropoetics.ucla.edu/ views/vw42.htm) or Nr. 80, 15 February 1997, "Triangular Utopias" (www.anthropoetics.ucla.edu/ views/ vw80.htm).

Notes to Chapter 4

1. Analogous to the theist God, who places humankind into an imperfect framework in which He then intervenes in unpredictable, unknowable ways. Like acts of God in general, theist devices appear to be pointless or unmotivated.

2. Readers familiar with deconstructive discourse will recognize this as the exact theological opposite of what is done by deconstruction. For deconstruction, such defects or lacunae mark the fatal nothingness lurking beyond signification. The whole point of occidental metaphysics, from its perspective, is to cover up, defer or deny these markers through the application of ever more discursive twists and turns. The melancholy, metaphysically pessimistic goal of deconstruction is to critique this cover-up or repression through the application of its *own* discourse, which in turn helps realize precisely that deferral which it itself is unmasking.

3. Cf. the discussion in Fritz Neumeyer, *Mies van der Rohe. Das kunstlose Wort. Gedanken zur Baukunst* [Mies van der Rohe. The Artless Word. Thoughts on Architecture] (Berlin: Siedler, 1986), esp. 147–174.

4. Colin Rowe and Robert Slutzky, *Transparency* (Basel: Birkhäuser Verlag, 1997 [orig. 1955]).

5. *Signs of Paradox*, 39.

6. *Signs of Paradox*, 40.

7. The Flatiron building in New York is the exception confirming the rule: occasionally, intersecting streets really *do* require acute angles. In performatist works, the acuteness is always optional.

8. One could oppose this to Heidegger's notion of the *Geviert* or fourfold as the point of architectonic origin, as outlined in his "Building,

Dwelling, Thinking," in *Rethinking Architecture. A Reader in Cultural Theory*, ed. by Neil Leach (London & New York: Routledge, 1997), 100–108. Whereas the performative threefold relation is pre-semantic and ostensive, the fourfold relation between "earth and air, men and gods" is necessarily already semantic or, as Gans and Derrida would say, metaphysical. In his own remarks on architecture in "Architecture Where the Desire May Live" (in *Rethinking Architecture*, 319–323) Derrida suggests two by now familiar patterns derived from his text analyses. Architecture may either be labyrinthine, a mark of the failure of the Tower of Babel to impose a universal language/architecture on humankind (322), or "an experience of the Supreme which is not higher but in a sense more ancient than space and therefore is a spatialization of time" (323) — in other words, an architectural incarnation of *différance*. In this last instance, Derrida is a hair's breadth away from generative anthropology's notion of the human and the sacred. What is missing, as always, is the causal nexus that would explain why this leap from time to space came about in the first place. Derrida's originary moment remains a brilliant, self-engendering act without any anchoring in the scene of the human.

9. Gehry himself considers these structures to be no longer postmodern. However, the Nationale-Nederlanden Building in Prague (popularly called "Ginger and Fred" or "The Dancing House") as well as the so-called "Horse's Head" conference room in the DG Bank contain anthropomorphic elements reminiscent of the postmodern habit of semanticizing architectonic relations. Moreover, the "Horse's Head" contains what look to me like large buckyballs, thus suggesting — by way of quotation — a double origin of undular organicity and angular crystality.

10. *Signs of Paradox*, 29.

11. *Signs of Paradox*, 29.

12. See Fredric Jameson, *Postmodernism or, the Cultural Logic of Late Capitalism*, (Durham: Duke University Press, 1991), 108–118.

13. For more on this technique see Fritz Neumeyer, "A World in Itself: Architecture and Technology," in *The Presence of Mies*, ed. by Detlef Mertins (Princeton: Princeton Architectural Press, 1994), 71–84; here 78.

14. Falk Jaeger, *Architektur für das neue Jahrtausend* [Architecture for the new Millennium] (Stuttgart: Deutsche Verlagsanstalt, 2001).

15. *Architektur*, 179.

16. See Claus Käplinger, "Monumentaler Raum der Stille" [Monumental Space of Silence], *Tagesspiegel*, 29 November 1998 (www2. tagesspiegel.de/archiv/1998/11/30/ku-ar-9330.html).

17. See the interview with Schultes "Die Republik muss sich wichtig nehmen" [The Republic must take itself seriously], *Der Spiegel*, Nr. 17, April 2001, 200–206 (also available at www.spiegel.de/spiegel/ 0,1518,130871,00.html).

18. Hanno Rauterberg, "Enthusiast des neuen Raums" [Enthusiast of the new space], *Die Zeit* Nr. 42, 12 October 2000, 51 (also available at www.zeit.de/2000/42/Kultur/200042_schultes.html).

19. The mainstream press's reaction to the Chancellery has been mixed. A positive view can be found in Rauterberg's "Enthusiast des neuen Raumes." For more on the standard criticism directed at the building see the above-cited *Spiegel* interview "Die Republik muss sich wichtig nehmen."

20. In Gans's reckoning, post-millennialism starts with the reunification of Central Europe and the victory of capitalism, rather than with the year 2000.

21. See "Die Republik muss sich wichtig nehmen."

22. See Jaeger, *Architektur für das neue Jahrtausend*, 68.

23. Mathias Oswald Ungers, "Der Entwurf für die Badische Landesbibliothek in Karlsruhe" [The plan for the State Library of Baden in Karlsruhe], *Buch. Leser. Bibliothek. Festschrift der Badischen Landesbibliothek zum Neubau*, [Book. Reader. Library. Festschrift celebrating the completion of the State Library in Baden], ed. by Gerhard Römer (Karlsruhe, 1992), 63–69.

24. "Entwurf," 68.

25. "Entwurf," 68.

26. "Entwurf," 68.

Notes for Chapter 5

1. *Life after Postmodernism. Essays on Value and Culture*, ed. by John Fekete (New York: St. Martin's Press, 1987).

2. See in particular *Against Theory. Literary Studies and the New Pragmatism*, ed. by W.J.T. Mitchell (Chicago: University of Chicago Press, 1985).

3. See Knapp and Michaels' critique of de Man in *Against Theory*, 22–23.

4. His recent book *The Shape of the Signifier. 1967 to the End of History* (Princeton: Princeton University Press, 2004), is a stinging critique of postmodernism and poststructuralism that, however, presents no positive alternative to them.

5. Groys is best known in America for his *The Total Art of Stalinism: Avant-garde, Aesthetic Dictatorship, and Beyond* (Princeton University Press: Princeton, 1992) a controversial — and, in my view, ultimately successful — attempt to reintegrate Stalinist culture into an epochal concept of cultural history.

7. *Über das Neue. Versuch einer Kulturökonomie* (Munich: Hanser 1992).

8. *Über das Neue*, 150.

9. See *Über das Neue*: "The successful, true description changes the boundary path separating the valorized and the profane and in succeeding robs itself of its own truth" (151).

10. *Über das Neue*, 48.

11. *Unter Verdacht. Eine Phänomenologie der Medien* [Under suspicion. A Phenomenology of the Media] (München: Hanser 2000).

12. *Unter Verdacht*, 7.

13. *Unter Verdacht*, 23.

14. *Unter Verdacht*, 73.

15. *Sphären I. Blasen* [Spheres I. Bubbles] (Frankfurt a.M.: Suhrkamp, 1998); *Sphären II. Globen* [Spheres II. Globes] (Frankfurt a.M.: Suhrkamp, 1999); *Sphären III. Schäume* [Spheres III. Foams] (Frankfurt a.M.: Suhrkamp, 2004).

16. See his *The Sacred and the Profane. The Nature of Religion* (San Diego: Harcourt, 1987).

17. *Sphären I*, 63.

18. *Sphären I*, 29.

19. *Sphären I*, 46.

20. *Sphären I*, 38.

21. *Sphären III*, 78.

22. In Martin Heidegger, *Basic Writings* (New York: Harper, 1993), 139–212. Sloterdijk, although not uncritical of dangers posed by technology, has none of Heidegger's rooted-in-the-sod, anti-modern bias. In keeping with his attempt to describe the "worst-best of all possible

worlds" (III, 878) Sloterdijk also accords considerable space to a treatment of what he calls "atmoterrorism" (III, 89–125).

23. See *Sphären III*, 78 as well as *Monadology*, § 61.
24. *Sphären I*, 32.
25. *Sphären I*, 41.
26. *Sphären I*, 40.
27. *Sphären III*, 872.
28. *A Thousand Plateaus: Capitalism and Schizophrenia* (London: Athlone Press, 1988), 3–25.
29. *Sphären III*, 302.
30. *Sphären III*, 302.
31. *Sphären III*, 303.
32. *Sphären III*, 298.
33. See *Sphären I*, 423–424 as well as the discussion of Olga Tokarczuk's "The Hotel Capital" in Chapter Two of this book, 44–53. The position of the synthetic *observator* injects a Kantian corrective into Sloterdijk's otherwise Leibnizian thinking.
34. See his main work, *The Laws of Imitation* (Gloucester, Mass.: P. Smith, 1962). Sloterdijk also draws on a work obscure even in its own time, *Monadologie et sociologie*, (Paris: Institut Synthélabo, 1999 [orig. 1893]).
35. *Thousand Plateaus*, 218–219.
36. *Sphären III*, 61.
37. As outlined in *Deceit, Desire and the Novel. Self and Other in Literary Structure* (Baltimore: Johns Hopkins Press, 1965).
38. *Sphären III*, 406.
39. *Sphären III*, 411.
40. *Sphären III*, 261–308. Sloterdijk titles this position "Neither Contract nor Natural Growth" [Nicht Vertrag, nicht Gewächs].
41. *Sphären III*, 876.
42. *Sphären III*, 877–8.
43. See Chapter One in this book, note 2, 230.
44. *Being Given. Toward a Phenomenology of Givenness* (Stanford: Stanford University Press, 2002 [French orig. 1997]).
45. *Being Given*, 40.
46. *Being Given*, 45–46.
47. *Being Given*, 43.
48. *Being Given*, 40.

49. *Being Given*, 47.
50. *Being Given*, 47.
51. *Being Given*, 48.
52. *Being Given*, 48.
53. *Being Given*, 48.
54. In conventional terms anamorphosis is a distorted image that requires an odd or unusual angle to be seen in proportion. For Marion's own definition see *Being Given*, 119–125.
55. *Given Time. 1: Counterfeit Money* (Chicago: University of Chicago Press, 1992).
56. *Given Time*, Chapter 2, passim.
57. *Being Given*, 81.
58. *Being Given*, 83.
59. *Being Given*, 91.
60. *Being Given*, 91.
61. *Being Given*, 91.
62. *Being Given*, 104.
63. *Being Given*, 99.
64. *Being Given*, 99.
65. See *Being Given*, 113.
66. For more on Goffman's relation to performatism see Chapter One, 10–12.
67. *Being Given*, 178. Here the relevant passage in full:

> [...] Couldn't we imagine, by contrast, that givenness admits variation by degree? On this hypothesis, the determinations of the given phenomenon, while remaining originary and definitively acquired, would modulate with variable intensity. As a result, thresholds of phenomenality in terms of givenness would define discontinuous strata of phenomena, which would then be distinguished by their level of givenness and no longer by their belonging to a region. [...]

68. For a discussion of keying, see Goffman's *Frame Analysis. An Essay on the Organization of Experience* (Boston: Northeastern University Press, 1986), 40–82.
69. For more on this see Randal Collins, "Theoretical Continuities in Goffman's Work," in *Erving Goffman. Exploring the Interaction Order*, eds., Paul Drew and Anthony Wooton (Boston: Northeastern University Press, 1988), 41–64.

70. To put this another way, it seems to me that Marion's phenomenological argumentation has less to fear from a confrontation with Goffman's frame analysis than does Derrida's deconstruction, which regards quotidian convention as a perhaps necessary, but nonetheless misguided, illusion.

71. *Being Given*, 193.

72. See *Being Given*, 194–195.

73. *Being Given*, 195.

74. *Being Given*, 195.

75. *Being Given*, 195.

76. *Being Given*, 198.

77. *Critique of Judgment*, § 57.

78. *Being Given*, 228.

79. *Being Given*, 229.

80. *Being Given*, 229.

81. *Being Given*, 229.

82. *Being Given*, 230.

83. *Being Given*, 230.

84. See the *Critique of Judgment*, § 22.

85. *Being Given*, 231.

86. *Being Given*, 232.

87. In other words, the dualist way of dealing with the body propagated most prominently by Judith Butler. For more on this in regard to performatism see also Chapter One, 23–29.

88. *Being Given*, 232.

89. *Being Given*, 232–233.

90. *Being Given*, 233.

91. *Being Given*, 233.

92. See, respectively, Chapter One, 24–25 and Chapter Two, 58–63 in this book.

93. See in particular Chapter 3 in *Sphären I*, "Humans in the Magic Circle: An Intellectual History of the Fascination with Proximity," 211–268.

94. *Being Given*, 285.

95. Ball, *American Beauty*, 96.

96. *American Beauty*, 100.

97. See Chapter One, 16 in this book.

98. In this regard Marion calls Kant's transcendental I "the countermodel of the gifted" (278).

99. *Being Given*, 282–283.
100. *Being Given*, 282.
101. *Being Given*, 270.
102. See the discussion of the originary scene in Gans, *Originary Thinking. Elements of Generative Anthropology* (Stanford: Stanford University Press, 1993), 8–9.
103. See the discussion of Derrida in Gans, *Signs of Paradox*, 148–149.
104. *Being Given*, 270.
105. *Being Given*, 270.
106. See his *Signs of Paradox. Irony, Resentment, and Other Mimetic Structures*, (Stanford: Stanford University Press, 1997), esp. Chapter 3, "The Necessity of Paradox."
107. *Originary Thinking*, 22.

Notes for Chapter 6

1. See his full treatment of this in *Originary Thinking: Elements of Generative Anthropology*. Stanford, Calif.: Stanford University Press, 1993, esp. the "Introduction," 1–27.
2. See *Originary Thinking*, 8–9.
3. Gans treats the Kantian affinity of his own theory in his "Originary and/or Kantian Aesthetics," *Poetica* 1–2 (2004), 335–353. The original Kantian concepts are summarized in *Critique of Judgment*, § 22.
4. See Jacques Derrida, *The Truth in Painting* (Chicago: The University of Chicago Press, 1987), esp. 83–118.
5. For more on this see my "Originary Aesthetics and the End of Postmodernism," *The Originary Hypothesis: a Minimal Proposal for Humanistic Inquiry*, ed. by Adam Katz (Aurora, Colo.: Davies Group, 2007), 59–82, esp. 60–64.
6. See, for example, Thomas McEvilley, *The Triumph of Anti-Art. Conceptual and Performance Art in the Formation of Post-Modernism* (New York: McPherson & Co., 2005), esp. Chapter 1, "Kant, Duchamp, and Dada," 15–35 or Arthur C. Danto, *After the End of Art. Contemporary Art and the Pale of History* (Princeton University Press: Princeton 1995), esp. Chapter Four, "Modernism and the Critique of Pure Art: The Historical Vision of Clement Greenberg," 61–78.
7. *The Abuse of Beauty. Aesthetics and the Concept of Art* (Open Court: Chicago, 2003), 15.

8. See *The Abuse of Beauty,* in particular the chapter "Three Ways to Look at Art," 125–142.

9. For more on this see Gans's historical outline of the ostensive in *Originary Thinking,* esp. Chapters 7–12.

10. This distinguishes it from the structuralist tendency to privilege the sign as icon and the poststructuralist tendency to privilege the sign as index. For more on this distinction see my "Originary Aesthetics," 61–64.

11. See also Chapter One in this book, 3–4.

12. See Chapter Two in this book, 57.

13. For more on the rationale behind the choice of "performatism," see "Originary Aesthetics," 64–65.

14. For a detailed study of performance art in postmodernism see McEvilley, *The Triumph of Anti-Art.*

15. A complete pictorial overview of her performances and other projects can be found at
www.vanessabeecroft.com

16. As reflected, for example, in the skeptical review of her Performance 55 by Hermann Pfütze, "Hundert nackte Frauen" [A hundred naked women], *Kunstforum* 176 (2005), 270–271.

17. Most notably as chronicled by Judith Thurman in "The Wolf at the Door: Can an Eating Disorder Be Turned into Art?" *The New Yorker,* March 17, 2003, 84–123.

18. Notable exceptions were VB 39 and 42, which used fully clothed U.S. sailors who had the approval of their commanding officers to participate.

19. See her description of this in her interview with Thomas Kellein in *Vanessa Beecroft* (Ostfildern-Ruit: Hatje Cantz, 2004), 123–124.

20. This creates problems for poststructuralist and/or feminist interpreters like Christine Ross, who in her treatment of Beecroft in *The Aesthetics of Disengagement. Contemporary Art and Depression* (Minneapolis: University of Minnesota Press 2006) speaks of a "preoccupation with homogenized body images and standardized ideals of femininity" (54) and of the "persistence of a desire to be feminine" (60). In the logic of late postmodernism, the position of not having an identifiable gender (i.e., being reduced to the female sex) is simply itself another standardized gender role. It seems hardly necessary to add that the result is a totalizing discourse oblivious to its own exclusion

of the human body as a source of originary significance. For more on the performatist critique of gender theory see Chapter One, 23–29.

21. For an analogous literary use of the uniform to achieve a positive, unifying loss of individuality see the analysis of Olga Tokarczuk's "The Hotel Capital" in Chapter Two of this book, 48.

22. Which consists of a black woman covered with evenly spaced vertical white cloth strips against a horizontal black-and-white striped background and a white woman covered with evenly spaced, vertical black cloth strips against a horizontal black-and-white-striped background. "Natural" race, in other words, merges with the artificial black-and-white pattern constructed by the artist.

23. See Pfütze, "Hundert nackte Frauen," 271.

24. *Aesthetics of Disengagement*, 68.

25. *Aesthetics of Disengagement*, 61.

26. *Aesthetics of Disengagement*, 61.

27. *Aesthetics of Disengagement*, 63.

28. Ross eventually does identify Beecroft's performances with a closed situation — namely with the aesthetic simulation of a clinical experiment: "What we have here is the perfect replica of a scientific laboratory in which subjects are asked to take part in an experiment that will test their reactions and coping abilities to a specific stressful life event" (*Aesthetics of Disengagement*, 80). As Ross quite correctly notes, the performers react to the stress situation by gradually giving up their uniform poses and affirming their own personal identities (82). This is precisely the goal of all theist narratives: individuation (and in ideal cases transcendence) is achieved by reacting freely to the force exerted by an outer "divinely" imposed frame (for more on this see Chapter One in this book, 19–21).

29. Beecroft, who appears to have no philosophical pretensions, consciously operates beneath the threshold of concept: "What I like about the performances is the live event, the moment where you don't know what's going to happen. It's a question of formalizing an idea without having it appear conceptually" (Kellein, *Vanessa Beecroft*, 130 [my translation from the German]).

30. Dave Hickey, *VB 08–36. Vanessa Beecroft's Performances* (Ostfildern-Ruit: Hatje Cantz, 2000), 7.

31. As documented in his *Frame Analysis. An Essay on the Organization of Experience* (Boston: Northeastern University Press, 1986), esp.

Chapter 10, "Breaking Frame," 345–377. For more on Goffman and performatism see also Chapter One in this book, 10–12.

32. This sort of deliberate frame breaking can incidentally also be found as a plot device in performatist narratives, most notably in the Dogma movie *Idiots* (discussed in Chapter One, 14–15). There is, of course, also real-life frame breaking in Beecroft's performances when spectators try to communicate with the models, provoke them, or take off their own clothes (as documented in Pfütze, "Hundert nackte Frauen").

33. This in contrast to Ross, who in *Aesthetics of Disengagement* interprets the lack of discourse peculiar to the intuitive state as a disengaged, depressive condition rather than as an originary, potentially positive moment of autonomous self-empowerment or individuation.

34. In Kantian thought the categories (quantity, quality, relation, modality) form a bridge between intuitive empirical experience (which is pre-conceptual) and the understanding (which is conceptual). In Beecroft and the other artists I will be discussing, the categories seem to emerge spontaneously out of the intuitively experienced material, which however has been organized beforehand by a theist artist. It goes almost without saying that this theist manipulation is foreign to Kant, whose thinking is explicitly deist (see in particular A 675/ B703 in *Critique of Pure Reason*).

35. This lack of postmodern discursivity has not been lost on postmodern artists like Vaginal Davis, who has put on queer burlesque send-ups of Beecroft's performances that supply the "missing" dimension of gender. For a lengthier discussion of this see Jennifer Doyle, *Sex Objects. Art and the Dialectic of Desire* (Minneapolis: University of Minnesota Press, 2006), 121–140.

36. In Gans's generative linguistics the imperative is the second basic linguistic form arising out of the ostensive (the imperative is, like the ostensive, still pre-conceptual, but is directed at an absent, rather than a present, object). Gans expounds on this relation at length in his *The Origin of Language: A Formal Theory of Representation* (Berkeley: University of California Press, 1981).

37. Kellein, *Vanessa Beecroft*, 129 [my translation from the German].

38. A representative English language edition is Bernd and Hilla Becher, *Basic Forms of Industrial Buildings* (London: Thames & Hudson, 2005). The influence of the Bechers on German photography

in general and Gursky in particular is documented in Peter Galassi, "Gursky's World," in *Andreas Gursky*, ed. by Peter Galassi (New York: Abrams, 2001).

39. A systematic catalogue documenting basic human types in hundreds, if not thousands, of photographs. For more on Sander see, for example, Robert Kramer, *August Sander, Photographs of an Epoch, 1904–1959* (Millerton, NY: Aperture, 1980).

40. The Bechers were presumably not trying to send a direct political message. However, the pictures were made around the same time that heavy industry in the Ruhr Valley, and in particular coal mining, was starting to lose its central role in the German economy, and they reflect a strong popular identification of Ruhr valley residents with the legacy of heavy industry. (This identification is so powerful even today that it has proven politically impossible to close down the highly unprofitable coal mining industry, which the German government is committed to subsidize until the year 2018.)

41. In his series *Interieurs*, for example, another Becher student, Thomas Ruff, did to petty bourgeois interiors what Struth did to urban exteriors: he photographed them in a way that made them look entirely desolate. See, for example, *Thomas Ruff. Fotografien 1979 – heute* (Köln: Verlag der Buchhandlung Walther König, 2001).

42. The crushing global dominance of capitalism has made Marxism into a kind of theory of internationalist localism in which the highest virtue is indigenous resistance to capitalism's homogenizing force. In art criticism, this position is propounded most eloquently by Julian Stallabrass in his *Art Incorporated. The Story of Contemporary Art* (Oxford: Oxford University Press, 2004), esp. "The New World Order," 29–72.

43. In *Andreas Gursky. Images*, ed. by Fiona Bradley (München: Oktagon 1995).

44. In *Andreas Gursky. Images*.

45. This massive constriction of both vertical and horizontal space is a feature encountered time and time again in the work of Struth and Ruff and fits in well with the Nietzschean motif of "wiping out the horizon" that will be encountered again further below (see 217–218 below).

46. Critics seem to agree on the optimistic outlook of the photo. Marie Luise Syring describes the human figure as being "between heaven and earth, alone and yet surrounded by protective architecture, small

and yet not lost." See her "Wo liegt 'ohne Titel'?," in *Andreas Gursky. Photographs from 1984 to the Present*, ed. by Mary Luise Syring (Munich; Schirmer/Mosel, 1998) [no pagination]. Greg Hilty goes even farther: he says the bridge "resembles a giant Japanese Shinto gate which frames the otherwise diminutive human subject. The man is miniscule, but potentially heroic; the image is minimal and mundane, but suggests a nodal point of infinite perspectives." See his article "The Occurrence of Space" in *Andreas Gursky. Images*, 15.

47. As quoted in Rupert Pfab, "Wahrnehmung und Kommunikation. Überlegungen zu neuen Motiven von Andreas Gursky," in *Andreas Gursky. Photographs from 1984 to the Present* [no pagination].

48. "I generally let things develop slowly...," in *Andreas Gursky. Fotografien 1984–1988*, ed. by Toby Alleyne-Gee (Ostfildern: Cantz, 1988), IX.

49. Andreas Gursky, "I generally let things develop slowly...," in *Andreas Gursky. Fotografien 1984–1988*, ed. by Toby Alleyne-Gee (Ostfildern: Cantz, 1988), VIII.

50. This manipulative grounding of the sublime in beauty avoids the metaphysical problems arising in Kant's own argumentation when he defines the sublime as immeasurable and incomparable — and is then forced to introduce terms of comparison into his argument all the same. For a critique of this see Derrida's *The Truth in Painting*, esp. the section "The Colossal," 119–148.

51. *Andreas Gursky. Fotografien 1984–1988*, X.

52. In *Thomas Ruff. Fotografien 1979 – heute* [no pagination].

53. In *Thomas Struth. 1977–2002* (Munich: Schirmer Mosel, 2002), 35.

54. Gursky's treatment of space has a direct parallel in performatist architecture's techniques of dematerialization and transparency; for more on this see Chapter Four, 122–123.

55. For a discussion of narrative centering, see Chapter One in this book, 17–18 and 24–26.

56. Susanne Gaensheimer, "Second-Hand Experience," *Thomas Demand* (Munich: Schirmer/Mosel 2004), 70.

57. Roxana Marcoci, "Paper Moon," *Thomas Demand* (New York: Museum of Modern Art 2005), [no pagination].

58. The inevitable poststructuralist objection — that Demand's supplementary outside explanations are as much a part of the photograph

as its supposedly discrete inner space — makes sense in epistemological, but not in performative terms. Why spend months painstakingly constructing and photographing a "traceless" scene in order to expose your own creation as a failure with a few short remarks? Here as elsewhere the point is not that Demand is "reinscribing" already existing discursive reality; he's creating a new reality of his own and reprojecting it categorically onto the consciousness of his viewers.

59. A good way of testing this is to go through a (previously unknown) collection of Demand's photographs and try to figure out just what media event they are about. My own personal identification quotient is around zero, although *Bathroom* (citing a very well known German magazine image from the 1980s) seemed vaguely familiar when I first saw it.

60. Michael Fried, "Without a Trace," *Artforum* 3 (2005), 202.

61. For examples of the visual representation of imperfect theism in architecture see also Chapter Four, 121–122.

62. "Without a Trace," 202.

63. See "Without a Trace," 202.

64. The painting was produced by carrying out a market analysis of what people like in a painting (colors, abstraction vs. representation) and then combining those wishes somewhat incongruously in a picture. The result is a painting done in the style of what appears to be the Hudson River school and containing, among other things, a large expanse of blue sky, George Washington, and a herd of deer.

65. *End of Art*, 195.

66. See *End of Art*, 199.

67. See his analysis in "The Lost Horizon" in Boris Groys, *The Total Art of Stalinism: Avant-Garde, Aesthetic Dictatorship, and Beyond* (Princeton: Princeton University Press 1992), 81–83. Groys's (and the conceptualists') basic thesis is that the utopian striving of modernism was always eminently political and hence also complicit in the totalitarian "total work of art" of Stalinism.

68. See *Unter Verdacht* (Munich: Hanser 2000), esp. the section "Der submediale Raum," 27–116 as well as the discussion in Chapter Five of this book, 164–168.

69. *Unter Verdacht*, 30.

70. If it would not hopelessly confuse the issue it would be tempting to label this position Apollonian. In Nietzsche's own words,

Apollonian form is enjoyed with a "direct or superfluous understanding"; "all shapes speak to us"; "nothing is indifferent," even as "the sense of its status as appearance still shimmers through" (*The Birth of Tragedy out of the Spirit of Music* [Oxford: Oxford University Press 2000], 20). Performatism, however, is no less reducible to a Nietzschean position than is, say, postmodernism, and the musical synthesis of the Apollonian and Dionysian envisioned by Nietzsche is nowhere in hearing range.

71. Lynne Cooke, among others, has noted the connection between Friedrich's *Mönch am Meer* and Gursky's *Düsseldorf Flughafen*. See her article "Visionäre (Per)Versionen," in *Andreas Gursky. Photographs from 1984 to the Present*, ed. by Mary Luise Syring (Munich; Schirmer/Mosel, 1998) [no pagination].

72. As noted by Annelie Lütgens in her "Shrines and Ornaments: A Look into the Display Cabinet. Andreas Gursky's New Pictures," in *Andreas Gursky. Fotografien 1984–1988*, ed. by Toby Alleyne-Gee (Ostfildern: Cantz, 1988), XVI.

73. See his remarks in *Andreas Gursky. Fotografien 1984–1988*, IX.

74. For examples see *Tim Eitel. Terrain*, ed. by Markus Stegmann (Berlin, Holzwarth Publications, 2004).

75. This is also in contradistinction to Edward Hopper's pictures of urban, isolated humans. Eitel's pictures lack the material volume and existential gravitas of Hopper's objects and people; they are emotionally "flat" without being stereotypes. Similarly, Eitel's paintings completely lack the feelings of distrust and malignancy that characterize the portraits of the Belgian Luc Tuymans, who in this regard remains a characteristically "Groysian," postmodern painter of suspicion.

76. The demeanor of Eitel's human subjects is strikingly similar to that of participants in Beecroft's performances, who are made to adopt neutral facial expressions while oscillating between the uncomfortable physical reality of the performance and its artificial, semiotic gesture. For more on the characteristic opacity of performatist subjects, see Chapter One, 8–9.

77. Interview in *Iskusstvo* 5 (2006), 54.

78. In his review "Erik Bulatov. State Tretyakov Gallery, Moscow," *Artforum* 1 (2007), 244 and 276, Tupitsyn suggests that after emigrating Bulatov entered into "a state of tranquility […] with zero-degree alienation" (244) and that "his paintings [after 1990] were

eligible for look-alike contests with promotional posters, sightseeing ads, and other 'life-celebrating' items [...]" (276).

79. See Hal Foster, *The Return of the Real. The Avant-Garde at the End of the Century* (Cambridge: MIT University Press), 1996.

80. In *Neo Rauch. Works on Paper. 2003–2004* (Vienna: Hatje Cantz Verlag, 2004), 5.

81. "'Night-Work' in Defence of Red, Yellow and Blue," in *Randgebiet. Ausstellung Neo Rauch*, ed. by Klaus Werner (Leipzig: Galerie für Zeitgenössische Kunst, 2000), 25.

82. Although performatism was not intended as an artistic program, at least one piece of art work has been inspired by it. Using Apple's text-to-speech software, an American artist living in Thailand, Dane Larsen, created *Performatist Piece with Embedded Text*. Physically, the piece consists of a black plastic pot filled with raw cotton with an MP3 player inside. Using Apple's text-to-speech software, Larsen set up the MP3 player to read my original essay on performatism ("Performatism, or the End of Postmodernism"). The software's distortion of the original text results in a kind of semi-understandable speech emanating "magically" from the cotton. The video of the performance can be viewed on Larsen's blog at:

http://nofolete.blogspot.com/search?updated-max=2007-01-12T13%3A33%3A00%2B07%3A00&max-results=50

Index

8826784R0

Made in the USA
Lexington, KY
05 March 2011